P9-ECP-750

'Guppy has integrated a whole lan ___ P9-ECP-750 own experiences so skillfully that, through her family, we come to know her country; through the country, her family.'
— **Rumer Godden, *Daily Telegraph***

'She has recreated Persia for us in loving, sensuous detail.'
— ***New York Times Book Review***

'Reading this absorbing book is a treat ... When Guppy describes growing up in Iran in the 50's, her narrative reads like a casual conversation with an old friend.'
Washington Post Book World

'A book of reminiscence drawn with warmth and affection, but also with intelligence and insight.'   — ***Chicago Tribune***

'One braces for horror stories about Islamic life for women. Instead, Shusha Guppy portrays a sunlit girlhood in pre-revolutionary Tehran, a world of ritual and intrigue peopled by philandering mullahs, dinner guests spouting poetry, learned grandfathers, gossiping yet wise aunts, matchmaking bathhouse attendants and dignified down-and-outs ... Lyrical memories of Ramadan fasting, New Year feasting and summer trips to the mountains remind us that the ancient land Ms. Guppy deliberately calls 'Persia' throughout once was the land of the nightingale and the rose'   — ***Baltimore Sun***

'A gifted weaver of tales with an artist's eye for sketching characters in context, Guppy evokes the magic, cultural traditions and social fabric of her growing-up years, which were greatly affected by both Reza Shah's efforts to westernize Persia in the 1920s and the ensuing brutal revolution led by bigoted Mullahs.'   — ***Publishers Weekly***

'This buoyant memoir re-creates Guppy's privileged Persian childhood in savory detail ... Guppy has captured a culture in transition with drama, imagination and zest.'   — ***Kirkus Reviews***

Shusha Guppy was born and brought up in Iran. When she was seventeen she was sent to Paris to study at the Sorbonne. She is the London editor of the American literary journal *The Paris Review* and she contributes to publications on both sides of the Atlantic. She is a well-known singer and songwriter and author of *The Secret of Laughter* (also I.B.Tauris) and *A Girl in Paris*. She lives and works in London.

Tauris Parke Paperbacks is an imprint of I.B.Tauris. It is dedicated to publishing books in accessible paperback editions for the serious general reader within a wide range of categories, including biography, history, travel, art and the ancient world. The list includes select, critically acclaimed works of top quality writing by distinguished authors that continue to challenge, to inform and to inspire. These are books that possess those subtle but intrinsic elements that mark them out as something exceptional.

The colophon of Tauris Parke Paperbacks is a representation of the ancient Egyptian ibis, sacred to the god Thoth, who was himself often depicted in the form of this most elegant of birds. Thoth was credited in antiquity as the scribe of the ancient Egyptian gods and as the inventor of writing and was associated with many aspects of wisdom and learning.

THE BLINDFOLD HORSE

Memories of a Persian Childhood

SHUSHA GUPPY

TAURIS PARKE
PAPERBACKS

Published in 2004 by I.B. Tauris & Co Ltd
6 Salem Road, London W2 4BU
175 Fifth Avenue, New York NY 10010
www.ibtauris.com

In the United States of America and Canada distributed by
Palgrave Macmillan a division of St. Martin's Press
175 Fifth Avenue, New York NY 10010

ISBN 1 85043 401 8
EAN 978 1 85043 401 6

A full CIP record for this book is available from the British Library
A full CIP record is available from the Library of Congress

Library of Congress Catalog Card Number: available

Printed and bound in Great Britain by MPG Books Ltd, Bodmin

For my brothers, Nassir and Nasser, and my sister, Badri, in memory of our parents

Sit down by the side of the stream
And in the rushing of water
Witness the transience of life.

Hafiz of Shiraz

Contents

Acknowledgements

In the writing of this book I have been helped by many friends, to all of whom I wish to express my gratitude. In particular I thank Michael Sagalyn and Jane Turnbull for their initial interest, Sue Freestone for her encouragement, Claude Roy and Loleh Bellon for their hospitality in Paris. Above all I am deeply indebted to Nicholas Guppy, my former husband, for his patient and invaluable guidance over the years.

The Blindfold Horse

It is winter. A narrow, muddy street, flanked by low mud-brick walls beneath a cloudless steely sky. The ground rutted deep by cartwheels, pock-marked with mule and donkey hooves, covered with a thin layer of ice that crunches underfoot. Dirty patches of snow linger here and there at the base of walls. At the end of the street the embrasure of a door in front of which hangs an indigo-blue patched curtain, like a single spot of colour on a fawn canvas. From behind it comes a regular, monotonous muffled thud, like a distant hammer, followed by a whining screech.

This is my first memory – I must have been two or three years old. An inquisitive child, I stop and lift a corner of the curtain apprehensively: a pungent, spicy smell wafts across the street; inside is a small, dark room filled with clouds of yellow dust; in the middle a huge circular stone with a mast at its centre is being dragged round and round by a large, emaciated horse on bending spindly legs. His eyes are blindfolded with a black cloth and, as he rotates the stone, a mustardy-yellow flour pours from under it into the surrounding gutter. The scene is lit by a single glass eye in the domed ceiling far above, which shoots a diagonal shaft of light and illuminates a column of dust whose yellow specks dance as if to the rhythm of the horse's hooves on the stony floor.

'Come along, child, we must hurry.' My mother. She takes me by the hand and pulls me away. I cling to the door, mesmerised, as the blindfold horse pulls round and round, its yoke screeching, its hooves thudding, its nostrils puffing jets of steam into the icy yellow air – turning, turning.

'Why are his eyes covered, Mother?'

'So that he doesn't see where he is, otherwise he would get dizzy going round in a circle all day, and he would balk. Blindfold, he can imagine he is walking in a straight line, in a field. But don't worry, at the end of the day they take off the cloth from his eyes and give him some lovely oats to eat. He is quite happy, really ...'

The image dissolves.

But it comes back, leaping into memory at odd times – in daydreams or nightmares, in moments of doubt and anguish, and every time I use turmeric in cooking: the skeletal blindfold horse, chained to its treadmill in a dark room, going round and round, day after day, year after year, all the while imagining that he is galloping in a daisy-dotted prairie, for a bag of oats at the end of the day ...

The blindfold horse, my earliest memory, *mon frère, mon semblable* ...

Haji Mahmood

There used to be thousands of such little mills in Persia, scattered through towns and villages. Long before petrol was discovered my great-grandfather, Haji Mahmood, owned one of them near the bazaar in Teheran. His mill extracted oil from a variety of seeds, mainly for domestic lamps, but also for medicinal uses. It was housed in a shed next to his house and behind his shop, so that he had easy access to both. A carpet was spread inside the shop to one side of which there was a dais, covered with a silk rug and a large cushion on which Haji Mahmood sat cross-legged all day, receiving clients and conducting business. At the far end a brocade curtain led to a closet which contained his ledgers, prayer book, a Qoran, and some personal papers. All around the shop, containers of oil were stacked neatly on top of each other, while larger barrels were stored behind the mill, labelled in his handwriting. He had an abacus by his side, and a rosary of amber beads in his hand, which he used for murmuring prayers and invocations, whenever he was alone.

That he was wealthy and reputable was indicated by his title of *Haji*, which means 'the one who has accomplished the holy pilgrimage to Mecca'. For the *Sharia* (Islamic Law) decrees that a man who goes must be rich enough to leave a whole year's provision for his family and an inheritance in case of his death while away. In those days the journey lasted several months and was fraught with all manner of excitement and danger. The ancient pilgrim roads were little more than stony tracks, going through high mountains and valleys, torrential rivers and deep gorges, across reptile-infested, lion-haunted deserts, until they reached Arabia and the Ka'ba, the House of God. Often the caravans of camels, mules, horsemen and men on foot were attacked by bandits who sacked their possessions and took their animals. Disease, epidemics of cholera and smallpox, snake and scorpion bites, old age and exhaustion would also take their toll. But these had their compensations: for if a pilgrim died *en route* he was sure to go straight to Heaven and be welcomed by no less than the Archangel Gabriel himself, who would lead him to the Garden of Eden where he would take his rightful place among the Prophets, Imams and the Righteous. As for the lucky pilgrims who returned home safely, they would receive a hero's welcome, and their safety would be considered due to the prayers and sacrifices they had made and the intervention of the Imam to whom they had been addressed.

An honest merchant would probably have to wait years before he became rich enough to be eligible for the haj, and Haji Mahmood was in his fifties when he finally accomplished it. When news arrived that the caravan of returning pilgrims was approaching the outskirts of the city, the entire bazaar went into a dizzy state of excitement and frenetic jubilation. Haji Mahmood's shop was decorated with tulip-shaped candlesticks and marble fountains full of goldfish; fine carpets were spread in his reception room, with silk and brocade cushions displayed along the walls to recline against; huge sacks of flour and rice, camel-loads of fruit and vegetables were delivered to his house for the banquets and meals that would follow his return, both for his guests and for distribution to the poor. And when he actually arrived two lambs were sacrificed – one at the entrance of the bazaar and another on his own threshold – and he was carried shoulder-high by youngsters amid great jubilation and mirth, accompanied by other hajis and notables of the district. For seven days a stream of visitors poured into his house to share the lavish hospitality, hear the pilgrim's tales and partake in the blessing of haj.

A man was supposed to be transformed by his experience at the House of God, whose grace would hit the pilgrim like lightning that would render the sinner righteous, the stingy generous, and the ignorant knowledgeable. Such dramatic metamorphosis seldom occurred in reality, but everyone tried to conform, at least in appearance, to the expected pattern of *noblesse oblige* and conduct himself with more *gravitas*. Apparently Haji Mahmood succeeded more than most: he gave freely to the poor and his reputation for piety and wisdom grew, spreading all over the town, and eventually drifted into myth. Nothing was known of his background but, long after his death, stories were told about, or attributed to him, that illustrated his exemplary evolution from poverty to riches, and from anonymity to fame.

I remember one of these anecdotes, which Aunt Ashraf, my father's younger sister, the inexhaustible and irrepressible chief-storyteller of the family, recounted one long winter's evening when I was a child, the story of Dash Jafar.

The Tale of Dash Jafar

The Bazaar was a vast maze of narrow streets, covered with vaulted ceilings whose apexes were punctuated by glass port-holes for letting in daylight. On either side of the criss-crossed lanes were arcades of shops and stalls, with behind them vast warehouses, loading yards and craftsmen's workshops. Each craft had its own quarters, gold and silversmiths, tin and coppersmiths, shoemakers, drapers; carpet-sellers, dyers ... You could find your way around by following the sounds and smells of the place: the cacophonic hammering of tin and coppersmiths, the swish and rasp of cobblers' tools and carpenters' planes, the pungent smells of perfumes, dyes and spices. From dawn till dusk the Bazaar seethed with a motley crowd of shoppers, pedlars, porters and errand-boys, brokers, layabouts and beggars, who bargained, pleaded, haggled and proclaimed their sincerity and honesty. Donkeys and mules, so heavily laden that they disappeared beneath their loads, their bells a-jingle, vied for space with human porters bent double under bales of cloth, sacks of grain, vats of dye or carpets. They said you could buy anything in the Bazaar, 'a hen's milk and a man's life'.

But the Bazaar was much more than just a shopping centre – it was the very heart of the community; commerce and industry, politics and religion depended on its prosperity and moods. For it was the rich merchants who kept the mosques and their legion of mullahs in funds; it was their taxes that filled the State's coffers and their support that kept the politicians in power.

At the entrance of the Bazaar was the Shah's mosque, where the King or his representative attended the midday prayer each Friday (the Muslim sabbath) and from whose tall blue minaret the muezzin called the faithful to prayer three times a day. The Shah's palace and Grand Vizier's residence were nearby, while the chief mullahs had their houses in the vicinity.

Like a healthy body that can tolerate germs and impurities without succumbing to disease, the bazaar harboured a legion of parasites – layabouts, con-men, thieves, brokers, urchins and beggars. The most important figure among those who lived off the Bazaar without working in it was the *Dash* (the word means 'brother' in popular idiom). He demanded and received from each shopkeeper a monthly sum called *baj*, or tribute, in exchange for 'protection' from vandalism and burglary. The *Dash* usually started his career in the *Zur-Khaneh* (House of Strength), a traditional gymnasium where young athletes learnt wrestling, weight-lifting, playing with lances, javelins and other props in graceful and stylised exercises that symbolised war activities, to the accompaniment of drum beats and epic chants from

Firdowsi's *Shahnameh*, *The Book of Kings*. The whole routine was performed in a sunken circular arena surrounded by benches for spectators. A *Dash* was the man who had beaten all his rivals at wrestling and weight-lifting, developed his muscles to bursting point and established his ascendancy over all others. He used his biceps the way Al Capone wielded his machine-gun, and no one ever dared refuse him the *baj*, since one swipe of his arm would land the foolhardy man in bed – if not in the grave – and expose his shop to pillage. At the same time the *Dash* had his own code of honour: he had to be generous and open-handed with the extorted bounty and give to the poor; he had to protect the honour of women and respect religious authority, especially that of his chosen mullah or guru. In short he modelled himself on the King, whose methods, after all, were not unlike his own, only on a larger scale and more institutionalised. If he conformed to the pattern and gained the respect of his peers and cronies, he was given the title of *Luti*, which had come to mean a lovable rogue.

At the time when Haji Mahmood had his oil-mill and shop in the bazaar, the chief *Dash* was *Dash* Jafar: a tall, extremely handsome youth, with thick curling mustachios and a short busy beard, who was too grand to stand at the entrance of the Bazaar and demand the *baj* himself and always sent one of his cronies instead. The only merchant who was exempt from *baj* was Haji Mahmood, for Jafar had taken a liking to him and tacitly adopted him as a father-figure. He visited him often and asked his advice on personal matters, and offered him help which was always politely refused.

One day, after an absence of many months, Jafar appeared at Haji Mahmood's shop, greeted him, kissed his hand and sat down on the carpet beside him, Haji Mahmood noticed that Jafar was not his usual, cheerful cocky self but seemed preoccupied and downcast. He offered him a cup of tea and sweets, and asked him what was troubling him. As if he was just waiting for a signal Jafar began to pour out his heart:

'To tell you the truth Haji Aqa [Aqa means "sir", "Master", "holy man" or plain "Mister", depending on context], I am tired of this life of dissipation and games. I am 25 years old and I have never done anything except playing at the *Zur-Khaneh*, being wild and living up to other people's expectations. I have never had a father and have regarded you as one, so I have come to you for advice, a solution that would get me out of my present way of life. I would like to repent for my wrongdoing and start a business of my own, but I have no money; everything I've "earned" has been squandered on loose living, and anyway you can't set up a legitimate commerce with illegitimate money because God would punish you by making it go bankrupt, as your Excellency would be the first to agree. So I can't see any solution.'

Haji Mahmood listened attentively, pondered for a few minutes, then got up and disappeared behind the curtain at the back of the shop into his closet, whence he emerged after a while holding a little silk bag which he handed to Jafar saying:

'This bag contains one hundred gold sovereigns. It is the money I have saved for a rainy day. Well, this seems to be the rainy day for you, so take it, give up your unlawful ways and start a new life. When you become rich and successful you can give it back to me if you wish.'

Dash Jafar was confused and overwhelmed. This was more than he had dreamt of; he knew Haji Mahmood was a shrewd and generous man, but not to the extent of parting with his life's savings. After a good deal of *taarof* (polite refusal on his part and insistence on Haji's), he took the silk bag of gold and left.

Years passed.

Haji Mahmood grew old and grey but carried on his business. One day he was sitting on his carpeted dais in the front of his shop and murmuring prayers on his rosary when he saw a tall, middle-aged, bearded man approach and salute him:

'Do you remember me Haji Aqa? Jafar? *Dash* Jafar! To whom you gave a hundred gold sovereigns all those years ago? I have come to pay back my debt.'

He then sat down to a cup of tea and sweets, and told his story: With the money he had received from Haji Mahmood he had bought a mule, some household goods – articles of toiletry and ornaments and small utensils – which he knew would be appreciated in the country, and he had gone to a village near Varamin, a town some hundred miles or so from Teheran, where he had set up a stall in the Bazaar and started selling his merchandise. Gradually he had made friends among other shopkeepers and tradesmen, and won the trust of the *kadkhoda* (the village headman), a wealthy grain dealer and the most respected member of the community.

One day, the *kadkhoda* had invited him to his house and after supper had told him that, since he had no son of his own, he would like to adopt him, Jafar, provided he accepted to marry his fourteen-year-old daughter who was his only surviving child and the apple of his eye. Jafar had heard that the headman's daughter was very pretty and modest – modesty being the highest attribute of a girl – and once he had caught a glimpse of her through the curtains when taking tea with her father, so he accepted the offer immediately, saying:

'If your Honour will accept this slave as son-in-law, he shall lay his life at your feet.'

A couple of years later, the headman had died and left his fortune to Jafar and his family. Suddenly Jafar was rich and eligible for haj, the pilgrimage to Mecca, which he had accomplished forthwith. In due course, the villagers had chosen his as their *kadkhoda*, a function he still carried out. But through all these events and adventures he had clean forgotten his debt to Haji Mahmood, until a few days before his visit, when he had a dream in which Imam Ali (the Prophet Mohammed's son-in-law and the first Imam of the duodecimal Shia sect) himself had come to tell him that he should not forget the hundred gold sovereigns he had borrowed and that it was about time he honoured his debt. Jafar had woken up shaken, convinced that this was no idle dream, the result of a heavy meal, but an actual visitation and warning, for he could feel the presence of the Imam in his room, even smell his scent of *atar* musk, which lingered long after the saint's departure. And so here he was, with *two* hundred gold sovereigns – the original debt plus one hundred as the interest it could have accumulated over the years.

Haji Mahmood took the silk bag, emptied it on his lap and divided the gold coins, saying:

'I accept the original sum so that you don't feel obligated towards me, for there is nothing worse than obligation which curtails freedom of conscience, but I cannot accept any interest as it would constitute usury and that is against God's Law.'

No amount of insistence from Jafar prevailed, so after a while he kissed the old man's hand, thanked him profusely, and left, 'To live a long life of virtue and prosperity,' added Aunt Ashraf to drive home the moral of the story.

Haji Seyyed Mohammad

Shortly after Jafar's visit, Haji Mahmood died of old age. His only son and heir, Mohammed, did not want to follow him in his trade, but wished to take the path of learning and become a theologian and a mullah. So the mill was sold and eventually disappeared, as petrol replaced vegetable oil for domestic lighting and more modern methods were introduced for extracting medicinal oils from seeds.

Mohammed had left home at 16 to become a *talabeh* (a theology student, a seminarist) at the nearby *madrasah* (college). In those days there were no universities in Persia in the modern, Western sense of the word, and those who wished to continue beyond elementary schooling had to enter one of these seats of learning which were the equivalent of Europe's medieval colleges.

The *madrasah* chosen by Mohammad was called Sheikh Abdollah, named after a famous Master and next to a grand mosque of the same designation. The students came from all over the country, attracted by the presence of celebrated teachers whose renown had reached them. They lived in small cells built around a courtyard with a pool in the middle, shaded by ancient plane and cypress trees, within the sanctuary of the mosque whose blue dome cast a blessed shadow over their residence and from whose minaret they were called to prayer at dawn, midday and dusk. Mostly they lived on a small grant provided by the mosque, though a few – among them Mohammad – supplemented this with an allowance from their fathers.

Their studies ranged over the whole gamut of traditional knowledge: mathematics, astronomy, philosophy, jurisprudence and, above all, theology. The majority left after a few years, having learnt the rudiments of theology, and became mullahs and prayer-leaders in mosques. Only a few stayed on for years, going from Master to Master, until they had covered all the aspects of their particular field. After some ten years, Mohammed became a *Mujtahid*: a learned man and a Grand Mullah who is entitled to interpret the *Sharia* and the Qoran, and pass judgement in religious courts. Years later, when the first Western-style university was established in Teheran and others gradually sprang up in other cities, the most famous of these *madrasahs* survived, notably in Qom, Mashad, Isfahan and Tabriz, to become theology schools for producing mullahs, prayer-leaders and religious dignitaries.

Once a man had become a *Mujtahid*, no matter what his origins he would move up the social ladder into the higher sphere of the clerical aristocracy. And that was where the real power lay, for in a country where an overwhelming majority of people were illiterate the mullahs, who could at least read and write, however ignorant they were otherwise, controlled education, the populace and its emotions, the bazaar and its money.

In the seventeenth century, the Safavid kings had declared Shiism, hitherto a minority sect, the official religion of Persia. Their principal reason for doing so was opposition to the neighboring Ottoman sultans with whom they were on and off at war. Shiism, which allows more room for manoeuvre than Sunnism (orthodox Islam) with regards to the *Sharia*, through the *Mujtahid* increased the power of the clergy until, in the nineteenth century, the Grand Mullahs became so powerful that even the Shah obeyed them and was wary of them, in the same way as, in the Middle Ages, European kings were afraid of the Pope. One anecdote illustrates the point: at the beginning of the nineteenth century, Fathali Shah, who ruled over an empire three times as large as Persia is today, begged his Chief Mullah for a special dispensation to forgo fasting during the Ramadan (the Muslim equivalent of Lent). He gave the reason that fasting made him bad-tempered and irascible, and apt to order harsh sentences, even unjust executions of innocent people, which was clearly not desirable. His Chief Mullah (Ayatollah) sent back a curt message which showed his displeasure by omitting all the elaborate courtesy titles by which the Shah was usually addressed, and simply said:

'Fathali *must* fast and he must *not* order the execution of innocent people!' And that was that.

But Mohammad had more modest aims: upon becoming a *Mujtahid* he acquired a mosque and a teaching post in the same *madrasah* where he had studied, set up house nearby and began his career as a mullah, a teacher and a scholar.

I have a photograph of him in middle age, in the company of his secretary, a young bearded mullah twice his own size. He is very short and fairly round, with a black beard, sharp humorous eyes, and the ghost of a sceptical smile. He wrote many treatises on the finer points of ritual and on medieval theologians' theories. Lately I have heard that the Oriental Department of some Canadian university is translating and publishing his works. Doubtless they will languish on a library shelf until one day a Ph.D. student will take them down for his thesis.

By all accounts the reason why he was not interested in too much power and politics was because he was a rather lazy hedonist who preferred the pursuit of pleasure – especially sexual ones – to social-climbing. He used his intelligence, charm and knowledge to lead exactly the life he enjoyed, within the limits allowed by religion: a large and magnificent household, a number of servants, children, and lots and lots of women.

My father was his third son.

Mohammad, my grandfather, was in his late twenties when he finished his studies at the *madrasah* and became a fully-fledged *Mujtahid*. In his last year as a student, a rich merchant from the bazaar took him to Mecca on pilgrimage, on the understanding that Mohammad helped him with the language – Arabic – and the religious rites. This meant that Mohammad became a haji much sooner than he would have done otherwise, at the tender age of 28, which added a considerable cachet to his already prestigious title of *Mujtahid*. As he was also a Seyyed (a descendant of the Prophet through his son-in-law Imam Ali) he became known as Haji Seyyed Mohammed.

There were a great number of Seyyeds in Persia, all claiming direct descent from the Prophet. The Seyyed mullahs wore black turbans to indicate their claim, while other mullahs had white turbans. There was usually no proof of the parentage, since such information was passed down orally from generation to generation. But I have a proper genealogy for our family which links us over thirty-five generations to Imam Hossein, the Prophet's grandson and Third Imam of the Shiites, through his marriage with a Persian princess, daughter of a Sassanian king. My own sceptical reaction to the matter is similar to the Duke of Wellington's when a man approached him in the street saying:

'Mr Smith, I believe?', to which he answered, 'Sir, if you believe that you believe anything!' Nevertheless somehow we were brought up to consider ourselves especially favoured, not only on account of our immediate ancestry but because of a much older spiritual and royal heritage.

On their way back from Mecca, Mohammad and his benefactor stopped at both Karbala and Nejef, in present day Iraq, which are the two most holy cites for Shia muslims, since they contain the tombs of Imam Ali and his son Imam Hossein (respectively First and Third of the twelve Imams), both martyred in the seventh century. Here Mohammad's task as companion and religious instructor came to an end, and he took leave of his older friend. The merchant continued his journey with the caravan of pilgrims to Persia, but Mohammad stayed in Nejef to study with a famous Master at the *madrasah* attached to the Imam's shrine.

It was on a trip to nearby Karbala that he met and married my father's mother, Halima – a young and beautiful widow, and a votary of Imam Hossein. Their encounter was the result of a miracle that became one of the foundation stones of our family mythology.

In those days a widow, however young and attractive, had

little chance of a good second marriage, since virginity was a guarantee of virtue and the highest prize every man was after. At best she could hope for a much older man, or an invalid, or someone below her own social standing. Yet Halima, on account of her reputation for modesty and piety, had several proposals, all of which she refused: she had decided to become a *tareke-donya* (a renouncer of the world) and devote herself entirely to securing a nice place in the next, through prayer and devotion to Imam Hossein. She and her two brothers had emigrated to Karbala from Persia, learnt Arabic and gradually melted into the local community.

Around every shrine, mausoleum, or *madrasah*, there were women – widows, divorcees, abandoned wives – who specialised in concubinage with students, mullahs and pilgrims. They 'married' for as short a time as a day, were called *sigheh* (temporary wife or concubine) and scraped a living thereby. Nowadays this would be considered legal prostitution, but Islam is a practical religion and works with the human material at hand, and the flesh being weak it has found accommodation with it in this way. Halima, however, was not weak, nor interested in such arrangements. For one thing she was sufficiently well-off not to need to, for another she clearly had a spiritual disposition and was given to piety more than to the pleasures of the flesh – unlike her future husband, I might add, as we shall see. In a Christian society she would have undoubtedly become a nun, a nurse, or a missionary, but no such course was open to an unmarried Muslim woman who had to follow the dictate of her father, or the nearest male relative, and whose role in life was supposed to be to please a man and produce children. Accordingly Halima had been married at 14, given birth to a son at 15 (who had died of fever soon afterwards), and become a widow when her husband had died suddenly of an unknown disease. She had vowed never to remarry.

But, a couple of years after she and her family settled down in Karbala, Halima had a dream: she was praying at the tomb of the Imam when, all of a sudden, the silver grid that surrounds it opened and the saint stepped out, wrapped in a full-length halo and looking splendidly regal. He told her that when she awoke at dawn she should go to the shrine as usual.

'And there at the foot of my grave you will find a young mullah, a descendant of mine, whom you shall recognise by his black turban and serene countenance. You must marry him for my sake.'

Halima had protested, saying that she wanted to devote her life to him and his pilgrims, but the Imam had put his index finger on her lips as a sign of silence, adding, 'As a reward for your compliance I will give you a special child,' and he had vanished.

The cocks were crowing under a pearly sky when Halima woke up. She performed her ablutions and went to the shrine for prayer. It was empty, the flow of pilgrims not having started yet, except for a young mullah standing at the foot of the tomb, lost in prayer. She waited for him to finish, then approached him and told him the story exactly as it had happened, adding that she would be willing to fulfil the Imam's commandment and marry him as soon as he wished.

Haji Seyyed Mohammad would not have given in easily and was shrewd enough to see through any stratagem, but it so happened that he also had seen the Imam in *his* dream the previous night, who had told him that early in the morning he should go to the mausoleum and meet a pretty young widow, a votary of his and a virtuous, gentle woman, whom he should marry.

Aunt Ashraf, who recounted the story, relished emphasising the word 'pretty', since women being veiled, Mohammad had no way of knowing what his future bride would look like. It was usually a marriage-broker, or go-between, a friend or relative who described a bride to her groom before marriage. The discrepancy between the dithyrambic praise of the girl's looks and the reality was so enormous that sometimes the poor groom fainted upon setting eyes on his hideous bride described as Venus. So it was rather thoughtful of Imam Hossein to reassure Mohammad on that score!

Anyway, they married and lived in Karbala, Nejef and Kazemein for several years while Mohammad studied with his Masters. On a pilgrimage to the shrine of Kazem, another Imam, in a nearby town, my father was born and named after the saint. He was the third son and the family was expanding. It was time to return to Persia and earn a proper living. Back home, Mohammad – by now Haji Seyyed Mohammad – acquired a mosque, a teaching post at his old *madrasah*, bought himself a house and began a long, happy and by all accounts totally fulfilled life.

Haji Seyyed Mohammad's house consisted of two buildings: the *andaroon* or women's quarter, where no males except close relatives were allowed, and the *birooni*, or men's quarter, where the study and reception rooms were – a male enclave for working and receiving visitors and students. Here Haji Seyyed Mohammad held court in an atmosphere of scholarship and devotion, surrounded by devotees, students and visiting colleagues. The two buildings were connected by a door and had communicating gardens. A high wall surrounded the whole edifice and ensured privacy, and this layout was typical of all seigneurial homes in nineteenth-century Persia.

The *andaroon*, the domain of children and servants, fortune-tellers and magicians, marriage-brokers and dressmakers, was a world of its own. There power resided, through intrigue, cunning and the wielding of sharp tongues; marriages were planned, intense friendships tied and broken, political fortunes made and destroyed. But the *andaroon* was also the sanctuary of feelings, where women developed and used their imaginations through the reading and memorising of poetry and tales, and the weaving of myths. They learnt the arts of good housekeeping and crafts such as sewing, embroidery, knitting and other 'dainty' activities. They refined cooking and pastry-making to a most delicate degree, and wove their dreams with the strand of their intricate brocades.

The *birooni* of an *Aqa* was an open house: visitors, friends and relatives, those with requests for a recommendation or a favour, called at all times. The samovar was kept on the boil from dawn till late at night, purring quietly like a contented cat in a corner of the vast kitchen, so that tea could always be served, accompanied by plates of sweets and biscuits. The *Aqa*'s personal valet was in charge of receiving the guests and serving refreshments, and keeping the two houses in constant touch with each other through his wife who had the same function in the *andaroon*. In short within the structured hierarchy of a feudal society every man's household was modelled, however modestly, on the King's court; every man's house was indeed his castle.

When Aunt Ashraf, my father's young sister, was only a year old, her mother Halima died. Once a week, a laundry woman came to wash the household linen. She would wash it in the back of the garden or the scullery, then spread it on the flat roof of the house to dry in the sun. The roof of a two-storey house was some 30-40 feet above the ground. One day at dusk, when the servants were lighting the oil lamps and bringing them in, Halima followed the laundry woman to the roof to make some arrangements for the following week. She gave her a hand with gathering the dried linen before darkness fell, while holding baby Ashraf in her arms. Her two younger sons, aged 5 and 8, were playing in the garden when suddenly she heard a scream. She looked down and saw Kazem, the younger boy, wrapped in flames, and instinctively she put down the baby and jumped off the roof, picked up the child and dipped him in the pool to extinguish the fire, and saved his life. The laundry woman rushed down the stairs, leaving the baby behind. Pandemonium ensued. The little boy was badly burnt, writhing in pain and crying; neighbours poured in through the door, everyone suggested a special oil or ointment, the *Aqa* was alerted and came in, eventually some old wife's ointment concocted of special plants and powders mixed with olive oil was spread over the burnt area of the child's body, and he was soothed and put to sleep. How baby Ashraf did not crawl to the edge of the roof and fall off to her death was yet another miracle.

The boys had found some matches, a rarity in those days, and had started playing with them when Kazem's shirt had caught fire. Whether from the shock of the accident or the effect of her tremendous leap, Halima fell ill that night and died a couple of days later. They said that she had wanted to die for some time, because she knew that sooner or later her husband would take a second, younger wife, and she did not know how to bear it, 'so

God took her to spare her the sorrow and disappointment,' concluded Aunt Ashraf.

Little Ashraf was clean forgotten during her mother's funeral wake, and the resulting *va-et-vient*. She nearly died of hunger. Fortunately a neighbour, a saintly middle-aged widow was 'inspired by providence' to come and look after the children. She moved in and saw them all through this period of confusion, and stayed to bring them up.

As for Kazem, my father, he carried the scar of that burn to the end of his life: his stomach was like a piece of shrivelled parchment, and there was always an almost imperceptible touch of melancholy behind his keen humour that came partly from that early suffering and bereavement.

Grandmother Halima's name means meek, gentle, soft: it was the name of the Prophet's nurse and, according to all who had known her, 'never was a name more apposite'.

Amineh – the Second Wife

❦

Within a few months of his wife's death Haji Seyyed Mohammad remarried. His new wife was the thirteen-year-old daughter of a *moreed* (disciple, follower). She was called Amineh, which means 'the trustworthy one'. Amineh found herself the mistress of a large household, with four stepchildren, the eldest of whom was almost her own age and resented her bitterly. He expressed it by being morose and bad-tempered, impervious to Amineh's potent charm.

Amineh realised that she had to learn the rules of the game, grow up fast or perish. With a strong instinct for survival, a shrewd and calculating mind, and an aptitude for intrigue and manipulation, she soon became as adept at *andaroon* Machiavellian politics and social games as a Renaissance courtier. She had her first son when she was 14, and thereafter another son and two daughters in fairly quick succession. She would have had many more children had her husband been more faithful and not shared his favours with other women.

Soon after her wedding, Amineh realised that there was no way her husband, who by all accounts had an insatiable sexual appetite, would be content with her alone. His temptations were numerous and varied: women admirers would offer themselves as *sigheh* (concubine), either because they genuinely fell for the easy-going, sensualist mullah's charm, or simply to receive the blessing of a descendant of the Prophet, while male followers would offer their daughters as second or third wife for the honour it would bestow upon them. Amineh could not bear the thought of having to share her authority in the *andaroon* with anyone else, and she hit on a compromise solution: she would herself organise and supervise her husband's extra-marital sex life. In this way her authority would remain unchallenged, and she would always be in control.

So it was that among the servants of her household Amineh always employed a young and pretty girl who would be personal maid to the *Aqa*. When a new young maid was hired she would be given a cup of mint tea to take to the *Aqa*'s bedroom late at night, and 'massage his legs'. As a priest, Haji Seyyed Moham- mad could perform the marriage ceremony himself and make her a *sigheh* there and then. He would murmur the few Arabic marriage formulae, then say in Persian, 'Do you agree?', to which the hapless girl would answer, 'Yes', out of politeness, and that would be that. The *droit du seigneur* dressed up in religious garb! The first time that a new maid went to 'massage the Aqa's legs', Amineh would sit up and wait till she came back to the *andaroon*, and from her confused expression, her ruffled hair, tearful eyes and flushed cheeks she would know that 'the deed was done'. From then on, it was a matter of routine, and for a year or so Amineh did not have to worry.

After a while her husband would become restless, fussy, less forthcoming with compliments, jokes and presents, and she would know that he was getting bored with the maid.

Whereupon Amineh would set out to find a husband for the discarded girl among the male servants and retainers, local shopkeepers and widowers, and once the arrangements were made she would buy her a trousseau, give a large party in the *andaroon* for her own friends, and proceed to find another maid for her husband. This pattern suited everyone, not least the girls who thus were guaranteed husbands and trousseaux.

In the meantime, Amineh was not idle either. She had a large and busy social life in the *andaroon*, and although it was never proved – how could it have been? – some said that she consoled herself with the young family physician, Dr Amran: a tall and extremely handsome Jew, who had studied medicine in France, wore elegant European clothes, carried a silver-topped walking cane and was very popular with his patients. His women patients loved him for his good looks and gallantry, and the men because of his exact diagnoses and efficacious treatments.

Dr Amran, and later his whole family, converted to Islam through my grandfather and were assimilated into Persian society. But at the time, to give him free access to the *andaroon*, Haji Seyyed Mohammad performed a marriage ceremony between Dr Amran and his own youngest daughter, a six-month-old baby, for the duration of one hour. According to Islamic Law, from then on Dr Amran was considered Amineh's son-in-law and therefore *mahram* (legitimate, lawful) and it was permissible for her to appear before him unveiled. This ploy was often used in *andaroons* to free the lady of the house from having to cover herself in front of a male retainer. As a child, I was myself 'married' for an hour to every new cook, valet, footman who came to the house, so that my mother could be free from the veil within the house. So Dr Amran was able to call at the *andaroon* and pay his respect to the *Khanoom* (Lady) whenever he visited the *Aqa*.

It was not long before servants and relatives caught glimpses of a fluttering eyelid, the ghost of a smile, of certain looks exchanged between the handsome doctor and the *Khanoom*. Amineh, veiled of course, was seen once or twice emerging from Dr Amran's surgery and recognised while getting into a droshky through a slight parting of the veil. Yet Amineh always managed to discredit her detractors, who were few, and silence her friends, who were numerous and loyal. She would tell her husband herself that she had called on the Doctor in his surgery while visiting friends nearby, to ask for a special medicine, or for advice about the children. And the old mullah was too cunning and easy-going to probe. Besides who was *he* to throw a stone?

When Amineh grew middle-aged, her eldest daughter, Aunt Etty, took her place in Dr Amran's heart and was able to sustain herself through an unhappy marriage by an occasional visit to his surgery. I doubt if anything concrete went on between those women and the gallant doctor – they were too devout and virtuous. But I'm sure waves of yearning and wistful sighs rippled through the air around them, and made their lives more bearable.

Haji Seyyed Mohammad died in his sleep at the age of 105: 'There was nothing the matter with him, just a candle that had burnt out,' said Aunt Ashraf. The night before he died, he called the young maid to his bedroom. She took him a cup of mint tea and an ointment for his knees, which had gone a little stiff of late. She stayed longer than usual, and when she returned to the *andaroon* she said that the *Aqa*'s legs were numb and cold, and that she had spent a long time massaging them ...

Haji Ali-Baba

The same year that Haji Seyyed Mohammad left the *madrasah* in Teheran and set forth for Mecca on pilgrimage, a young seminarist came from the north of Persia to study in Isfahan, another seat of learning. Isfahan had been the capital of Persia during the era of the Safavid dynasty in the sixteenth and seventeenth centuries, when it had been expanded and built up to become one of the most beautiful cities in the world. The Safavids had declared Shiism the State religion and turned their capital, with its innumerable mosques and *madrasahs*, into a centre for religious studies.

The young *talabeh* (seminarist) was called Ali-Baba and his family were smallholding farmers in Mazandaran, by the shores of the Caspian Sea. He had the fair complexion, high cheekbones and black eyes of northern people who were of Caucasian origins. He was an only son, because the rich rice fields and waterways that produced his family's livelihood were also the breeding ground of mosquitoes and other parasites, and all his brothers and sisters had died in infancy of regional diseases – malaria, rheumatic fever, tuberculosis, etc. ... When his father tilled the land, Ali-Baba went with him, but in winter he had gone to the local school, learnt to read and write, and caught the bug of literacy. At 14, he announced that he did not wish to become a farmer but wanted to leave home, go to Isfahan, and study with some famous Masters, at the Shah's *madrasah*, whose reputation had reached even this far region behind the high mountains and deep ravines that separated it from the rest of the country.

Ali-Baba's parents had been shattered at the thought of losing their only son, for it was clear to them that he would never come back – children who left the country for the city seldom did, and anyway what would an *Alem* (a learned man, a savant) and a mullah want to do with a patch of earth? No amount of pleading and reasoning prevailed, and after a couple of years they gave in to their son's ambition. They bought him a white turban, a brown coat and a black cloak – the outfit of a fledging mullah – and delivered him one autumn dawn to the leader of a caravan *en route* for Isfahan.

Would he ever get there? The road across the mountains was fraught with dangers: many a traveller fell into the bottomless chasms and snow-covered canyons around which the tiny stone track wound like a thin serpent. There were packs of starving wolves, fearful avalanches, and other unforeseen hazards. They wept and sighed and prayed for his safety and eventually resumed their daily life.

Ali-Baba stayed in Isfahan for many years, going from Master to Master studying various subjects of the traditional curriculum, specialising in the *Sharia* and jurisprudence. He then moved to Teheran armed with certificates and recommendations. He ended up as a High Court Judge and a Law Professor, but that was much later, under Reza Shah's rule. Meanwhile, like Haji Seyyed Mohammad, he bought a house near the bazaar, started his career, begat six children – three girls and three boys – became a haji, etc. ... Soon the two households met and made friends, and some years later they intermarried: Ali-Baba's eldest daughter, Azra, was my mother.

While still a student in Isfahan, overcome by homesickness and need, Ali-Baba had married a young girl whom one of his Masters had found for him. Her name was Agha Begum and she had a fair complexion, blonde hair and grey eyes – all highly appreciated qualities in the South. The Isfahanis are supposed to be converted Jews, and certainly they have the reputation in Persia that Jews have elsewhere: of having charm and a sense of humour, of being shrewd, wordly and 'good at money'. There were countless jokes to illustrate these characteristics, mostly put about by the Isfahanis themselves. One which has remained in my mind is the following: On the first night after a man has died and been buried two angels come to his grave, wake him up and ask him his catechism:

'Who is your God?'
'My God is Allah Almighty.'
'Who is your Prophet?'
'Mohammad, his messenger.'
'Who is your Imam?'
'Ali, God's minister,' etc.

If the dead man answers correctly, the angels escort him to Paradise. If, however, he does not know his catechism or answers wrongly, then he is led to Hell. An Isfahani dies and then two angels duly arrive at his grave to question him. Not knowing his catechism he avoids giving himself away by a cunning piece of lateral thinking:

'Who is your God?' ask the angels.

'I know it, but I'm not telling!'

'Why on earth not?'

'Because I'm wilful!'

No matter how much the angels insist, the Isfahani is adamant. In the end they have to leave him alone and he finds his own way to Heaven. There is a variant on the story today: A man dies and is buried, the angels come to question him, he gives the right answers until they ask him who his Imam is, and he answers, 'Ali, God's minister,' whereupon they pull out two machine-guns and shower him with bullets: he is supposed to have answered, 'My Imam is Khomeini!'

I don't know if my grandmother was of Jewish origin or not, but I recall my father teasing her about it, and her laughing, because she was the opposite of all it implied – guileless and hopeless with money; she was repeatedly swindled by shopkeepers and often ruined herself through excessive largess to relatives and friends.

When Reza Shah came to power in 1925, he started to modernise the country. An important part of his plan was the creation of a proper judiciary, supervised by a Ministry of Justice, with courts and judges and lawyers. Until then, justice, like education, was in the hands of the mullahs and their religious courts. He entrusted the task of preparing a Civil Code for the new Persia to my grandfather Haji Ali-Baba. In the next couple of years, Ali-Baba headed a group of eminent jurists, including an expert from France, and produced a Civil Code which remained the basis of Persia's legal system until the fall of the late Shah in 1979.

The new Civil Code was the brain-child of my father, for by then he had married my mother and his father-in-law enlisted his help to make sure that nothing in the new Code would go against the *Sharia* and incur the wrath of the big mullahs in Qom. This was tantamount to squaring a circle – 'You either chop a thief's hand, and stone an adultress to death, or you don't!' – yet Father somehow managed it, and the result was acceptable to the Grand Ayatollahs. This Civil Code is supposed to be one of the most remarkable legal documents ever produced, comparable only to France's *Code Napoléon*, in its ingenuity and comprehensiveness.

Since 1979 attempts have been made to discredit and destroy it, to go back to religious courts, and the strict application of the *Sharia*, but luckily it has so far been impossible: the edifice has proved too solid, and although, in a post-revolution period, justice is summary – to say the least – at least there remains a basis on which to build a decent judiciary once the mayhem is over. The Civil Code retains the spirit of the *Sharia* while providing a judicial system suitable for a modern society.

Ali Baba's reputation spread not only because of his position but also on account of his extravagant living and eccentric ways. He was scrupulously honest and did not tolerate the slightest infraction of the Law. He would walk through the bazaar with some disciples and issue curses and admonitions to those merchants who had been reported to him as being iniquitous or having overpriced their goods, saying that the wrath of God would fall upon them. Everyone was afraid of him and his violent outbursts, yet loved him for his generosity and his willingness to shoulder responsibility for others. He would weep openly in the middle of the street while preaching justice and charity. Some thought him 'quite mad', others 'just a little eccentric.' His entire life was based on the principle of *noblesse oblige* – for he considered himself a nobleman, even though he was born on the land and had no wealth to back such a claim. He believed that only knowledge conferred authority and led to power, especially in a country where historical cataclysms changed the social structure frequently and drastically.

In the end, he broke under the burden of too much self-imposed responsibility; his stomach ulcers turned cancerous and he died at the age of 60. My mother adored him and mourned him till the end of her life. She used to say a special prayer for the salvation of his soul every sabbath eve – Thursday. She had a photograph of him on her mantelpiece, taken in 1932 on the steps of the Faculty of Law of the new University of Teheran. He is sitting in the centre of the front row next to his French adviser and his assistant, with some fifteen students standing between them. He is the only man still wearing the traditional priestly costume of turban-and-cloak while all the others are in European suits, by then *de rigueur* for all civil servants and university staff. You can tell the French man by his goatee and rimless glasses. My mother knew every one of the fifteen students, the first Law graduates of the university, and would tell me about them: how they had gone on to become important political and legal personalities – Senators, MPs, Ministers, judges and lawyers. 'And now all of them are dead!' she would conclude, with a sigh of regret at our inevitable end and the transience of life.

That photograph, like everything else, was lost in the upheavals of 1979 when houses were ransacked by 'revolutionaries'!

Haji Ali-Baba's Line

If Haji Seyyed Mohammad's progeny were endowed with charm, cunning, social manipulation and sophistication, Haji Ali-Baba's lacked these qualities – except perhaps a certain charm. Instead they were guileless, honest, generous and temperamental, with a streak of eccentricity often verging on madness: the South versus the North, Balzac versus Dostoevsky!

'They are too clever for me,' my mother would say of certain members of my father's family. She meant devious, two-faced, wily, and said so when she was in one of her less charitable moods. 'You never know what they really think; they say one thing and mean another!'

When Reza Shah came to power in the 1920s and began to modernise Persia, he decreed that all citizens adopt surnames and obtain birth certificates. Until then, no one registered the births of their children and everyone had just a first name, followed by some indicative such as a patronym, a title, the profession he practised or the village he came from. Similarly people referred to their birth dates in relation to some memorable event: 'Ahmad was born the year of the earthquake'; 'Mahmood arrived in the spring when late hailstones destroyed the fruit', and so on. A countryman who had made the pilgrimage to the shrine of Imam Reza, the eighth Shia Imam, in Mashhad, was known as *Mashdi*, while the one who had gone as far as Karbala, to the shrine of Imam Hossein, the Third Imam, was a *Karbalai*, and the grandee who had amassed sufficient wealth to visit Mecca was a *Haji*. These titles were followed by the first name and were enough to identify the bearers. Girls were of course invariably daughters or wives or sisters of somebody whose name followed theirs: Fatima-sister-of-Ahmad, or wife-of-Mahmood. Daughters of patrician families were given titles – my mother was 'the Dignity of the *Sharia*', my two maternal aunts 'the Pride of the Age' and 'the Pride of Kings' respectively!

When it became compulsory to have a surname most people adapted their existing patronyms or land titles, or their royal honorifics if they had any. Certain professional callings became famous surnames too, but poor peasants in the country were often at a loss as to what name they should adopt when they were summoned to the nearest town hall for 'name-registration'. They often left it to the clerk at the notary's office to put whatever name he wished, but he soon ran out of ideas and began to invent things according to his whim and mood. Thus some bizarre surnames were in circulation when I was a child: Mr Old was so called because on the day his father had been to see the village notary for the purpose of registering his birth he had looked old and worn out, while Mr Wretched had looked the part when *he* had gone to put down his name.

The scene must have been something like this:

The Notary:	Have you chosen a surname?
The Man:	No, sir, but whatever your Honour will put down will be alright by me.
The Notary:	Well don't make such a miserable face – what's the matter?
The Man:	Nothing, sir!
The Notary:	Alright then; we'll call you Mr Wretched!
The Man:	As you wish your Honour …

Without a trace of humour, my maternal grandfather, Haji Ali-Baba, took the surname of Alem, which means savant, learned, sage. This was less a vain reference to his own qualities as to his scale of values in which knowledge, erudition, wisdom and enlightenment occupied the highest echelons and conferred true nobility. Meanwhile, my paternal grandfather, Haji Seyyed Mohammad, adopted his forebears' professional name of oil-maker, Assar. Little did the two men know that History would scatter their seed all over the world within a couple of generations, and that near the end of the twentieth century there would be Assars and Alems in telephone books from Vancouver to Capetown.

When Haji Ali-Baba died at the age of 60 – before I was born – the grand social edifice he had built by the force of his personality and professional achievements collapsed like a house of cards. It was revealed that his largess and extravagance had accumulated an unmanageable mountain of debts whose interest payments alone were twice his income as an academic and High Court Judge. He had been given unlimited credit by Bazaar merchants and money-lenders (there were no banks in Persia as yet), who had never dared ask to be paid back, for fear of being exposed to his searing wrath and indignation, and to accusations of meanness and usury, since after all he did not spend the money on himself but mostly on public benefaction: all those tons of rice, pulses, preserves; those bolts of cloth and sacks of coal and tins of paraffin, with which half the district's poor had been fed, clothed and warmed, were mostly bought on credit and conveniently forgotten forthwith: 'If a man came to him and said he needed money badly because creditors were at his throat, he just couldn't say no,' Grandma recalled. 'He went and borrowed the necessary sum, gave it to him, and forgot the incident!'

Haji Ali-Baba's body was barely in the grave when all his creditors, who had not dared to come forward before, descended upon his heirs with a vengeance, demanding capital and interest, there and then. His eldest son, Uncle Alem, then a young lawyer, took his body to Karbala, buried it in the blessed grounds of Imam Hossein's sanctuary, and returned home to face the music.

He sold everything to pay off his father's debts: the grand house, the coach and horses, the crystal chandeliers, the antiques, everything ... He dismissed the younger servants by finding them other positions and kept only a couple of old retainers whose livelihood depended on him, and he moved the household into a smaller house uptown.

With his mother, unmarried sister, two younger brothers and a few servants, Uncle Alem was responsible for a still fairly large household. So he began his law practice with all the energy and determination of ambitious youth, and was soon famous both for his ability and his pugnacious championship of worthy causes. But the pressure of work and responsibility took its toll, and as the years passed he became more and more irascible, harsh, subject to bouts of deep depression and hypertension which worsened as he became ever more successful and busy.

Uncle Alem was exceptionally good-looking. His dark almond-shaped eyes, always glittering with intensity and passion, dominated a face of classical proportions akin to those on the ancient friezes of Persepolis. He was tall and slim, and he dressed like a very elegant dandy. His suits were made of the finest English cloth by the town's best tailor; his silk and cotton shirts and ties came from Europe; his shoes were made to measure from his own designs. He had the reputation of never having lost a case, had more clients than he could handle, and made great quantities of money which – like his father before him – he squandered at a phenomenal speed. He kept open house and provided the best food and most lavish hospitality for his guests; he lent money to all and sundry and was never paid back; he organised poker games at his home (there were no casinos in Persia then), at which he invariably lost.

In between money-making cases Uncle Alem took on clients who could not afford his fees; as a result he often ran out of cash and was forced to borrow at high interest and worry himself ill about it.

The tragic flaw in Uncle Alem's character was an uncontrollable, almost insane anger, which made him violent, capable of hitting, maiming, nearly killing anyone within reach. No one knew what triggered off these fits except that he hated hypocrisy

28

and lies – even the harmless, white variety. Unfortunately Persians often withhold information, or say something to please their interlocutor, which strictly speaking would be considered untrue but is in fact an example of wise discretion, designed to placate hostility or bring about accord. A cursory glance at Persia's history is enough to understand this ambivalence towards strict adherence to truth-telling: thousands of years of despotism, both native and foreign, have created a defense mechanism in the Persian psyche, whose varied manifestations include the blurring of fine lines between certain concepts and their opposites! Uncle Alem would have none of these Levantine subtleties; to him, statements were either true or false, and if the latter they would touch a button in his unconscious that would cause him to see red. Paradoxically *everybody* lied to him, out of fear, even otherwise perfectly truthful people, which created a vicious circle. Once he got so angry that he tried to set fire to his house and burn it down with all its precious contents and inhabitants, himself included. The tragedy was averted in the nick of time by my father's intervention, as he was the only man in the world capable of exorcising Uncle Alem's demon and soothing his tormented soul.

Uncle Alem's attacks of violence were usually followed by searing, pitiful remorse. He cried bitterly, made amends with abject *mea culpas*, and by dispensing charm and lavishing presents on his victims. 'You would think it would never happen again!' wailed his devoted, long-suffering valet after his death, 'but, alas, it did, soon enough!' Some unforeseeable provocation would trigger off a new chain reaction and in a split second Mr Hyde would take over from Dr Jekyll.

Yet everyone loved and admired him: my mother worshipped him, and in her eyes he could do no wrong – though it is true that she herself had never been a victim of one of his rages. His relatives, servants and friends loved and feared him in equal measures. To me, he was the first example of a species of human beings I have since met everywhere, who have everything in life to be perfectly happy yet are profoundly discontented, as if existence itself were a burden to them.

Uncle Alem built several houses which he furnished with

impeccable taste, felicitously mixing Persian rugs and antiques with Western furniture made by local artisans to his own designs and specifications.

'What a pity he is not married!' friends commented. 'All this luxury and no wife or children to enjoy it,' and they pressed their daughters, sisters, cousins upon him. Many of the girls in question were secretly in love with him, on account of his good looks and confident manners, but he always found some reason for not marrying. Instead, he kept a mistress, a divorcee, whom he saw at irregular intervals, to the utter disapproval of my grandmother.

Then, all of a sudden, Uncle Alem got married. His bride was an unlikely choice for one of his reputation and temperament, for she was no beauty compared with some of the other candidates, and she was a 'free girl', a 'modern girl'. One of the first graduates of the new College of Midwifery, she worked as an assistant to one of the town's most distinguished obstetricians, at the maternity hospital of the university's Medical College.

'No wife of mine is going to work,' Uncle Alem declared upon proposing to her, and she agreed to give up her career. She produced three sons in quick succession and was content to be a wife and a mother. Aloof, level-headed and wise, she turned out to be the best wife for someone of his fiery disposition. She was forever pouring the cool water of her placidity and gentleness upon his burning heart. Gradually his demon was reasonably tamed, if not completely under control, and his financial affairs were put in order. He loved his sons and found some peace and happiness in watching them grow.

As the head of my mother's family, Uncle Alem played an important part in our lives. Remote and unwordly, my father left all practical matters to my mother who in turn asked her brother for help and advice. But he died fairly young, of a heart attack. When his 'heart condition' – it was angina pectoris – was detected his doctors advised him to follow a strict diet and lead a quiet life, give up smoking and, above all, never, never get angry or worked up to one of his periodical paroxysms of rage. He ignored their advice, continued smoking and eating rich food, and generally behaving as though there was nothing wrong with him. But somehow he was not angry any more, and everyone thought that his demon had been exorcised for good. Then, one evening, he was watching a current affairs programme on television and suddenly he blew up:

'Lies! Lies! Nothing but lies! Bunch of demagogues and hypocrites! They lie through their teeth to fool people and get their votes: why bother, since the elections are rigged and the list of candidates come from foreign embassies? Scoundrels and . . .'

He was dead. His wife tried resuscitation, chest massage, the kiss of life, everything, but he was gone. Luckily he had just won an important case and had not had time to squander or gamble away the money, which his wife invested prudently to bring up and educate their three sons. She sent them to the Lycée and thence to universities in the West, and went back to work herself. Grandma and Aunt Batool, my mother's sister, moved to our house to be with my parents, since they were getting old and we had all left home.

Uncle Alem's death finished my grandmother who went mad with grief and became seriously old. She withdrew into herself and sat on a prayer rug, in a corner of my mother's sitting-room, quietly muttering prayers or simply lost in thought.

'May God forgive my sins and take me!' she would sigh, longing to cease.

'She lays down conditions!' Father would joke, though now more for our benefit than hers, since she no longer could hear or relish his teasing. Her eyesight deteriorated until in the end she was almost blind, which gave her gaze an even more withdrawn, inward expression. Occassionally she had a moment of lucidity: once I had gone home for a visit and suddenly she recognised me and began to ask questions about Europe. I told her that I lived in Paris, in a studio flat, studied, had friends, was reasonably happy.

'Where does your maid sleep if you have only one room?' she wished to know.

'I don't have a maid, Grandma. People don't any more in the West, except if they are very very rich,' I explained.

She looked puzzled and worried for a moment, and then switched off again, as if the matter was too complicated for her to understand. In the end, death came to her as a friend, in her sleep, early one winter night. Her youngest son, Uncle Hassan, sat at the foot of her bed and recited the Holy Qoran from cover to cover, by way of food for her journey to Heaven, tears pouring down his face. When he had finished, it was dawn, her body was taken away and a week later, the mourning ceremonies and rituals completed, she faded away to become just another memory.

My mother's younger sisters, Aunt Batool and Aunt Zarry – Pride of the Age and Pride of Kings – had been married off young to unsuitable husbands; but while Zarry, the youngest, a vivacious optimist of irrepressible gaiety, had made the best of a bad thing and created an adequate life for herself and her family, Batool, the most beautiful and gifted of Haji Ali-Baba's children, had been relentlessly pursued by ill luck. Her husband had been imposed on her by her mother and the pressure of a whole social network, and she had found him utterly repellent from the moment she had set eyes on him on her wedding night. Her whole being had rejected him outright and irrevocably. Plain, effeminate and puny, her groom, a Bazaar merchant, was totally dominated by his powerful mother and two spinsterish sisters known as 'the Two Old Toads'. On her wedding night he had clumsily tried to kiss her, and the touch of his lips had provoked such a violent attack of nausea in her that she had vomitted into the silver chamber-pot by her bed. Nonetheless he had managed to fumble around with her and make her pregnant. Thereafter she refused to be 'touched' by him and they lay side by side, 'like brother and sister', without the slightest attempt on his part to force the issue, hoping that in time she would accept him and submit to her fate. But she never did: passive resistance was not a conscious scheme on her part to get rid of him but an instinctive reaction.

'Oh, but she's a virgin!' exclaimed the midwife nine months later, when she was called to deliver her baby daughter. Apparently this was a common occurrence – virgin girls often got pregnant without complete penetration. 'What a shock! And all the while everyone had assumed that the newly-weds were leading a normal married life!'

A few weeks after the birth of her baby, Haji Ali-Baba died and Aunt Batool went home for her father's funeral and wake ceremonies. She never returned. She requested a divorce, and although women had no right to initiate it and her husband could have refused to grant her one till the end of her days, he was persuaded by Uncle Alem to let her go. He never remarried.

Aunt Batool told me the story of what happened next:

'One day, a few months later, there was a knock on the door – it was the Two Old Toads. They had come to take the baby for a day or two to see her father. I did not even pack any clothes for her, thinking she would be back soon, but when three days passed and there was no sign of the baby, I sent Nanny with the coach to bring her back. The Two Old Toads and their mother refused to hand her over, saying that the baby belonged to her father by law and that nothing could make them part with her. I raged and cried and pleaded and offered bribes, but all in vain. They had hearts of stone and wouldn't relent. It would have meant a lengthy law-suit and in the end they would have won – the law was on their side.'

Generation after generation of Persian women lived miserable lives, locked up in hopeless marriages, in order not to lose their children:

'Once you have children you just sit and bear it, whatever *it* is,' my mother used to say to my sister and myself. Even after the country was modernised and women were emancipated, the laws relating to marriage and divorce remained biased in favour of men for decades, for fear of popular revolt provoked by the mullahs. Eventually, in 1966, the late Shah introduced a Family Protection Law which enabled women to obtain a divorce under certain circumstances without automatically losing their children. As was expected, of all his reforms this one caused the biggest controversy, as it hit the heart of patriarchal supremacy, but he was then at the height of his power and could defy opposition.

'The tears women have shed over centuries of tyranny and bullying by men would run in rivers! Is it not time that some justice be introduced?' he asked in a television speech. Everyone agreed that it was – no one would have dared do otherwise. Who would have believed that only twelve years later the women on whose behalf he had run the gauntlet of disapproval would pour into the streets and clamour for his abdication! Since then these same women have lived to regret it, but 'what is done cannot be undone'.

Aunt Batool was 18 when she divorced, before I was born. Many years later, she received an invitation to her daughter's wedding. After some deliberation she decided to go and take lavish presents. From then on, mother and daughter saw each other regularly as two loving friends. But that early brutal deprivation and subsequent unhappiness had left an indelible scar on Aunt Batool's soul which was reflected in her huge, beautiful eyes, her languid allure and wistful expression.

Aunt Batool was too lovely and accomplished to remain unmarried for long, yet she did, for the rest of her life. 'The thread of her fortune has been knotted by witchcraft,' lamented Grandma, or, 'The Two Old Toads have blackened her fate.' She knew for certain, having been told by Mirza Saleem, the most reliable and skilful of fortune-tellers and magicians in town. It was a complex tale of dark nights in cemeteries and menstrual blood being burnt in skulls, and a dead monkey procured and buried in an empty grave, and endless other recherché machinations, the details of which I have forgotten. Grandma cursed the Two Old Toads night and day and called the fire of hell upon them, but since their fate was no better than Aunt Batool's, it was not easy to assess the efficacy of her imprecations.

Occasionally it looked as though 'the knot' on Aunt Batool's 'luck-thread' was getting unravelled of its own accord, and that the evil spell she had been cast was being removed, but always something happened at the last minute which maintained the unhappy *status quo*: her suitors withdrew, or she decided against them, or an unforeseen event occurred to stop the marriage. She once fell in love with a handsome Army officer who had become a friend of her brother's, Uncle Alam, and frequented their house. It looked as though everything would work out and that they would marry and live happily ever after. Then, inevitably,

Uncle Alem picked a quarrel with the dashing officer and he withdrew his proposal. He did want to marry her, he let it be known, 'but could not cope with her brother's insanity.' Another time a middle-aged aristocrat, recently widowed, saw her at a wedding, fell madly in love with her, and asked for her hand immediately.

'I can't find any fault with him – he is perfect!' declared Uncle Alem, adding, 'And I've accepted his proposal.'

Arrangements for the wedding were made in record time; we were all excited, Grandma was over the moon, Aunt Batool glowed as if a cloud had been lifted from her countenance. But, two days before the marriage ceremony, her fiancé dropped dead with a massive heart-attack.

'You see, when fate is adamant, there's nothing anyone can do,' commentated Aunt Ashraf, who had submitted to her own unfortunate destiny with serenity, in a spirit of Islamic surrender to the will of God. She quoted the poet:

'When misfortune strikes, what is good turns bad;
One disaster becomes ten, and ten is followed by a hundred more;
Fire loses its warmth, the sun its light;
Philosophy becomes erroneous and Logic a lie.'

After the death of her fiancé, Aunt Batool gave up hope; yet she still cared about her looks and spent hours in front of the mirror making up her face, curling her abundant dark hair, adjusting her ornaments. She bought beautiful clothes and European accessories; she plucked her eyebrows pencil-thin and smoked cigarettes in long holders in the manner of the movie-stars of the day; but it was all for the benefit of the mirror and her day-dreams ...

When Uncle Alem died and his three sons went to Europe, Grandma and Aunt Batool moved to our house, and once again our home became the centre of our family life, where we converged as often as we could from all over the world and enjoyed the delicious food, the warm noisy atmosphere and the loving solicitude we could get nowhere else.

Aunt Batool died a couple of years after the events of 1979:

suddenly her generous loving heart just gave out – she had used it too much!

To me, as an adolescent, Aunt Batool, with her forlorn beauty, her tall, graceful figure and her dignified resignation, epitomised multitudes of Persian women of her generation and class: abused virgins, long-suffering wives, deprived mothers and desperate spinsters, all victims of iniquitous laws and antiquated customs based on perverted religiosity, whose beauty and gifts were lost between the Charybdis of emancipation and the Scylla of traditional securities.

My mother's youngest brother, Uncle Hassan, was 14 when his father died. As the youngest of six children, he had been much cherished and spoilt by his father, at whose death he went demented with grief. He mourned him inconsolably and gradually became morose, apathetic, subject to violent mood changes. His eldest brother and guardian, Uncle Alem's reaction to his erratic behaviour was to whip him and beat him into obedience and discipline. But it was of no avail: harsh treatment only pushed the young boy into deeper paranoiac gloom and psychosis, until, one day, soon after he had passed his baccalaureate at the *lycée*, he could stand it no more and just vanished. Grandma was beyond herself with worry. I see her walking about the house wringing her hands and muttering prayers for his safety. She dispatched a messenger everywhere to search for him and bring him back, but he was nowhere to be found. After a while he sent word that he was in Qom, at a *madrasah*, and had become a *talabeh* – a seminarist. His eldest brother was furious, as by then the career of a mullah had become discredited, almost an opprobrium, and held no prospects for a young man of his class, but he could do nothing about it. At the *madrasah*, Uncle Hassan lived the ascetic life of a seminarist, very occasionally showing up in town to visit his old mother: 'He is a little light in the head,' they said about him. 'Not quite right up here!' In fact, he was mildly and harmlessly eccentric, with an aristocratic disdain for 'what-will-people-say'. Grandma worried for him and suffered silently but pretended that there was nothing wrong with his unusual behaviour. We were always pleased to see him: he was gentle and courteous, full of good will towards his fellow men and generous to a fault. He never became a mullah, nor, I think, did he ever wish to. His move to the *madrasah* was more a flight from the harshness and humiliation he had suffered at home than a striving towards an acceptable career. In the West, he would have been a Franciscan monk, for that is how he lived, to the end of his life.

By contrast, Uncle Hassan's elder brother, Haji Ali-Baba's second son, Uncle Hossein, was the real black sheep of the family. Indeed, the consensus of opinion was that he 'had no redeeming features', that 'he was wicked through and through', and that 'he had a tongue like a viper's'. It seemed a miracle that he had avoided inheriting any of his parents' good qualities – he was not even good-looking – but only their defects, plus several nasty characteristics from 'God knows where' – he was *sui generis*! He was ignorant, fanatical, violent and vindictive, duplicitous and mean, without any charm or sense of humour. Yes, I'm afraid you've guessed right: he was a fundamentalist *avant la lettre*! The embodiment of that obscurantist fanaticism which had lain dormant for fifty years, like a deadly virus in incubation, and suddenly burst forth in 1979 to devastate Persia. Needless to say, Uncle Hossein was the only member of the family to welcome the advent of the reactionary mullahs, though by then he was too old and ill to enjoy taking part in the conflagration, and he died shortly afterwards.

'This world is full of sinnnnn!...' Uncle Hossein would declaim stentorianly upon entering our house, usually at mealtimes and uninvited. He would then proceed to criticise everyone for their lack of religious zeal, their less than perfect observance of God's commandments:

'I saw some sheep being led to the slaughterhouse. And what were they doing? They were copulating! Yes, perfectly, that's what they were doing! Climbing on each other's backs as they were being pushed forward, unaware that Death was a few seconds away! I tell you, human beings are no better than sheep – they go on doing it and sinning and sinning and sinning until their last breath, as if there was no Judgement Day, no Retribution! . . .'

'Good for the sheep!' my brother Nasser would wink at us, while we tried to suppress a giggle.

'Look who's talking,' Grandma would mutter under her breath, and go back to her rosary.

'You!' Uncle Hossein would point a finger at me or my sister. 'You are not a child any more, you know. At 9, a girl becomes an adult and is fully accountable for her sinnnnnnns. You should cover your hair when you go out and not look at boys! . . .'

We were bored. Whenever Uncle Hossein came round and started ranting we left the room quietly, one by one, until there was no one left except Grandma, who ignored him completely, far away in her own world. Yet once he had started his sermon he had to complete its trajectory whether anyone listened or not. Everyone tried to keep away from him; even the servants mysteriously vanished. You might think that we should have got rid of him, but in the traditional family structure of Persia that is easier said than done, for one simply cannot discard close relatives just because one does not like them; rather one has to accommodate them, make allowances and accept them, like misfortune.

Uncle Hossein had been a keen sportsman in youth and had frequented the *Zur-Khaneh*, where he had built up his muscles and learnt wrestling and weight-lifting. So, on the very rare occasions that he was in a good mood, he told us tales of famous wrestlers and *pahlavan*s (heroes) of the past. He ate tremendous quantities of food, and looked upon our small consumption with a mixture of disbelief and pity:

'If you eat one spoonful less at each meal, eventually you'll kick the habit altogether!' he once joked to me. It was the only time I ever heard him say anything funny. On the contrary, he usually managed to spoil family gatherings, by arguments and verbal bullying which sometimes degenerated into rows; where-upon he would storm out of the house cursing and swearing and vowing never to return. Alas, return he invariably did, usually to borrow money and treat us to yet another moral lesson.

As luck would have it, he was married to a lovely, sweet,

devoted woman who forever made up for his nasty tongue with her own courtesy and kindness. We all liked her, and put up with him for her sake and for the love of their ravishing little daughter, aptly called Angel.

In my teens, I began to read European literature and soon discovered that the Persia in which I lived was very much like the nineteenth-century Russia described by its great authors. Not only our way of life and the settings, but also the characters were the same: Aliosha, Prince Myshkin, Masha, Natasha, Nina ... down to Gogol's petty bureaucrats and Chekhov's country folk. Later, among the political activists of my generation, I also encountered Stavrogins, Bazarovs, et al. But nowhere were the similarities as pronounced as in my mother's family, while my paternal relatives came straight out of Balzac and Flaubert.

We were much closer to my mother's family than to my father's – except for Aunt Ashraf and a few of our innumerable cousins. But most of my parents' social life was with friends, some of whom became closer, and certainly more cherished, than any relative. But then the cult of friendship, like its corollary – hospitality, is so much part of Persia's ancient and deep-rooted traditions that it deserves a separate story.

Kazem

One of Aunt Ashraf's proverbs was: 'The nightingale produces seven chicks, but only one becomes a nightingale, the others are just starlings.'

Of Haji Seyyed Mohammad's eight children, Kazem, his third son from his first marriage, was to be the Chosen One, destined to become a thinker, seeker and sage.

He was born near the end of the last century in Kazemein, in present day Iraq, and named after the Imam whose tomb in that city is an important Shiite shrine and a magnet for pilgrims. Soon after his birth, the family returned to Persia and settled down in Teheran. He was 4 when his sister Ashraf was born, nearly 6 when his mother died and his father remarried. His stepmother, Amineh, was only 13 and a child herself, but providence intervened in the shape of a neighbour, a childless middle-aged widow, who came and took over the running of the *andaroon* and brought up the children with tenderness and care, all for no material gain, just *ad gloriam dei*.

Lost in a large household with a young, cunning stepmother, Kazem quickly perceived that the keys to survival were discretion and charm. Quiet, obedient, obliging, a keeper-out-of-intrigues, he was nicknamed 'Kazem the Meek', and soon became Amineh's favourite.

By all accounts, Haji Seyyed Mohammad's attitude to his children was that of benign neglect – he left them to fend for themselves in the *andaroon* while leading his own public life in the *birooni*. He married off his children as soon as possible – to get rid of them – the boys between the ages of 16 and 18, and the girls at 12 or 13. This stunted their emotional and intellectual development and, in the case of the girls, even their physical growth. Aunt Ashref, for example, had been married at 12, to a much older widower. By the time she was 22, she was already a widow, with two sons to bring up on her own. Rather than go back to her father's house, as custom required, and put up with Amineh's domination, she had managed to earn a living by teaching, reading the Qoran for people, writing letters, and other such chores. She had retained the physique of a twelve-year-old, so tiny that she had to buy her shoes from children's shops. In those days, people took off their shoes before entering the room, to keep the carpet on which they sat clean. We immediately knew Aunt Ashraf had come to stay when we came back from school and saw her shoes outside my mother's drawing-room: they were the size of a child's shoes, but had a grown-up allure. She herself was like a little girl who had been made up to look like an old woman.

Haji Seyyed Mohammad noticed his youngest son's eagerness to learn and sent him to the local *maktab* (elementary school), where he quickly learnt to read, write and do arithmetic. Soon Kazem was earning his own pocket-money by teaching the same things to other children, and even adults, writing letters and doing accounts for the local shopkeepers, and other such chores. His only other source of income was the one penny a day which he got for heating the bath before dawn for his father and stepmother's Grand Ablutions. Ablution is the ritual washing of hands and face which muslims have to perform before their daily prayers; the Grand Ablution is the immersion of the whole body in water and is obligatory in certain circumstances, notably after sexual intercourse. Given Haji Seyyed Mohammad's penchant for it, he had to perform the Grand Ablution every day before the dawn prayer. Indeed, a man or a woman's sex life could be measured, and would be known to the whole neighbourhood, by the frequency of their visits to the *hammam* (public baths) for the purpose of performing the Grand Ablution. Otherwise, one visit a week was considered sufficient to keep clean. A young bride would be seen at the *hammam* daily until her first baby was born, then gradually her visits would be spaced, and finally, somewhere in middle-age, cease to be a barometer of her husband's energy or affection.

'Mrs X still *gets close* to her husband, you know! She was seen *twice* at the *hammam* last week!' a neighbour would say, and all the other middle-aged women would go green with envy.

Haji Seyyed Mohammad had a private bath and Kazem was assigned the task of heating the water with coal in the middle of the night so that the *Aqa* and his lady could make their Grand Ablutions before the prayer at dawn:

'The servants were up from sunrise to late at night and Kazem was glad of this extra penny with which he bought books and stationery,' Aunt Ashraf recounted, 'but it was hard on him. It meant that he never had a whole night's rest. I used to stay up with him and tell him stories to keep him awake. He would buy me a packet of watermelon seeds and I would shell them for both of us. Sometimes he put his head on my lap and fell asleep; I had to wake him up now and then to stoke the fire. That was the beginning of his long *riazat*.'

Riazat is the austerity, hardship and suffering attendant upon the acquisition of knowledge and enlightenment, the regimen of a seeker-after-truth. All mystics, prophets and saints have had to suffer *riazat* to acquire vision – the inner eye – which sees deeper and farther than any other:

'Didn't the Prophet, peace-be-on-Him-and-His-people, live in caves and eat nothing but a few dates to receive God's message?' enquired Aunt Ashraf, lifting blackcurrant eyes from her darning, creasing her tiny nose to hold her granny glasses, and waiting for a dramatic moment to hear our positive response.

'Not like today, when you are sent to glamorous schools in fancy uniforms, learn foreign languages and everything is done for you, and you behave as though you were doing your parents a favour!' she concluded, a jerk of her elbow expressing all her indignation at the sorry state of affairs in the modern world.

A friendship grew between brother and sister during those nights of vigil that was to last all their lives. It was undemonstrative and found expression in small details: Aunt Ashraf would bring a packet of a special tobacco and light a *qalyan* (water pipe, hubble-bubble) herself, and they would share it over a cup of tea after siesta. She would sew all Father's underclothes and shirts herself, while he discreetly helped her financially and kept an eye on her life.

At 13, Kazem enrolled at the new prestigious Polytechnic College which had been founded on the model of the Ecole Polytechnique in Paris, by an enlightened nineteenth-century Grand Vizier, the first statesman to perceive that Persia had to catch up with the modern world in order to survive as an independent nation. At the Polytechnic, Kazem studied mathematics, philosophy and astronomy. Upon graduation, he started teaching there – mathematics and theology – while continuing his own study of philosophy. Then came the break with his father.

One day Haji Seyyed Mohammad, who had heard of his younger son's success as a scholar, summoned him to his study in the *birooni*. After Kazem had kissed his father's hand and

42

exchanged the usual pleasantries with him and was congratulated on his success, Haji Seyyed Mohammad came to the point:

'Well, now you have a teaching post and a regular salary, it is time for you to get married and settle down. You need a woman to look after you and some children to give you joy.'

Kazem went pale and lowered his gaze. His piety forbade him to disobey his father, yet the prospect of being fettered down with a family, as his two older brothers already were, was too horrendous to contemplate:

'Thank you, sir, for concerning yourself with your humble slave's well-being, but I wish to remain single at present and continue studying. I would like to travel and visit other Masters in various parts of the country, even go abroad, and it would be impossible with a family.'

Haji Seyyed Mohammad knitted his brow and pretended not to have heard:

'We have found you an excellent girl, a niece of your stepmother's, and we will give you a large room in the *andaroon* and a study here. Don't worry about money, I can supplement your income ...'

'No, sir, thank you,' broke in Kazem, this time with a shade of firmness in his tone. 'I simply don't wish to marry.'

Haji Seyyed Mohammad could not believe his ears: Kazem the Meek, the gentlest and most pious of his children, dared to disobey him? He was so taken aback that he did not know how to react, and to give himself time to ponder the situation he dismissed his son with a movement of his hand and a frown of displeasure.

No one asked a girl whether she wished to get married or not, but a boy had to consent. But then, they always did, pressed by biological imperatives and the absence of higher goals. Besides, no man could disobey his father, especially a father of such standing as Haji Seyyed Mohammad. The incident exploded like a bomb and stunned the household.

It was time for Kazem to leave. He packed a few clothes in a bundle and his books in a case, and took lodgings at the nearby *madrasah*. He supplemented his meagre grant from the college with private tuition, and saved all he could to travel later.

In those days, the great Islamic *madrasahs* had a collegiate system, similar to that of medieval colleges in Europe, or indeed the tutorial method at Oxford and Cambridge today. Between the tutor and the student, there grew a bond of love and trust, a Master-disciple relationship which was often closer and more affectionate than that between sons and fathers. The student would work on a subject with his chosen Master, be given a certificate when he had completed the course, and move on to the next Master to study another subject, or a different branch of the same. According to contemporary memoirs, Kazem was always his Masters' favourite, 'on account of his intellectual brilliance, his diligence and courtesy. He combined seriousness with a keen sense of humour, always ready with a joke or a witty remark that diffused tension, yet rigorous and respectful.'

One day he opened his heart to one of his Masters and told him about the quarrel with his father:

'My soul is in torment, because I know I have committed a grave sin by disobeying my father, yet I know that I could not have done otherwise.'

The Master had soothed him with the story of the Prophet Jesus, God's Beloved, who had told his followers to leave their mothers and fathers and follow Him:

'Nothing should impede the soul's pilgrimage towards its goal. One day, your father will be proud of you, for you will surpass him in learning and renown. In time your children will leave you to follow their own paths, which will be different from the ones you would have chosen for them; you too will suffer for it, and that is all in the natural order of things.'

I heard this story one day when I was returning to Europe after a visit to Persia. My mother was crying and my father told her this anecdote to console her. At least now there were things like telephones and aeroplanes ...

At the time of the Constitutional Revolution of 1905–6, the hitherto all powerful clergy were divided into two camps: the Progressives, who saw change towards a more modern, Western model as inevitable and wished to rise with the tide in order to control it, thereby retaining their power, and the Absolutists, who thought modernisation would lead to Westernisation, break down the Islamic fabric of society, and unleash a process which would eventually take power out of their hands. The leaders of the Progressives, or Constitutionalists, were two Grand Ayatollahs, Behbahani and Ashtiani, while the Absolutists followed Ayatollah Kia-Noori. It was their progenies who were to become the educated élite of the country in the decades to come – none was a mullah and nearly all were educated in the West. Even the future leader of the Communist, Tudeh Party was the grandson of Ayatollah Kia-Noori. As the top clerical families had often intermarried, the feud caused havoc in personal relationships. Sons turned against fathers, brothers against brothers, while their womenfolk were caught up in their enmities. My paternal grandfather, Haji Seyyed Mohammad, was progressive and a Constitutionalist, friend and colleague of Ayatollah Behbahani, while my maternal grandfather, Haji Ali-Baba was an Absolutist and supported Ayatollah Kia-Noori, whose three eldest daughters were my mother's best friends all her life.

One day Haji Seyyed Mohammad was walking home from his mosque, accompanied by some followers, when a man jumped in front of him and attacked him with a knife. He was cut in the chest and shoulders before the terrorist – a fanatic Absolutist – was overpowered. A crowd gathered and the victim was carried home on a makeshift stretcher to the cries of *Allah Akbar* (God is great) and 'the Master has become a martyr', etc. Fortunately, his life was saved by the care and skill of Dr Amran, and he was kept in bed while the Revolution raged outside to the ultimate victory of the progressive, Constitutionalist faction. In time, wounds healed, enemies became friends and Reza Shah emerged, like Napoleon after the French Revolution, to unite the country and build up a modern Iran.

As the British had backed the Constitutionalists and the Russians their opponents, Persia became part of the British zone of influence in the struggle between the two superpowers, until the Americans supplanted them after the War.

Meanwhile, Kazem had packed his couple of bundles and joined a caravan for Tabriz, where he was to start studying with a famous Master, who was also the leader of the Constitutionalists in the region. He took lodgings in the *madrasah* and presented his credentials to his new Master. It was not long before a bond of friendship and trust developed between them; Kazem was asked to meals at his Master's house, where he met other notables of the city and took part in intellectual and political discussions.

One day, his Master asked him for lunch alone. After the meal, he confided to him that he had heard of the Russians' plan to enter Azarbayejan in support of the Absolutist faction:

'If they do come, they will arrest and probably kill me, in which case you might get caught in the middle and be harmed too. I think it is time for you to leave for Europe, as you were planning to do later. I will get you a passport and give you some money, and you can join a caravan that is leaving for Tbilisi in a few days. From there you can take a train to France. Come back when things have quietened down.'

Kazem thanked his Master, and said that he would rather stay and share his fate, whatever it might be, but the Master would not hear of it:

'You have a different destiny from mine, which it is your duty to fulfil. But, just before you go, I want to show you something.' He opened the door of a closet filled with books and manuscripts, and from inside a cupboard took out a box. In it was a beautiful flute, wrapped in velvet, which he began to play. So musical was his rendering of the melancholy tune, so warm and sensitive his tone, that Kazem was moved to tears:

'You are amazed that I can play this instrument? I would not dare to do it except in the strictest privacy. As a *Mujtahid*, I would be acused of laxity, if not heresy; yet one must always cultivate the gifts that God, in his munificence, has bestowed upon one. When you become a *Mujtahid*, you will also come up against ignorance and bigotry, and you will have to steer a cautious path so as not to provoke animosity and yet carry out God's will. If you wish to remain a free spirit, a dervish (Sufi), you would do well to avoid becoming a mullah. If you must earn a living, then teach. It's more honourable. A mullah depends for his living upon the contribution of the common people, who are often ignorant and fanatical. I am glad life is almost over for me, but I wanted to warn you against the snares ahead, even though I'm sure you will always know and do the right thing. Now, go, and God be with you.'

The Master said prayers of protection in his disciple's ears, made him cross the threshold of his study under a Qoran he held above his head, and Kazem left with a heavy heart for an unknown future.

A day or two later, the Master sent him a passport and a bag of money by a messenger, and Kazem left the city with a caravan bound for Tbilisi. Soon after, the Russians entered Tabriz, arrested the Master, and hanged him in the Central Square.

Journeys

Il voyagea. Il connut la mélancolie des paquebots, les froids réveils sous la tente, l'étourdissements des paysages et ruines, l'amertume des sympathies interrompues. Il revint.

Gustave Flaubert, *L'Education Sentimentale*

There is a gap in Kazem's story. There were no witnesses and he seldom talked about his past, except when pressed by us, the children, or in anecdotes used judiciously to illustrate a point or make a joke. We know that he travelled by train through Russia to Vienna, where he stayed for a few days in 1906, and thence to Paris:

'You are all so wild about Paris,' he would say in later years. 'I don't know why. Now Vienna – that was a beautiful city!'

'That was fifty years ago, sir?' we would reply.

Perhaps the memory of Vienna was sweet because of a pretty

young woman he met on the train and made friends with. Perhaps she showed him her town, took him to those famous cafés frequented by artists and intellectuals. What an effervescent place Vienna must have been in those days, teeming with creative genius which was to help shape the twentieth century! Perhaps the atmosphere it generated imbued the city and got through to the heart of a lonely young traveller. Whatever it was, the memory of Vienna remained vivid and lovely for him.

In Paris, Kazem improved his French quickly and started his studies of philosophy at the Sorbonne. He struck up a debating friendship with Georges Clémenceau, whose lectures at the Collège de France he attended. But, unlike his Masters in Persia, the great statesman was too busy to see him in private and take him under his wing. Money was the big problem, as always. Nothing from home, and what he earned from private teaching was insufficient for anything but the most precarious living.

In Persia meanwhile, the Revolution had ended in favour of the Constitutionalists. A Parliament – *Majlis* – was created, and order was gradually returning. Kazem thought he could go back and sort out his finances, perhaps get a grant, and return to Paris for good. Upon arrival, he went straight to his father's house, kissed his hand and asked forgiveness for his past disobedience. He was received as the prodigal son: his father had not been insensitive to Kazem's reputation and the praise of his Masters. The nightingale among the starlings of his progeny had flown away, but it had sung in other glades and the strains of its melodies had floated back home from time to time.

Haji Seyyed Mohammad now found that he enjoyed intellectual discussion with his younger son, something he had never indulged in with any of the others. Anxious to get rid of them as quickly as possible, he had only succeeded in stifling their natural gifts. Luckily one had slipped through the net, as sometimes happens, for History shows that civilisation and progress often gain through the achievements of 'the one who strays'; freedom flourishes on heresy.

On the eve of his departure for Paris, Kazem had a dream which changed the course of his life radically: he dreamed that

Imam Ali came to visit him and said: 'Why go to Paris? Why not come to me and be my votary?' Great statesman, philosopher and warrior, Ali is the patron saint of the Sufis and occupies a special place in the heart of Muslims of all sects. The *madrasah* of his shrine in Nejef, Iraq, has always been a great centre of traditional learning. In those days, some of the most learned Masters taught there, and Kazem joined the first caravan of pilgrims leaving for the holy cities of Iraq.

Dreams and omens played an important role in people's lives in those days, and my family was no exception. They were instruments of vaticination, used as guidelines for conduct and decision-making; they provided hope and an escape from the rigid frame of bigotry; they were agents of free will against the forces of determinism and predestination; they were part of an apparatus of varied devices used by the Persian psyche to accommodate a religion that was fundamentally alien and uncongenial.

In later years, people would bring their dreams to my father for interpretation. According to traditional knowledge, there are two kinds of dreams: false or true. False dreams are the result of indigestion or debris of the day's events, while true dreams are a guide to the depths of the psyche and, as such, portents or directives. Together, they encompass both modern and ancient dream theories, including the latest, put forward by certain behaviourists, that dreams are the refuse discarded by the mind during sleep and have no meaning at all. Only an *Alem* – learned man – could distinguish between true and false dreams and see through barriers of superstition.

For the next decade or so, Kazem led the life of a seeker at the shrine's *madrasah* in Nejef, and obtained the highest qualifications. Although soon he was a *Mujtahid*, he stayed on to lead a monastic life, and concentrated on philosophy. Eventually, he was to be considered Persia's last great traditional philosopher, in the line that ran from the Greeks through Avicenna and the Islamic Neoplatonists to their successors in the nineteenth century.

At the *madrasah*, Kazem led a life of *riazat* – asceticism: he lived in a small cell, with a mattress and a pillow, the rudiments of cooking facilities, and his books. He could afford one candle a month, which he used at dusk to consume his frugal supper. He slept during the dark hours and woke up when he heard the muezzin's call to prayer at dawn. He read, wrote and prayed; he taught and his reputation spread; he was content. Years later, when I visited some monasteries in France, I realised how happy he would have been as a monk, had he been born in a Christian country. As it was he became a dervish – a Sufi.

Tales of his *riazat* were told to us by Aunt Ashraf, and occasionally he alluded to it himself: once when our table was laden with a variety of delicious dishes whose colours and aromas dazzled the eyes and whetted the appetite of our guests, he said:

'When I had the appetite of youth, there was nothing to eat. Now that I have no appetite, there's all this display!'

Why did he return to Persia? I never learnt:

'Perhaps just to produce *you!*' he joked once, when I insisted on knowing. By the time he arrived back in Persia, the country had changed. The Qajar era was over and the new Pahlavi dynasty founded. Reza Shah, who had risen in the ranks of the Army to become first Chief of Staff, later Prime Minister and finally Shah, was in power. He had emerged during the years of post-Revolution chaos, pacified the rebellious tribes, secured Persia's territorial integrity, wrested concessions from the British and the Russians, and begun to rule the country with an iron fist. He wanted to shake Persia out of centuries of stagnation, build a new society on a Western model in record time, and educate the largely illiterate population. He decreed that Persians should look back not to their recent past but to the glorious pre-Islamic era of Persian empire – Firdowsi's *Shahnameh* (*The Book of Kings*) should be their source of inspiration. The first obstacle to remove from his path was the power of the clergy; from now on, they would have to render unto Caesar and concentrate on their religious duties. Their traditional costume became a symbol of reaction, and all but a few professionals discarded it. The veil would soon be abolished, women would be emancipated, and endless other reforms would drag the country out of the Middle Ages into the twentieth century. He declared that Persia be called Iran – the land of the Iranians, which is what Iranians themselves had always called their country. Persia was the name given to Iran by ancient Greeks and later by other Europeans.*

With his qualifications, Kazem could have made a meteoric career in the religious hierarchy and rapidly reached the very top to become the Grand Ayatollah, especially since he was one of the very few *Mujtahids* in whom Reza Shah believed, being not only a theologian but also a philosopher and an *Aref* (Sufi):

'He is a learned man and a sage, not like the other mullahs, who are a bunch of frauds and parasites,' the Shah is reported to have said.

But Kazem did not want power, nor did he wish to accept the compromises it inevitably entailed. He wanted to lead the contemplative life of the Sufi and the philosopher. Luckily, soon the University of Teheran was founded – the country's first Western-style university, modelled on the Sorbonne. It gathered Persia's intellectual élite, many of whose members were graduates of Western universities. Kazem was invited to take the Chair of Philosophy.

Later Reza Shah established the Royal Academy – modelled on the Académie Française – my father was one of its founder members. One of the tasks the Academicians were assigned was to find words for the new concepts, scientific expressions, technological terms, that had entered the language. They looked through classical Persian authors and poets, and whenever they could not find a suitable word for a new concept, they devised one. They purified the Persian language from unnecessary foreign imports and from all the Arabic formulae introduced by the mullahs for the purpose of obfuscation and mystification of their flocks. Many words in current usage in the Persian language were found by my father – im Saadi, Hafiz, Nezami, et al. . . .

Decades later, when he retired, his Chair was taken by an

* Throughout this book I have used Persia in preference to Iran, because of its linguistic and cultural connotations. We speak about Persian language, poetry, carpets, miniatures, cuisine. Alas 'Iran' and 'Iranian' at this particular juncture, evoke nothing but negative images. The Persia I recall is no more, but it is closer to 'The Land of the Nightingale and the Rose' than to that of the Hezbollahis, in Teheran or Beirut.

eminent philosopher, Dr Hossein Nasr, author of numerous books on traditional Islamic philosophy. It is a measure of how things changed within a generation that he was not a product of the *madrasah*, but a Harvard graduate who did not write his books in Arabic or Persian as philosophers had done for centuries, but in English!

The Wedding

❧❧

Haji Seyyed Mohammad and Haji Ali-Baba: two more different men could hardly be imagined, the one intelligent, shrewd, hedonistic, the other imbued with the Northerner's simplicity of mind and heart – the cunning and sophistication of the bazaar versus the candour and nobility of the land. Ali-Baba wore the white turban of the Sheikh, while Mohammad sported the black one of the Seyyed – the descendants of the Prophet.

Haji Ali-Baba's eldest daughter, Azra, was 17 when Kazem returned to Persia. She had unusual looks: blonde hair, grey-green eyes, high cheekbones and a very fair complexion, 'just like a *Farangi* [European]'. In reality she looked rather Russian, an impression enhanced by her intensely emotional and fiery temperament. She had had many suitors but her father had refused them all – they were 'not good enough for her!'

As soon as the two men met, Ali-Baba fell completely under Kazem's spell; he was impressed by his erudition and captivated by his charm.

'I have found Azra's husband,' he declared upon arriving home that evening. The snag was that Kazem had no wish to get married. On the contrary, he planned to lead the life of a celibate, ascetic philosopher and Sufi.

'I'm honoured by your generous interest,' he rejoined, when

his future father-in-law offered him his daughter's hand, 'but I am in no position to marry, as I have no proper job and no money.'

'Nonsense!' retorted the Sheikh. 'I will give you both!' He was not a man to be contradicted, the offer was tempting and timely, and Kazem's resolve was broken.

'Oh, it was the grandest and loveliest wedding of the year!' recounted Aunt Ashraf. The story of my parents' nuptials was one of my favourites when I was a small child, and I often begged Aunt Ashraf to tell it.

'The preparations took months, at the end of which she had a fantastic trousseau – the finest rugs from Kerman and Kashan, gold-studded leather chests containing her clothes and linen – all finely embroidered – brocade spreads and wrappings, glass from Bohemia, china from France, and a large samovar from Tula (in Russia). She had enough for a whole house, although at first they were going to live at your grandfather, Haji Seyyed Mohammad's house.'

'Then what happened?'

'Then came the wedding which lasted three days and three nights. The first day was devoted to the *Aqd* [the marriage ceremony and registration]. At dawn they brought the *Ghoncheh*. Now you probably don't know what that is, because it is going out of fashion among you modern people, but in those days it was part of the festivities. It consisted of two big trays, one containing coloured seeds arranged in decorative abstract patterns, the other a long flat bread, equally decorated with saffron and other vivid colours, and together they symbolised prosperity and fertility. The *Ghoncheh* was ordered from specialists in the Bazaar, and sent over with trays of cakes, biscuits, sweets and fruit arranged on silver dishes. Porters carried the enormous trays, precariously balanced on their heads, in a procession through the streets, followed by crowds of noisy urchins. It was displayed in the drawing room, around the bridal seat. When everything was ready and the guests arrived, they brought in the bride and sat her in the middle of the room on a *soozani* [an embroidered mat] in front of her wedding mirror, flanked by two candelabras and a glass lamp, to give light and happiness to the couple's life together.

'Then the groom's party arrived, headed by Haji Seyyed Mohammad, his secretary, and the mullah who was to perform the ceremony. Your mother sat there reading the Qoran while her younger sisters rubbed two pieces of block sugar above her head on a scarf. The sugar is supposed to make her life sweet ever after. Presently the mullah read the marriage contract from behind the door, and asked the bride if she agreed to it. When she said, "Yes," everyone cried, "God be praised," and the party began, for the women in the *andaroon* and for the men in the *birooni*. It wasn't like today when men and women are all mixed up together!'

'What happened the next day?'

'The next day was the public feast, when all the poor of the district were invited to a meal. They brought their containers, which were filled with delicious rice and stew, and went away to eat it with their families and pray for the couple's happiness and good health.'

'And the third day?'

'Ah, that was the wedding proper! There was a sumptuous dinner for family and friends. Again outside caterers were hired – cooks, assistants, waiters. They arrived with cartloads of huge pots and pans and serving dishes. Smoke from the charcoal braziers drifted high above the roof of Haji Ali-Baba's house, streaked the turquoise-blue firmament, and filled the air with the aromas of barbecued lamb, spicy stews and saffron rice. The whole neighbourhood was abuzz with excitement and shared in the festivities. It was wonderful!'

On the wedding day, the *hammam* (public baths) had been rented exclusively; the women went in the morning and the men in the afternoon. My mother had been taken there, washed, rubbed with rosewater and made up with powder and rouge. She was dressed in white satin and lace, and wrapped in her black *chador* – it was several years before the veil was abolished. Her father had covered her in gold and jewellery, as an investment to be used in emergency or later to buy a house. Bangles jingled on her wrists and forearms; gold necklaces and chains, hung with sovereigns and half-sovereigns covered her chest, and her fingers flashed with rings. Her father ordered the most beautiful four-horse coach from the royal stables, complete with liveried footmen and grooms, and a fleet of lesser vehicles and droshkies for the guests to ride the short journey to the groom's house:

'I can see him standing outside his front door,' went on Aunt Ashraf, 'tears pouring down his cheeks, throwing fistfuls of *noql* [tiny pieces of almond coated with sugar] and silver coins to the crowds that lined the street. Urchins scrambled to pick up the coins while he showered more and more handfuls on them, until the bag was empty and the cortège had disappeared round the corner.'

At its destination, the nuptial room had been prepared with the bride's trousseau. She sat on a brocade mat, ready to receive the groom. One by one the female guests kissed her goodbye:

'May God give you many sons,' 'May your household be blessed,' 'May God's shadow never leave your heads,' were some of their valedictory blessings.

It was customary for an elderly relative – in this case, the old nanny – to remain outside the nuptial room. Sometime during the night, the door would be opened and the groom would give her a blood-stained handkerchief, proof of his bride's virginity. If, by any chance, the bride had turned out not to be a virgin, she would be sent back to her father's house, the marriage contract would be annulled, and her life thereafter blighted by opprobrium and dishonour. At other times, there would be cover-ups: stories were told of the knightly gallantry of husbands who had cut their own fingers to produce the necessary few drops of blood and save the honour of their wives. Other tales told of bloody battles that had resulted from a girl's dishonour and engulfed whole families for generations. Sometimes the bridegroom would be too nervous, chivvied by the presence of the old woman waiting outside and the rest of the family not far off, and would fail to 'perform'. His excruciating misery and humiliation the next morning can be imagined. But such customs were already considered barbaric by the educated people and the upper classes, and my father had sent the nanny to bed with a tip before entering the nuptial room, certain of his wife's virtue.

Left alone, Azra began to pray. Presently the door opened and the groom entered. My mother had never seen him, of course, except once, when she had caught a glimpse of him through a window as he was entering the *birooni* to visit her father. She had exclaimed: 'Oh but he's so *old*!' Sharp glances had darted towards her like poisoned arrows and put an end to her comments. Nor had she ever been consulted about her wishes as to her future husband. At the wedding ceremony, the mullah had spoken the marriage formula, Will-you-take-this-man-as-your-husband, etc. and she had answered, 'Yes,' but then no bride in known memory had ever said, 'No.' There were instances of the bride being quite adamant – if the groom was a relative she had seen and disliked, or if she secretly desired another. But surrounded with threatening parents and relations, the prospect of dishonour and scandal, she had always ended up by saying, 'Yes,' only to regret it for the rest of her life. Why anyone bothered to ask the bride at all was only because Islam, in fairness to women, had insisted upon their consent, and so consent was duly extracted by hook or crook.

My mother told me the rest of the story herself . . .

'Father came in and greeted me with a *salam* [hello – peace be on you]. I was supposed to say it first, being his wife, but I could not open my mouth with nervousness. He then sat beside me on the mat, and took my hand, kissed it and said:

'Well, young lady, what brings you to our part of the world?'

That made me laugh and the ice was broken. I thought well what if he's a bit old? He *is* kind and charming, so perhaps I will like him . . .

In fact he was 23 years older than her, but she fell in love with him that night and loved him single-heartedly for the rest of her life. He died a few years before her, but she continued communicating with him through dreams and prayers: every night he came to her while she slept, as ever soothing, consoling, guiding her as he had done throughout their lives together.

My mother's old nanny stayed on with her for a few weeks to show her the ropes and give her moral support, then she returned home, leaving her to manage on her own and be absorbed into the *andaroon* life.

Eventually my mother sold her gold and jewellery, and with the proceeds my parents bought their first house. By then no one had separate *andaroon* and *birooni*, just one house divided into two spheres:

'We were so happy then,' mother used to reminisce wistfully. 'Your father helped me to cook as I learnt by trial and error, before we could afford a proper cook, and he shared the chores. Nowadays you modern people think it is natural for your husbands to help you, but in those days it was unheard of! Everybody was jealous of me, seeing how lovingly he treated me. He taught me everything I know about the world.'

Of all the beautiful objects my mother had in her trousseau the finest was a filigree gold and tortoise-shell toilette set – Haji Ali-Baba's personal gift to his son-in-law. It consisted of a gold tray, with three gold bowls of varying sizes fitting into each other, a shaving brush of tortoise-shell decorated with gold, a mirror and a tortoise-shell comb framed with gold, all most delicately made. My mother did not display it, but kept it hidden in a box, and locked in a cupboard with other family documents, photograph albums, and a few objects of sentimental value. She kept the key to the cupboard always in her handbag. Twice she showed me the toilette set, and I remember marvelling, even as a small child, at the beauty of the design and the delicacy of its execution. Of all family heirlooms that disappeared in the events of 1979 – stolen, looted or sold for a pittance – it was the loss of that gold and tortoise-shell set that I most regretted, for in my memory it symbolised my parents' union.

On my last visit to Persia in 1977, my mother gave me a few pieces from her trousseau: her French wedding lamp, painted with cherubs whirling among the clouds, a Bohemian glass water-pipe which I have converted into a lamp and which was made specially for the Qojar king, Nasserudin Shah, and her samovar from Tula. Everything else has gone. But it matters not, compared to the loss of innocent life other families have suffered from the revolution. I have often wondered where the filigree gold and tortoise-shell set now is. I was told that, soon after the revolution, Japanese antique dealers came to Persia and bought everything cheaply from those who had looted the houses. So I would like to think that today it is displayed in a Japanese home among other beautiful works of art.

The Blind Midwife

❦

*El mayor delito del hombre es haber nacido.**
Calderón de la Barca

'It was one of those harsh winters when the snow stays on the ground until *Norooz* [the spring equinox on 21 March, which is the Persian New Year].' Aunt Ashraf was recounting the circumstances of a family event which had taken place some ten years earlier.

'It was a yard deep, and where people had swept it off their roofs it had formed little white hillocks in the streets. We had to dig tunnels to go out.'

Persian houses had flat roofs then, built of timber, clay and straw. The rain ran over them and spilled from the edges, but snow settled and had to be cleared away before it froze, lest it should seep through the clay when it thawed and cause cracks, even collapse. Men climbed on their roofs as soon as snow stopped falling, armed with *paroos* (long-handled wooden shovels), and swept it off on to their gardens and the street. Then they ran a *qaltac* (a heavy cylindric stone with a handle) over the surface to tighten the wet clay. If you walked in the streets at dawn, and looked up, you could see a man on each roof-top, frenetically 'snow-sweeping' the white powder which showered like a cloud, tinged into a rainbow by the rising sun. The traffic

---

* Man's biggest crime is to have been born. (From *Life is a Dream*)

of coaches and carts – and, in later years, cars – melted the snow on the roads and furrowed the ground with deep muddy ruts; at night these froze solid, and made walking difficult and hazardous. When eventually roads were asphalted, the situation improved, but in those days nobody ventured out after sunset following a snowfall.

'We had to send a droshky to fetch Zivar, the midwife. But where to find one on a night like that? Eventually we saw one in the Army Square. There it stood, on the far side, like a ghost coach, with its owner wrapped in a black cloak sprayed with snow, nodding in his seat, and the horses chaffing and exhaling jets of steam into the frozen air. We had to pay him treble the usual price even for that short distance. The ground was solid ice and the poor horses slipped and got frightened and neighed and baulked, but we finally got to Zivar's house near the South Gate, where she lived with her eldest son and his family.'

Zivar was the most famous midwife of the day. Nobody knew where she came from or how she had trained, doubtless the way everyone learnt his or her trade in those days – through apprenticeship. A young woman who wanted to become a midwife would follow an older one around, help and observe her perform, and gradually learn the skill. When the older woman retired or died, the younger one would take over her clients.

But no midwife had ever achieved Zivar's reputation, although, by the time of Aunt Ashraf's story, she had become old and blind:

'Yet she was so experienced that she did everything by touch. She ran her hand over a pregnant woman's tummy and predicted exactly what day, even what hour on that day, the baby would be born. Sometimes, when the birth seemed imminent, she would say, "Don't panic, there's plenty of time." At other times, when the pains had barely started, she might order: "Quick! Quick! Get me some boiling water and a towel. I've got a couple of minutes." What is more, you knew that, in her hands, both mother and child would be safe. She had never delivered a stillborn baby, nor had any mother in her care ever died of post-natal fever.'

Childbirth at that time was a spectators' sport. Close female relatives came and sat around the labour room, and went through the parturient woman's contractions with her, offering prayers, invocations and encouragements: 'May God deliver you from your pain ... May Imam Ali, the Commander of the Faithful, give you forebearance ... May the Prophet's daughter come to your rescue ...' Extra hands were called in to provide meals and serve refreshments; neighbours would send their servants to enquire, and a general atmosphere of drama pervaded the house.

'Persians turn every event into a drama and every drama into a crisis,' was one of Aunt Ashraf's aphorisms. Meanwhile the baby's father would be waiting anxiously for news in another room, or in the old days the *birooni*.

I witnessed a traditional childbirth in the 1970s, when I was travelling with the Bakhtiari tribes of southern Persia on their spring migration from their winter quarters in the plains to their summer pastures in the mountains. Tucked away in the high hills of the Alborz Range, far from city amenities, tribeswomen gave birth as Persian women had done from time immemorial, as my mother had given birth to me.

I was woken up one night by the sound of footsteps outside my tent – someone hurrying past with a hurricane lamp, women whispering and rushing. I came out and enquired what was going on, they told me that a woman was giving birth nearby and asked if I wished to be present. Of course I did.

The tribeswoman was in advanced labour: she was crouching in the middle of the tent, over a layer of ashes and was pushing hard, supporting herself by pressing her hands on her knees. The ashes provided an antiseptic soft cushion for the baby to fall into and a sponge to absorb the fluids. The tribeswoman pushed and pushed, encouraged by the 'midwife' – just an older neighbour – until the baby's head appeared, which the midwife held while the rest of the baby slithered out. Soon came the afterbirth, and within a few minutes the umbilical cord was cut and bandaged with a strip of cloth torn from an old rag, the baby was wrapped up and put to the breast, the ashes were cleared away and everyone went back to sleep. The next morning at dawn the tribes moved on. I came across the young mother on the brow of a hill as she was climbing the rocks nimbly, carrying her newborn baby in a cradle on her back, as agile and gay as a little deer. I wondered how she was feeling, after her ordeal of the previous night:

'Oh *that!*' she said. 'I've forgotten all about it!' and giggled off, her voluminous tinselly skirts swishing and flashing, like a butterfly fluttering in the sun.

City women were not so close to nature, and for them childbirth was a much more hazardous adventure. It was assumed that mother and baby might perish in the process, or as a result of later complications – and they often did, hence the ominous, dramatic atmosphere.

'This baby has no wish to get out!' declared Zivar, upon feeling my mother's tummy. 'I can't say I blame it, the way the world is changing and on a night like this! I'll have a snooze next door and come back when it's time.'

It was around midnight that Zivar reappeared, asking for boiling water and some hot ashes, and with her deft healing hands eased my way into this world:

'You yelled heartily and we all said you were a cheeky noisy little girl, but from then on you were the quietest and happiest baby in the world!'

It seems that the rest of my life has been an apology, and an attempt at justification, for that first *faux pas*!

During my mother's labour, my father was in his study, praying for a safe and speedy delivery. Nanny rushed in with the news and was given the traditional tip – a gold sovereign. Later, when the room had been tidied and Mother put to bed, he came in to see her. My parents had already three children, two boys and a girl. When the boys were born, Father congratulated Mother with a quotation from Firdowsi's *Book of Kings*:

'Sufficient unto women is the art of

Producing and raising sons as brave as lions'

My sister was a welcome variety, and 'such a pretty little girl'. I just happened.

Would Father have preferred a boy, as men always did in those days? I once asked him: 'Not because boys are better, but because women suffer more. One worries about their future; one wonders into whose hands they will fall ...'

I was born into a new and rapidly changing Persia. The veil had already been abolished and women were emancipated; they could go to school and university and take up professions. By the time I grew up, other freedoms and equalities were taken for granted and more reforms were planned to balance the law in their favour. Yet many found it hard to accept these improvements and adjust their attitudes.

'God knows how far women will go once they start enjoying their liberty' was the reason for apprehension. Certainly I caused my parents endless trouble, with my radical adolescent politics, my settling in Europe and subsequent marriage to an Englishman. Perhaps my father foresaw all this at the time of my birth; perhaps it was all 'written on my brow'? Ah, that writing on the brow! They said that, when a baby was born, an angel wrote its destiny on its forehead with an invisible ink, and that nothing anyone later did could alter it.

Fortune-telling charlatans played on this belief and claimed that they could read what was inscribed 'on the brow' and change it with potions and talismans. As a philosopher, my father was no Determinist, and did not believe in any of this superstition; nothing was 'written' and no one could foretell the future since we make it as we go along. Naturally, such factors as heredity and circumstance play a part, but basically we shape our own destinies. And, of course, there is always prayer, communion with He who ultimately decides everything: the perennial problem of reconciling human free will with the will of God.

'Man is free and has no excuse'; 'You are not born a woman, you become one,' etc ... Twenty years later, like many of my contemporaries in France, I found Existentialism the most congenial of the prevalent ideas. Sartre, Camus, Simone de Beauvoir, et al. became our gurus, shaped our minds and influenced our behaviour. Of course, over the years we would modify our attitudes, but at the time we were totally captivated. Man is alone and free! We thought that it was a hard philosophy which left no room for alibis, but that it was also optimistic, favoured hope for change and improvement, and spurred to action.

But, in Persia, the 'writing on the brow' was considered irrevocable. A famous story, of which several versions exist, illustrates this belief. Here is Aunt Ashraf's:

'At the time of Khalif Haroon-Al-Rashid in Baghdad, a man saw the Angel of Death in the Bazaar. As no one sees the Angel except at the moment of death, the man realised he was about to die. Yet the Angel had a very quizzical expression on his face and motioned to him with astonishment, as if to say, "What are you doing here?" The poor man panicked and ran to the Khalif's palace, crying:

"Oh, Commander of the Faithful, send me away from here by your flying carpet so that I can escape from the Angel of Death. I have just seen him in the Bazaar, and he beckoned to me, but I ran away and came to you for help." Haroon-Al-Rashid felt sorry for him and ordered his flying carpet to take him to Samarkand, several thousand miles further east, in the confines of Persia. A few minutes later, he arrived and went straight to the caravanserai, where he rented a room. Presently the muezzin called to prayer and he went to the nearby mosque to pray. There, to his horror, was the Angel of Death, waiting for him at the entrance. The Angel smiled and said: "I'm glad to see you! I was told to come and take you away at this hour in this place and, when I saw you in the Bazaar in Baghdad an hour ago, I wondered if I had not made a mistake. How *did* you manage to keep your appointment?" '

Over the years, scholars and mystics came to see my father from all over the world, among them a famous Indian yogi, when I was a year old. Apparently he did have an extraordinary power to foresee the future, for he gave a broad outline of every member of our family's destiny. When my turn came he shook his head and said:

'She won't stay with you long … her life is elsewhere.'

My mother laughed incredulously:

'Oh yes, she'll marry the Governor of a Province or an Ambassador and travel …'

The Yogi smiled and said no more. Perhaps it is all 'written' after all!

Soon after I was born, the first College of Midwifery was founded by Reza Shah, and its graduates took over from old-fashioned midwives, at least among educated classes in cities. Maternity hospitals mushroomed all over the country, staffed by locally trained or Western-educated obstetricians and nurses.

Uncle Alem married one of the first graduates of the College of Midwifery, and her boss at the hospital, a celebrated Professor of Obstetrics at the University and a surgeon, offered to deliver her first baby at home.

The baby was late, forceps were applied a fraction too late, and it was dead on arrival.

'Oh, where is Zivar!' my mother lamented. 'She never delivered a dead baby!'

'Yes, it's these *Farangi* doctors with their grisly instruments, who kill babies,' Aunt Ashraf was convinced. 'What is wrong with human fingers that God has made soft and malleable for the purpose of easing the baby's passage? If God wanted metal hands to be used, He would have made our hands of metal!'

The great obstetrician evidently learnt his lesson for, many years later, he delivered the Crown Prince – the present young Shah in exile – safe and sound, this time applying the forceps before the baby had stopped breathing!

My father wrote down my name and date of birth on the last page of an ornate Qoran, below those of my brothers and sister. That Qoran disappeared with other family heirlooms in the events of 1979 when my brother's house was looted. Ostensibly they were confiscating ill-gained goods, but nothing was more pure and innocently acquired than that Holy Book.

I was Zivar's last baby. She was old and already retired – I was 'a favour'. Her reputation endured long after her death, and was embellished with many stories of miraculous births and spectacular resuscitations and uncanny healings. Eventually she entered that twilight realm where myth and reality merge. Not surprisingly her name, Zivar, meant 'ornament'.

The First House

After their wedding, my parents had joined the household of my grandfather, Haji Seyyed Mohammad, where my mother was given a room in the *andaroon* and my father a study in the *birooni*. But she was too guileless, as well as independent, to fit well into the complex structure of women's quarters, and it was not long before she was totally bewildered by its web of intrigues, jealousies and subtle power games which she neither could or wished to play. She became mutely unhappy and one evening, feeling slighted in a parlour game by her stepmother-in-law, Amineh, she retired to her room and cried bitterly. Exhausted, she fell asleep and was woken up by her husband when he came in. Noticing her swollen eyes and kohl-streaked cheeks, he asked what had upset her so, and she told him.

'We'll move,' he said, and meant it.

The very next day they set about looking for a house and found one behind the bazaar. They paid for it by selling her gold and jewellery – except the filigree gold and tortoise-shell toilette set and her prayer ring of no great value. This was a green agate set in gold and carved with the first verse of the Qoran, 'In the Name of God the All-merciful and Compassionate'. (Traditionally prayer rings are made of agate, it being suitably hard for carving.) She gave it to me last time I saw her. It is too big for me and I never wear it, but I cherish it and in my dreams of her she is always wearing it.

The house they bought was fairly small, with a courtyard and a central round pool. Soon after they moved, my parents had their first baby who died within a year, of what sounds like diphtheria. Smallpox vaccination was beginning to spread among the better-off people but no other immunisation was yet available. As a result, infant mortality was extremely high, but if a child survived beyond the age of 7 it meant that his immune system was robust enough for a long life.

My parents were inconsolable at the loss of their first baby, yet as devout muslims they submitted to the will of God and saw loss and pain as part of a higher design. But acceptance does not alter suffering, it merely averts rebellion, and while my father allowed his sorrow to express itself against a background of surrender to God's will, my mother's pagan soul rebelled at the fundamental iniquity of the human condition – she cried profusely.

One night she had a dream (yet another one!) in which Imam Ali came to visit her:

'I knew it was Him because he had a halo and light shone from his countenance. He put his hand out and touched my eyes saying, "Grieve no more! God will give you another son soon, and he will be good and make you proud." I woke up still feeling his touch on my face and his perfume in the air, as if he had just left the room. Sure enough I was pregnant within a month and your brother Nassir was born safe and sound.'

True to the Imam's promise, Nassir turned out to be everything that an eldest son should be: intelligent, kind, dutiful; he was the only one of us to remain with our parents, except when on diplomatic missions, and at the end risked his own life and lost all he had by staying in Persia for as long as possible after the events of 1979.

By the time I, the last of four children, was born a decade or so later, my parents had decided to move to a larger house in a better area of the city. So I remember very little about the first house – only a couple of sepia-coloured images remain, one of which relates to the circumcision ceremony of my younger brother, Nasser.

According to Islamic and Jewish laws, all baby boys have to be circumcised and this is usually done in the first couple of weeks of life. In those days, the man who performed the operation was not a doctor but the village barber, who also extracted teeth and executed other minor surgery, such as lancing a carbuncle or pulling out an ingrown toe-nail. But in towns and among the educated classes a specialist was called in who, although not a doctor, was a skilled craftsman and a thorough professional. He would arrive with his bag of tools, spread a leather mat on the floor, cover it with fine ashes, spreadeagle the boy on it and cut off the foreskin in one clean swift movement. Then he would roll it up, tie a piece of cloth around it, and sprinkle some warm ashes on the wound to help it heal. Warm fine ashes were the penicillin-powder of folk medicine, an antiseptic drying agent to be used in all circumstances.

If for some reason, such as post-natal illness, circumcision was postponed, it was considered better to wait till the boy was old enough to be talked into it and accept it willingly. The boy would suffer for about a week and go around in a loincloth instead of trousers for a month until the wound healed. Nasser was not circumcised as a baby, perhaps because of my mother's post-natal illness. He was 8 or 9 before he was 'done', and much too clever to be talked into something so painful and disagreeable. He was told he would not be a *real* man until he was circumcised, that it was a religious duty, that it was not difficult, etc. but he would not hear of it. On the day of the ceremony he just vanished. Servants were sent out to search for him but they could not find him anywhere. He had taken refuge in the house of a friend whose father betrayed him and he was brought back, kicking and screaming. My father talked to him and soothed him, but at the last minute, when he saw the blade approach his 'vital parts', he wriggled himself free and bolted. Finally he was caught, held down and circumcised. In a few minutes, the ashes-covered mat was cleared away and the party began. Nasser was showered with presents and complimented on his becoming 'a man', and a brave one at that!

Certainly this was to be the first of a series of tribulations, the beginning of Nasser's *riazat*. The most intelligent and gifted of the four of us – the nightingale among the starlings – he was to suffer from numerous childhood sicknesses, and later, as a young struggling artist in Paris, he had to pay his dues with poverty and hardship before recognition came.

I can see him in his loincloth, thin and wiry, dashing around like quicksilver, playing in the courtyard, brimming with concentrated, irrepressible energy. Then the image dissolves and we are in the new house.

Our House

❧

*Ô Maison, Maison, pourquoi m'avez-vous laissé partir!**
Oscar Milosz

In the first decade of his reign, after subduing the rebellious tribes and unifying the country, Reza Shah began a programme of modernisation designed to make Persia a modern, sovereign state. He started by improving the capital, Teheran. Streets were widened and surfaced, electricity replaced oil and gas lamps, squares were laid out with statues and fountains and flowerbeds, and gradually the physiognomy of the city was transformed. One artery near our house was called Electricity Avenue, because electrification of the town had started there. It had previously been Avenue of the Gas Lamps, having been the first to be fitted with them. Telephone and telegraph systems were installed, and the town began to spread beyond its ancient gates. Soon, better-off families moved northward to the foot of the mountains where the air was fresher and water more abundant. The big mullahs who had opposed Reza Shah's plans were silenced and the Bazaar, which was their power-base, began to lose some of its importance. Those *Bazaaris* who could afford it moved uptown, building themselves new houses in fashionable and salubrious areas, leaving the hot and dusty quarters behind the Bazaar to the poor and the disenfranchised.

My mother, who had soon discovered that my father 'couldn't handle anything except books', took all the practical aspects of life into her own hands. She dealt with staff, workmen, shopkeepers and, having been swindled repeatedly by crafty merchants, soon became ruthless at bargaining. I recall being embarrassed as a child when out shopping with her. For example, she would ask the price of a yard of silk crêpe de Chine.

'Two pounds,' would answer the salesman, adding 'for your Ladyship only, otherwise it would be three pounds and is in fact worth four.'

'Two shillings,' Mother would pronounce somewhat indignantly, and start walking out. The salesman, aghast, would call her back, plead with her to be reasonable, swear by the Holy Prophet and the Twelve Imams that it had cost *him* a pound a yard, and ask if she did not wish him to make a small profit and feed his poor family.

'Alright then, four shillings,' Mother would respond, pretending to relent. Eventually a compromise would be reached and she would buy the cloth for ten shillings a yard – a quarter of the original asking price and apparently at a considerable loss to the merchant!

'Don't you believe it!' she would say later. 'These shopkeepers would take the skin off your back if you let them. I *know* them!' This should have taught me how to bargain, but I was too shy to attempt it and am still hopeless at it. Later on, prices were marked on goods as in the West and bargaining disappeared in fashionable shops, but it continues to this day in markets and bazaars all over the Middle East.

As soon as my parents decided to move uptown – Mother went house-hunting and soon found one, much larger and prettier, behind the *Majlis* near the University's Faculty of Letters where Father held the Chair of Philosophy. It was in a cool leafy residential area named after a nineteenth-century nobleman whose mini-palace was now the Swiss Embassy.

The High Street was bordered with plane trees and watered by a stream. Water, always a rarity in Persia, was the most sought-after commodity: it implied coolness and lush vegetation and shade against the torrid heat of summer. The colour blue in Persian is *abi*, literally 'watery colour'. Perhaps the unique translucent turquoise-blue of Persian tiles and faience is the expression of a deep longing for a necessity always scarce and often unobtainable. Perhaps the precious turquoise stone itself is related to the climate, since nowhere else in the world has turquoise the deep warm luminosity of the Persian variety. An English traveller (Robert Byron, in *The Road to Oxiana*) relates how, thirsty and tired while crossing the Central Desert in Persia in the 1920s, he came upon a man carrying a blue water jug on a donkey: the touch of scintillating blue on the prevailing fawn made him understand why blue is *abi* in Persian – the colour of water.

Our new house was a two-storey building with ornate wrought-iron windows and high outer walls decorated with brick patterns at the top. It had spacious rooms and high ceilings, downstairs vaulted in the Persian classical style, upstairs flat and decorated with painted plasterwork, from which hung crystal chandeliers. Its inner walls were thick, and insulated the rooms from extremes of heat and cold. There was a long loggia supported by slender Corinthian columns along the front of one section of the house, which was set back from the rest and overlooked the large garden whose ancient trees soared above the walls. The reception rooms and my father's study were upstairs, the living quarters downstairs, and in between near the entrance door was a room for my father's valet, Ali, who answered the door and received visitors.

The Chief Mullah of Teheran lived nearby in a house similar to ours, while other notables – diplomats, university professors, high-ranking officials, an Army general and a couple of Qajar princes – many of whom were friends and acquaintances of my parents – lived in the surrounding streets. Families of the lower bourgeoisie had smaller and more modern homes.

My mother decorated the house with beautiful carpets, lace curtains, coloured crystal shades and chandeliers, a few antique ornaments, and some beautiful objects for the eyes to rest on.

At the beginning, like most peoples who have evolved from nomadism and are used to carrying their possessions from place to place, Persians lived in uncluttered homes: you sat on the carpeted ground and, at mealtime, spread a tablecloth on which you placed the food, sat around it and consumed your meal. At night you spread your mattress and slept, and in the morning you rolled up your beddings, wrapped them up into large cushions which were placed around the room – or the tent – to lean against. Thus the same space was used for a variety of functions – sitting-room, dining-room and bedroom. I have often wondered if this is not a more rational way of using space, now that it has become so scarce. Certainly in Japan I noticed that many families are discarding their Western furniture in favour of the traditional Japanese variety, dividing their living-space with curtains and mats. But in our house, as far back as I can remember, the furniture was Western-style, with tables and chairs and sofas. Although Aunt Ashraf and Grandma still preferred sitting cross-legged on the floor, I never learnt to sit cross-legged and still can't.

From her room, the focal point of our family life, my mother ran the house forcefully and efficiently, though with much fretting and wringing of hands, like a capable general with a big regiment and scant amunition. She had to sustain the way of life of a *grand seigneur*, keep open house and provide unstinted hospitality, all on a professor's salary – a miracle she somehow managed to perform fairly smoothly. My father meanwhile stayed in his study, often invisible behind piles of books, and was called down for meals. He was a warm, affectionate but remote godhead we all worshipped and relied on.

As we grew older, we children were given separate rooms upstairs. My sister and I shared a large room overlooking the garden, while my brothers occupied another room, behind the loggia. Our room had a closet which we used as a wardrobe, and to store our expanding stock of books and, much later, gramaphone records.

My parents lived in that house for the rest of their lives and I lived there until I left for Europe in adolescence. But over the next two decades our district changed: the grand families moved further north, to the new rich suburbs at the foot of the mountains, while the lower bourgeoisie moved in. The old houses were subdivided, or pulled down and new ones built on their sites, in a variety of hybrid Western styles – depending at which European or American university their architects had trained. In the end, only three houses remained – of which ours was one and the Chief Mullah of Teheran's another – as a testimony to an authentic Persian style of architecture amid a horrendous welter of pseudo-Californian villas, many-storey appartment blocks and lesser dwellings, all utterly unsuited to the climate of the country and the way of life of its people. The hundred-year-old trees were cut down to provide more building

71

land, each house was replaced by several, and the green canopy formerly seen over garden walls disappeared. But that was due largely to over-population and not peculiar to Persia.

After 1979, our house was occupied by 'sitting tenants', mostly relatives of servants who had joined the bandwagon of the so-called revolution, and finally, after my mother's death a year later, it was sold for a pittance. Soon it was pulled down and I am told that several characterless boxes have been built on its foundations.

For me that lovely house is the very setting of Memory. It was the focal point of our large and varied family and circle of friends. Had we kept a visitor's book during the years of my childhood it would read like a roll-call of Persia's historical figures: prime ministers, parliamentarians, academics, Army chiefs, students, as well as humble folk who came to see my father, brought him their problems and sought his advice and help. They always left happier and richer than when they arrived. He put his knowledge, wisdom and position at the disposal of whoever was in need of them.

But we did not keep a visitors' book, and now we are left with nothing but memories.

The Garden

I said that when I reached the
Rose Garden I would pick an armful
of blooms to present to my friends.
But when I did reach it the perfume
of the Rose made me so drunk that
I forgot my promise.

Saadi

The most attractive feature of our house, and the one that had
won my mother's heart when she had first seen it, was its large
and beautiful garden. It had a rectangular pool in the middle and
a smaller, round one on the side, beneath the loggia. Grassy
expanses surrounded the central pool, bordered with flowerbeds
fringed with old box-hedges and an abundant variety of climbing
roses of all hues. Ancient pine and plane trees spread their
swaying shade over the display in every-changing patterns. In
spring, the roses and sweet brambles in full bloom foamed over
the hedges, curled round the tree trunks and spilled over the
lesser plants in exuberant abandon, like diaphanously veiled
dancers in a frenzy of movement. They filled the air with subtly
varied perfumes and harboured a population of bees and
butterflies and birds. A paved path weaved around the house and
garden, opening out in the front to a wider area where rugs were
spread in early spring so that we could sit and savour the balmy
air, the ravishing roses and the warm sunshine.

Beyond the main garden was an orchard with cherry,
greengage and apple trees, and, on the ground, beds of mint,
chives, parsley and other herbs. Opposite the kitchen window an
old grapevine twisted its gnarled trunk around a pine tree and
spread its foliage over a trellis. In spring and summer, cooking
preparations were often done in the shade of the vine which
produced a rich crop of the most delicious musk grapes in
autumn. My sister and I used to wrap the bunches of green grapes

in newspaper bags we made ourselves to protect them against the birds until they were ripe.

All over the grassy expanses, large earthenware pots of jasmine and smaller pots of gardenias were strategically placed so as to exhale their exquisite scent over the whole garden during the summer; the jasmines yielded a daily crop which the breeze scattered over the lawns like little white bows on a green velvet dress. Every morning, my father would gather some in a blue plate and bring it to my mother at the breakfast table, where the steam from the samovar enhanced their scent. My sister and I used to string them into garlands which we hung around our necks or wove in our hair.

My mother, whose artistic talents had not been cultivated in a formal way, became an artist of life, and among other things made our garden. She had a greenhouse built on one side, near the smaller pool, to protect the delicate gardenias and geraniums in winter. She chose the plants and flowers in the spring and the bulbs in the autumn, and had her design executed by our gardener. He was one of the gardeners of the University who charged very little for his services and got on well with her. They shared a love of plants and of growing things, and he did not mind her exacting standards. The result was that blend of wildness and control, achieved by subtle hands gently guiding nature, which the lovliest gardens alway have.

In most European languages, the words 'garden' and 'paradise' are related to the ancient Persian word '*paradaiza*', meaning 'the Lord's Enclosure'. In Persia, where rainfall is limited to a short season and water is always scarce, making a garden traditionally meant creating a personal paradise, a reflection on earth of the Garden of Eden. It expressed the soul's aspiration to eternal peace and beauty. Persian rugs, with their stylised birds and plants, were originally a representation of Paradise, and even the Flying Carpet of fairy tales was related to the longing for return to Eden.

The Persian gardener's aim was to produce an atmosphere of *safa*, which means 'serenity', but has connotations of coolness, relief and beauty. The traditional Persian garden, home of the nightingale and the rose, celebrated by poets and writers throughout the centuries, was the expression of a national genius whose other manifestations were rug-making, miniature-painting and poetry. Alas, few of the great gardens of the past remain today. More fragile than verse or painting, they have not survived the country's turbulent history. Yet, even today, everyone tries to make his or her own *paradaiza* as best he can.

In summer, our garden was watered every afternoon late, when the sun had left the ground and a cool breeze tempered the heat. The precious water came from a reservoir beneath the lawn and was used parsimoniously to feed the plants, and sprinkle the grass and paving stones. The gardener filled his two watering-cans at the pool which was connected to the reservoir by a hand-pump. Sometimes we children, with our friends and cousins, would pump the water, giving a hundred strokes each, to help him and have fun. In those days, the city had no underground supply system and water came from the mountains in open tunnels, called *joobs*, through the streets. People diverted it to their houses through tiny openings. When dry, the *joobs* filled with litter and next time the 'water came' you had to let it run for a while to clear it away. Reservoirs were filled at night, when the water was at its cleanest.

Once a day, the 'waterman' brought our drinking-water from a mountain spring near the city. He had a huge barrel on a horse-drawn cart and filled our earthenware narrow-necked pitchers at its tap. Some people said that the 'waterman' never went to the mountain spring but filled his barrel at a reservoir in town. But Mother didn't believe it. Certainly we never caught typhoid or any of the other infectious diseases which were rife in those days.

On the whole, the sharing of water was very civilised; no one took more than was needed to saturate the garden, fill the pool and the reservoir. Yet it was not unknown that, in less patrician neighbourhoods and in the country, quarrels broke out over water among those whose survival depended on it. Even cases of manslaughter were sometimes reported.

The *joobs* water was anything but germ-free, and epidemics of different sorts broke out periodically – typhoid, diphtheria, gastric flu ... Then, in the 1950s, when money from oil began to flow, the government embarked upon the construction of an underground water system which would bring clean spring-water from the mountains to the city. No one believed it would actually happen – cynicism about government promises was the bedrock of jokes and satirical sketches – and 'the water system' became a euphemism for lies and false pledges:

'Oh it's a load of water system!' people would say, or, 'Don't you believe so-and-so, he talks a lot of water system!' But it was eventually built and suddenly every household had a supply of germ-free delicious mountain water permanently on tap.

There was no longer any need for deep pools and reservoirs. They took away the hand-pump and filled our pool with cement, turning it into an ornamental blue-tiled pond only a foot deep, and filled it with goldfish. The reservoir was redundant and got rid of too. The garden was watered with a hose and sprays, the lawns were kept dew-fresh with sprinklers. But by then I had left the country.

So much of our time was spent in the garden that it is the scene of some of my happiest memories. I rode my tricycle – an imported novelty – endlessly along the paved paths; I played with the kitten under the vine trellis and day-dreamed behind the hedges; I made up stories about exotic places and strange creatures to entertain my sister and our friends. We skipped and raced, played hopscotch and ball games, hide-and-seek and marble games – we had not a care in the world.

From the tall windows of my room, I watched the parade of seasons as reflected in our garden. In winter, heavy snow covered the trees and hedges, and most of the birds disappeared, leaving only the crows, with their nests hidden among the high branches of the pine and plane trees. Sometimes, the garden itself vanished beneath a thick blanket of snow which had fallen silently all through the night. We made 'icebergs' with bowlfuls of clean snow shot through with fruit essences or molasses; we played snowballs; we fed the odd sparrow rummaging around in the orchard after the thaw.

Spring arrived with *Norooz* – the New Year. Snowdrops and crocuses peeped through everywhere, swallows began to return from the South and rebuild their nests in our eaves. Soon, flowerbeds were covered with strong-scented narcissi and flamboyant tulips, irises and asphodels. Water came once a week and filled the little channels by the roots of the box-hedges; trees were teeming with birds – sparrows and robins and thrushes. Sometimes, in late spring and early summer, we had a visit from the nightingale: suddenly, amid the chatter of garrulous birds, its sweet trill would ring through the air. Mother would lift her index finger to her lips and hush everyone; we would listen in rapt silence until the song was over, then slowly resume our conversation. But spring is a short season in Persia, lasting only a few weeks: 'Like youth, it's over before you can bat an eye,' as Aunt Ashraf often quoted.

In summer, daises were put on the lawn at dusk, covered with rugs and cushions, and we spent the evening in the garden. We always had guests for dinner and sat up late consuming quantities of fruit and soft drinks before putting up the mosquito-nets over the daises, spreading the mattresses inside and going to bed. Sometimes in June, before we left for the country, even the garden was too hot and we slept on the roof, which was always pleasantly cool. At four thousand feet, the sky was so close and luminous that we could see by the light of the stars. We would sit up and talk, or listen to Nanny tell us stories. I used to think that if I put several long ladders on top of each other I could reach the Milky Way, and follow it to the end of the world.

During the day, you had to stay indoors, let down the blinds and switch on the electric ventilators to keep cool. Before they filled up the pool and made it shallow, we often bathed in it before lunch. My father had taught my brothers to swim and my sister had learnt to dog-paddle by herself, but I was terrified of water and watched them from the side. Drowning in pools was a major cause of infant mortality in those days. The scenario was always the same, with slight variations: everyone in the family would go to sleep after lunch; but soon The Child would wake up, get bored, and go to play with the goldfish in the pool. After a while he or she would slip in and drown. To avoid such a calamity in our house, my mother had instilled the fear of water in me. It was so strong that I have never managed to get rid of it completely, although years later I taught myself to swim.

Autumn was also a short season, with dusty winds, violent storms and heavy showers. Suddenly the trees lost their leaves, the swallows left for the South, and the gardener took in the pots of geranium or gardenia. He cleared away the dead leaves, planted bulbs and covered the pool with planks to prevent it from freezing through and cracking. His daily visits stopped and he just dropped in twice a week. The garden looked sad and denuded, the sparrows rummaged anywhere for food. There was melancholy in the air and anticipation of a long cold winter.

One autumn day, when I was 11 or 12, an event occurred which in retrospect has acquired a metaphoric dimension: Uncle Alem, my mother's eldest brother, came to visit us. In the course of the conversation, he suggested that we change the design of our garden, make it more spacious by cutting down some of the trees and taking out the box-hedges:

'Make it less dense, more open, like a French garden,' he summed up. He had seen photographs of what in France is pejoratively called 'municipal gardening', with conventional flowerbeds and patches of grass, and wanted to create something similar for us. My father, who was one of the few men in the whole country brave enough to stand up to Reza Shah, never dared contradict my mother! He acted on the belief that one should stand firm on certain essential principles but be flexible and give in on less important matters for the sake of peace and harmony. So he did not interfere with the running of our daily life and left it all to my mother. In this case, he knew that the plan would be irreversibly disastrous – those hedges had taken fifty years to grow, those trees a hundred years to reach their height – and he mumbled a few words advocating caution, but he met with deaf ears and did not insist. My mother herself was dubious, but she adored her brother and could never say no to him.

Soon workmen arrived with saws and axes, cut down trees, including all the fruit trees in the orchard, leaving just a few pine and ornamental trees to stand guard over the desolation, like sentinels above a battleground. Then they uprooted the box-hedges and rose-bushes and sweet brambles. Instead of looking bigger and uncluttered the garden looked smaller, bare and helpless, like a naked body. My mother regretted her decision immediately but said nothing; my father shook his head but tactfully held his tongue, and Uncle Alem looked peevish. Suddenly a piece of gratuitous vandalism had destroyed fifty years of growth, like a random bullet cutting down a young life. And it was done with the best of intentions, in the name of 'modernity'. My mother immediately set to work, with the help of the gardener, to try to rectify the damage. The old hedges and rose-bushes had gone, but she laid down lawns and flowerbeds, planted new roses and ornamental trees. Over the years, whenever I went home for a visit, the garden looked better, prettier and more luscious, but it never regained its past splendour. It was like looking at a loved face that had altered. Years later, I found gardens in England, whose mixture of wild, poetic abandon and sophisticated design, reminded me of our old garden in Persia.

To me, the destruction of that garden is a metaphor for the negative aspects of rapid Westernisation, just as its positive side has enabled me to sit here today and tell the tale. Why did my Uncle think that a French 'municipal patch' was better than an authentic Persian garden, similar to those that had inspired poets and mystics for centuries, unless the sudden strong impact of an alien culture had shaken his native judgement?

Over the years, I have seen far grander and more beautiful gardens, mostly in Britain, yet to me that first garden in Persia remains unique, the lost paradise of childhood. I do not have a garden now, only a terrace, but I seem to have inherited something of my mother's green fingers, for the jasmines, roses and gardenias I have planted in tubs flourish, and together with honeysuckles and geraniums produce the colours and smells of those far-off days – they are my '*petites madeleines*'!

Sometimes, on summer evenings, I sit alone among my plants to savour the mild air and watch the moon rise over London. I remember the old garden, the blue pool, the swaying pine and plane trees. I can almost hear the sweet trill of the nightingale, the magical bird who came so rarely and one day left never to return, as I did.

The Household

By the time we moved to the new house, our family had reached its final size: my parents, their four children and a permanent staff of four. My father believed that, with every new child, an extra hand was needed to help my mother. It would be pejorative to use the word 'servants' in relation to our staff. Rather, they were members of the family and so much part of our lives and affection that I have no memory without them. They loved us and we loved them; they did their work and we did ours; there was no conflict of interest, though there were, of course, plenty of quarrels and scenes.

Nanny, who took over the cooking when we grew up, was a widow who came from Damavand, a valley in the mountains where we spent our summer holidays. She dressed in traditional peasant costume: a flowery dress over baggy trousers and a white kerchief pinned under her chin. She donned a light *chador* when she went out, which was seldom. She had the rosy complexion and keen eyes of mountain people, a sweet smile and an angelic temperament. She was simple and devout, in constant wonderment at God's ingenuity and the world's beauty: a bumble bee, a flower, the sweetness of a melon, everything would elicit 'Wows' and 'Ahs' of appreciation from her.

In summer when the rose-bushes were in full bloom, Nanny used to go round the garden looking at them, smelling them and praising God for His munificence. There was a heavy-scented pink variety called 'Mohammad's Rose' from which rose-essence and rose-water were extracted. She would put her nose to the most luscious bloom, breathe in deep the heady perfume, and exhale a pious invocation: 'Praise be to the Holy Prophet and His People!' At that very moment, a bee, hidden among the petals, would sting the tip of her nose. Her screams would resound through the garden, followed by pandemonium. Someone would try to extract the poison by squeezing her nose – more cries of pain, more general fuss. For the next week or so, Nanny's nose would be the size and colour of a beetroot, with the porous texture of a heavy gin-drinker's:

'Every year the same thing happens, Nanny. Why do you do it?' we would ask.

'Don't you marvel at God's canniness? The way He puts scent in the rose so that the bee is attracted to it and produces honey? You eat the honey at breakfast but you don't want to praise the Honey-Maker?' Soon she would forget the incident and the following spring repeat the performance, overcome by the flamboyant luxuriance of the rose-garden and its inebriating scents.

Ali was my father's valet and general factotum. Whenever Nanny was away or unwell, he took over the cooking as well. He came from a village in Azarbayejan which was famous for its pomegranates, and spoke Persian with a heavy Turkish accent. We teased him about it and exaggerated his malapropisms and inarticulacy. He was bad-tempered but good-natured, bossy but loyal, and he ran the house efficiently though grumpily. When he eventually married and left us, he brought over a cousin from his village and trained him to take over his job. By chance, he too was called Ali, and so over the years we had a succession of Alis (because if they had different names we changed them to the simple Ali), who would arrive as uncouth country lads and leave a few years later as trained and well-spoken service staff.

Ozzie was Nanny's daughter and the general maid. She was pretty and simple-minded, shy and relentlessly pursued by bad luck in later life. Her first marriage to a cousin ended in divorce: her mother-in-law suddenly remembered that her son and Ozzie had been breast-fed by the same wet-nurse and were, therefore, siblings. Their marriage was consequently incestuous and against the *Sharia*. The village mullah, a particularly bigoted specimen, had decreed so, and nothing my father or any other *Mujtahid* could say would make a difference. Ozzie was sent home. Without her virginity and no dowry, her chances of a good second marriage were almost nil. Nanny wept and 'chewed her heart' and lifted her arms to Heaven in supplication. Eventually her prayers were answered, and Ozzie remarried. Her new husband was a baker and very 'good to her', but Ozzie's spirit was broken and she became sickly. She was always complaining of some ailment or other, so in the end Nanny left us to live with her and look after her.

Zahra was my own young nanny and later our general housekeeper. She came from the Caspian region and was remotely related to my maternal grandfather, Haji Sheikh Ali-Baba. She was an orphan, having lost her father before she was born and her mother when she was 10. When her mother had realised that her illness was fatal, she had brought Zahra to Teheran, left her with my mother, and gone back to her village to die. At first Zahra had been devastated by her mother's 'desertion', but gradually she had accepted her fate and got attached to the family. When I was born, she immediately adopted me as the object of her affection and care. She used to tie me to her back as she went about her chores, cuddle and kiss me, clean and dress me, and play with me. At night, she told me endless stories – of jinnis and ghouls, princes and princesses, dragons and mythical birds. She it was who first told me about the *Seemorgh*, the all-seeing, all-knowing ruler of the birds' kingdom who dwells on the summit of Qaf Mountain and whom the great Sufi poet Attar describes in his *Conference of the Birds*. There were other, more sinister creatures she knew about: the *Pa-lees* (foot-licker), for example, who was like a horrible hairless dwarf and licked the feet of sleeping travellers in the desert until they bled, then he drank their blood until they died. There was also the *Bakhtak*, a heavy bear-like humanoid who crept up to you while you were asleep, lay on top of your chest and pressed it hard until you died, then he ate you! I believed every word she said and visualised the horrible, bloodthirsty creatures; many a night, I woke up in terror, feeling the *Bakhtak* in the room, about to jump on my chest and squeeze me to death. I would scream and Zahra would come:

'I won't tell you any more stories if you're going to be silly and cry!' But it was all so irresistibly exciting when the lights were on and she was sitting beside me ...

Zahra often talked about the Caspian region, its mild climate and orange groves, its vast forests that covered the mountains behind the shore, above all the sea itself, so mysterious in its immensity. She also told me her mother's story:

'When my father died, my mother sold our patch of land and became a coolie, a farmhand in summer and a hawker in winter. She bought household goods in a market town and went selling them from village to village. She walked miles and miles every day, sometimes even through the night, with me tied to her back, a thick walking-stick in her hand, and two baskets of goods hanging from her shoulders. She became known in the whole region as 'the Lioness' on account of her fearlessness and strength. In those days, the whole region was covered with dense forests teeming with wild animals – leopards, panthers, bears, wild boars, snakes ... But 'the Lioness' was not afraid to take short-cuts through the woods, even at night when the animals were out prowling. One night, she came face to face with a black panther; it was pitch-black, and all she could see were two huge green eyes scintillating like emeralds. She froze and stared at the beast. After a couple of minutes, which seemed like an eternity, the panther turned round and ran away ...'

I adored Zahra and felt sorry for her being an orphan and all alone in the world. She set me an example of devotion and loyalty as hard to find as to renounce. She married one of our Alis who died a few months later in an accident, leaving her pregnant. After her daughter was born, she remarried, 'for her sake', and produced two more sons. Soon she was widowed again, but, undaunted, she trained and practised as a nurse, brought up her children, gave them a good education, and, when they were all happily settled, she retired.

Apart from these four, we had a number of other, part-time helpers. They came to give a hand with spring-cleaning, with the flood of visitors at *Norooz*, or if we had large parties. None worked for money alone: they always claimed that it was an honour to work for my father and turned down better-paid jobs to do so. In later years, after I had left Persia, the oil boom and new industries created a large and rich middle-class for whom the shortage of domestic staff was a permanent problem – and a very boring subject of conversation. In the end they would import Filipinos, Afghanis and Pakistanis, paying them vast salaries. My mother had great difficulty in finding staff she could afford, and was forced to employ 'new people', 'people who work for money!' Some of their relatives became 'sitting tenants' after the revolution of 1979. Only one was persuaded to leave on the principle that his prayers would not be acceptable if performed on unlawful ground. The others were less scrupulous, and for them revolution was a licence to loot. But is that not what most revolutions are all about these days: power and possessions changing hands, evil shifting grounds?

Ali Gets Married

When Ali first came to our house from his Turkish-speaking village in Azarbayejan, he hardly spoke any Persian. He knew nothing about city life and, like ninety per cent of the country's population, was illiterate. By the time I was born, he had become an accomplished cook – trained by my mother – an efficient valet/butler, and he practically ran our house. In his drive for literacy, Reza Shah had decreed that all schools be open in the evenings as adult education centres, and Ali, like countless other young men, availed himself of this facility.

By the time I went to school, Ali was in his twenties and getting more and more bad-tempered. He was irascible and blew up at the slightest provocation. He bullied everybody and even began to tell off my mother for 'wasting too much money on entertainment' and *his* precious time!

'You know what's the matter with him, don't you?' Aunt Ashraf quizzed my mother one day. 'He wants a woman. Of course he is too shy to say so in so many words but he is letting you know through ill-humour and volatility.' She offered to broach the subject with him and Ali agreed immediately that, now she happened to mention it, he would like to get married!

Soon word got round that Ali was looking for a wife, and several girls were suggested to my mother through the usual channels of information – the local shopkeepers, the staff of the *hammam*, marriage-brokers ... As Ali had no relatives in town, my mother undertook to sort out the candidates and make the necessary arrangements. She saw a few girls and eventually chose the sixteen-year-old daughter of a shopkeeper, to whose parents she proposed on Ali's behalf. She sent word to the family to expect her visit and asked Aunt Ashraf to accompany her. Ali's envoys were received with the utmost courtesy and warmth, and after the preliminary exchange of pleasantries, the girl was called in to be given the once-over. Mother told the family that Ali was a good man, honest and hard-working, though somewhat autocratic and stubborn, which was 'not surprising in a Turk!'

It was clear that the girl's parents were delighted to give her away and would have accepted the proposal if Ali had been Jack the Ripper! Their daughter was 16, far from being an oil-painting, and it would be a calamity if she stayed on the shelf. A pink-and-white complexion was valued above all else in a young girl – the whiter the skin, the higher her price. But, as it turned out, Ali's future wife had an exceptionally dark complexion, hence her parents' eagerness to get her married. Many years later, when sunbathing and acquiring a tan became fashionable, a dark complexion ceased to be a handicap: if Swedes and Germans cooked themselves in the sun to acquire the brown skin that God had given to most Persian girls, it couldn't be too bad, people thought.

'What's she like?' Ali wanted to know, when Mother and Aunt Ashraf came home.

'She is very modest, that's for sure, because she didn't utter a single word! She never even lifted her eyes from her toes – not once!'

'That's good! Who wants a wife who talks? She might get it

into her head to answer back!' said Ali, timidly adding, 'Is she pretty?'

'Well, with a bit of powder and rouge she could be ...', Mother ventured cautiously. 'Her skin is a bit dark, but I suppose it'll improve once she puts on a bit of weight ... Anyway, I've warned them against your filthy temper, so that they can't blame me later for misleading them! I hope marriage will improve your character Ali; you're a bully and a tyrant!'

Ali's room was between the two floors of the house, near the front door, whence he could monitor all comings and goings, and hear Father call. It was refurnished for his nuptials with a new rug and the bride's modest trousseau of bedding, a chest, a small samovar, a few ornaments ... Mother gave a party and invited family and friends; we were all very excited and Ali could barely contain his happiness. He had supervised the cooking himself and, when everything was ready, he had gone to the barber and thence to the *hammam*. He had dressed in his new suit and splashed himself with rose-water and donned a tie. He was ready.

'How handsome you are!' Aunt Ashraf teased him. 'Pity your temper doesn't match your looks! I dare say it'll be different tomorrow! ...'

The bride wore a pink satin dress, silk stockings and a chiffon stole – all presents from my mother. She sat motionless, her chin in her chest, and never lifted her eyes or uttered a word. She consumed nothing at dinner and afterward shed a couple of token tears when her departing family kissed her goodbye.

In the morning, Ali announced to my mother that he did not like his wife and had no intention of keeping her: 'I don't want her! Send her away, please!'

My mother was dumbfounded: 'Whatever do you mean? What happened? What's wrong with her?'

'She's as black as an Abyssinian! And she's covered with spots. I didn't say I wanted a negress, did I? You said she was a bit dark-skinned, but she's pitch-black!' he spluttered bitterly.

Mother was panic-stricken and did not know what to do. She went to see the bride, who was sitting in a corner of her room, knees pulled up to her chin, shivering like a wounded bird and whimpering softly, 'I'm not going back! I'm married to him and that's that. I want to stay here, with your Ladyship!'

'Well at least you can talk! I was beginning to think that maybe your tongue was chopped off!' Mother made a half-hearted attempt at joking the problem away. She comforted the girl and promised that whatever happened she would see to it that no harm came to her. But the girl knew that if she were sent back, not only she, but her entire family would be dishonoured, and that she would never find another husband. Mother knew it too, and she went back to Ali to try and reason with him, saying that it was a grave sin to break the girl's heart and destroy her hopes, that she had come to him in good faith, that her looks would improve once her spots cleared up with regular married life – she meant sex life – etc.

Ali was adamant: 'I don't want her! I haven't touched her and no harm has been done,' meaning she was still a virgin and could find another husband. In desperation, Mother appealed to Father and Ali was duly summoned to the study. He spent twenty minutes in tête-à-tête with Father, at the end of which he was persuaded to give the marriage a week and, if he still found his wife repulsive, arrangements could be made for an honourable separation.

And that was that. What happened in the nuptial room, the following night, is part of love's mystery; suffice it to say that Ali never mentioned sending his wife away again, and that nine months later she produced a baby daughter. As time passed, Ali became quieter and meeker while his wife revealed the self-confidence and authority of a born matriarch. Soon she was ruling him completely: now it was Ali who never talked or answered back, his wife who never stopped talking and bossing him around.

After the birth of their second child, it was obvious that Ali needed a different job. Father dispatched him to a friend, then the Minister of Justice, with a letter of recommendation, and Ali was given the job of a courier, delivering writs and court summonses.

Ali and his wife were a devoted couple and produced seven or eight children – I lost count after the fifth.

'God is not a carpenter, but He sure knows how to match two

pieces of wood.' Aunt Ashraf quoted the proverb regarding harmonious marriages. It certainly applied to Ali and his wife.

They came to see us often, each time bringing a different assortment of children. Sometimes Ali came on his own, to give a hand whenever it was needed. He was always there when I went home for a visit. He would slip back into his old role as soon as he arrived in the house, answering the doorbell, serving tea, ordering around the staff. He would bring the cream buns and ice-cream we used to like when we were children, bought from the same shops.

I have no direct contact with old Ali now, but I know he thinks of us and asks after us whenever he meets someone who has recently returned from the West.

Street Life

From beyond the high walls of our house came sounds and smells that told of a rich and varied life going on in the streets. From dawn till dusk and beyond, an assortment of hawkers and pedlars chanted the praise of their wares in elaborate, poetic images, heralding each season's first fruits and vegetables. Our house being at the intersection of two streets, we heard them for a long time as they came down the larger road, turned the corner and proceeded along the garden wall towards the High Street or the *bazaarcheh* (little, local bazaar). People opened their doors and called to them, and after lengthy negotiations and haggling bought a little of what they offered. Some set up shop for the day by opening a simple wooden trestle, topped with a round tray on which they presented their goods. At dusk, they lit a paraffin lamp and stayed on until the last householders returned home from work and the streets became deserted, then they folded their trestles, put the trays on their heads and moved away.

All day long, we heard a ceaseless flow of exhortations: 'Give your heart a treat with a glass of ruby-red pomegranate juice!'; 'Cleanse your liver with these juicy blackberries!'; 'Build your muscles up with a skewer of liver-and-kidney kebab!'; 'Purify your blood with these black mulberries, nay sugar lumps!'; etc. etc.

In winter, they brought citrus fruit and fresh fish from the Caspian Sea. For some reason, most of the salesmen were Turkish-speaking Azarbayejanis. They carried the oranges and sweet lemons in carpet-bags hung from their shoulders or tied to their necks. Families that had servants had no need for the hawkers, but they were useful in providing a kind of delivery service for single-handed housewives. Ali went to the Main Market, near the South Gate of the city, and bought quantities of seasonal fruit and vegetables which he stored in a cool basement recess. But sometimes we ran out between his trips, usually due to extra guests, and he called the street-sellers to the door to replenish the larder. He spoke Turkish with them, drove a hard bargain and only when he was satisfied that the price was fair did he agree to it.

In those days, fruit and vegetables were seasonal: citrus fruit disappeared at the end of the winter, and my mother wanted us to have enough while it lasted: 'You'll never catch colds if you have oranges and lemons every day,' she would say and make sure there was plenty in the house. Thirty years later, Linus Pauling said the same thing and won the Nobel Prize for it, but that is by the way! She had large quantities of Shirazi limes – small, thin-skinned and very juicy – squeezed and bottled for making lemonade in summer; orange peel was cleaned, and cut into strips to be used in cooking; marmalade, chutney and orange compotes were made and stored while the fruit was in season.

Sea bass was the main fish from the Caspian, sold either fresh or smoked. Often it froze in the itinerant fishmonger's bag as he walked all day through the streets. Cut into steaks, seasoned with lemon juice and fried, the fish was served with a special herb pilau. It was one of the traditional New Year dishes, symbolising fertility at sea and on land.

At the first sign of the short-lived spring, came the herb-seller: 'Wild herbs ... wild herbs from the woods! ...', he clamoured. These were the wild varieties of parsley, coriander, chives, onions, garlic and other herbs, whose names we did not know but the peasants recognised as edible and beneficient. Country-women went into the woods as soon as the snow melted and the first bluebells and violets peeped through the undergrowth, picked the mushrooms and herbs which their men brought to sell in town. Zahra and Ozzie took hours to sort out and clean, wash and finely chop the mounds of herbs to be used in pilau or stew. We could hear the rhythmic sound of their sharp little hatchets as we played, and our mouths would water in anticipation of the culinary delights it promised.

Summer, long and munificent, was the season of hawkers *par excellence*. It was heralded with the first greengages and fresh almonds. We were not allowed to buy them in the street for fear of germs. It became fashionable to wash fruit and salad in permanganated water, as if germs, like an irresistible army of mortal foes, had suddenly invaded the country, or at least the consciousness of its educated classes. We ignored the interdict and bought the fruit on our way to school, often paying for our greediness with gastric troubles.

Apart from fruit and vegetables, ice-cream, toys and household goods could be bought at your doorstep during the summer months. Many hawkers had donkeys, loaded heavy with honeydew and water melons, aubergines and courgettes, kitchen utensils and crockery. From a little window of a cool basement-room, where we took refuge from the midday heat, we could see them go past, followed by their masters. One morning early, we heard a knock on the door and there, by the doorstep, was a camel, loaded with melons and watermelons. Camels had disappeared from town, having been replaced firstly by horse-drawn carts and later by delivery vans, and we were astonished to see one so close. My mother had placed the order with a wholesaler who had sent it by this old-fashioned means of transport. We were fascinated by the animal, but Nanny said we should not get close to it:

'Haven't you heard of the expression "grudgy-as-a-camel"? It's because the camel has the longest memory in the whole animal kingdom, and keeps a grudge for ever! Once it has seen you, if you do anything to hurt or even tease it, he'll never forgive you and some day, somewhere, it'll kick you to death!'

So we kept our distance as the camel was made to kneel down for unloading. Relieved of its burden it started chewing its cud slowly, without taking any notice of us or the urchins who had gathered around it. Every move from the peaceful animal, every side-glance, was interpreted as a sign that it wanted to memorise our faces in order to wreak revenge at a later date:

'There is no grudge in the camel or any other animal, only in human beings,' Aunt Ashraf assured us, never missing an opportunity to vent her deep suspicion of her fellow man.

Soon our attention was diverted from the camel to its load: the smaller watermelons could be used for playing ball, and eaten once they fell to the ground and cracked open. The bigger ones, the size of rugby balls or bigger, would be stored and consumed as we went along. In later years, when the increase in population reduced such careless lavishness, we would reminisce about those days of abundance, 'Do you remember how we played ball with melons? We ate a dozen a day like that! ...', as if centuries had passed. There was a melon shop in the *bazaarcheh*, which consisted of one big room, open on the street side, filled from floor to ceiling with several varieties of melons of all sizes and shapes. It stayed open till midnight, long after all other shops had closed, and if we came home very late we would see the owner dozing on a bench at the back of his shop, wrapped in his cloak, surrounded by mounds of green and golden globes. A paraffin lamp, hung on a hook from the ceiling, spread a ghostly glow over the oneiric scene. If we stopped and woke him up with a salaam, he would jump down briskly and offer to choose us the very best. He would survey the mounds of fruit with the eyes of a proud connoisseur, pick out a large one, and say, 'This'll be like melted sugar, Lady.' For not all melons were equally sweet and crisp, and some people had a knack for selecting the best. Evidently he did.

For important parties, Mother went to a market uptown, accompanied by Ali, and bought the best and most expensive fruit: sweet white peaches, creamy apricots, several varieties of grapes – the 'ruby', with little red grains tightly clustered around the stem; the topaz-coloured 'musk'; the grainless green ... She arranged them all in a huge bowl as a centre-piece for the table, like a cornucopia in an old painting – a *nature vivante*!

Even poultry was sometimes sold in the street. There were no battery chickens then, and poultry was a luxury reserved for special occasions. 'Hens and cockerels! ... Chicks and chickens! ... We sell the birds of paradise! ...' chanted the poultry-man.

Once, when I was very small, I went with Ali to the door to watch him negotiate and buy a pair of chickens. A dozen birds were imprisoned in a long basket, their spindly legs tied together like a bunch of twigs. They cackled and fluttered their wings impotently as their owner took them out and laid them on the ground. They darted suspicious side-glances and growled as Ali examined them:

'This one is too scrawny,' he commented, 'that white one seems a bit more like it,' while the poultry-man protested and invoked God and the Prophet to be witness to his sincerity and fairness. Finally, a bargain was struck and Ali bought the white hen and the rainbow-tailed cockerel. He took them to the back of the orchard, pinned their legs to the ground with his foot and, with a neat swift movement of a kitchen knife, slit their throats. The blade flashed in the sun, blood spurted out and the birds went on struggling and flapping their wings furiously for a while before lying still.

I had never seen a chicken immolated in this way, nor associated the delectable dishes made of it with such a scene, and I was horrified! I cried bitterly and punched Ali's legs as high as my hands could reach, ordering him to stop at once! He just laughed.

'We'll see who will eat chicken tonight!' he chuckled cynically, and took the birds to the kitchen to have them plucked. I ran to my mother, howling with pity and rage, and she admonsihed Ali for 'frightening the child'. That evening, the two chickens, cooked in a rich succulent sauce, were brought to the table. It did not occur to me not to eat my portion, but Ali would not let me get away with it:

'Is the little lady still crying for chickens?' he teased, and everybody laughed. I admire vegetarians who abstain from meat out of compassion for animals, but I am wary of trying to match theory with practice myself.

By the time I left Persia, the first battery chickens had appeared on the market. One farmer opened a shop on the high street of our area, and we tried one:

'It tastes like cotton-wool!' was Mother's verdict. 'Better the genuine thing less often than this rubbish every day.' I have tried to follow that piece of advice whenever possible – and not only in relation to chicken!

With the warm weather, the ice-cream man appeared. All over the Middle East, from Greece to India, you can find a special ice-cream which contains mastic and rose-water. The former gives it an elastic texture, like melted toffee, while the latter adds a delicate aroma to it.

For a penny, you could buy a dollop pressed between two thin wafers. We were not allowed to buy any because, if the milk was not properly pasteurised, you could get anthrax, a painful lethal disease which was transmitted to human beings from sheep. There was a reputable ice-cream merchant far away, near the Bazaar, and from time to time Ali was sent to buy us some. The specialist made his ice-cream by putting the ingredients into a metal cylinder which was inserted in a barrel of ice and churned around until the liquid solidified.

Later on 'machine-made' ice cream invaded the tea-rooms and pastry shops of the newly affluent districts; a chic café opened on Parliament Square which sold this, and on our way back from school we would sometimes stop there with our friends to enjoy a cupful. Gradually, traditional ice-cream became a rarity, as did sherbet, an Edenic soft drink made with just fruit essence and iced water. Once, on a visit home, I sat at a café and asked for a glass of cherry sherbet. The waiter looked at me as if I had dropped from Mars:

'We don't have any, Madam,' he said indignantly. 'Coca-cola, Pepsi, Seven-up, anything ...'

I said, I had not come all the way from Europe to drink Coca-cola in Teheran!

He looked at me in amazement; 'How old-fashioned can you get!' he seemed to be thinking. Here was an idea for an entrepreneur: bottling traditional sherbet, even exporting it to other countries in the region and beyond. Amazingly, no one took it up! Now you can find bottled sherbets in Greece and Turkey, and fruit essences in supermarkets everywhere.

You could always tell the toy-seller was around by the sound of his *vaq-vaq-sahab* (yap-yap-master), a tiny concertina made with a piece of white paper stretched between two round clay discs which made a noise like a yapping puppy. All the urchins would rush with their pennies to buy something and to be given demonstrations of various toys. Our toy-seller had clay whistles, windmills, streamers ... He stopped at the crossroads until his box was depleted and the street loud with the competing barks of his *vaq-vaq-sahab*s and bright with colourful whirring windmills.

But, of all the hawkers, the most popular was the *Shahre-Farang* (a City in Europe) man. He pushed his big black box on a wheelbarrow shouting:

'Come and see the *Shahre-Farang*! Travel with me to the land of the *Farangi* and see its marvels! ...; *Farang*, originally meaning France, was a generic term for Europe. Persia's cultural contact with the West in the nineteenth century was first with France, and *Farangi* came to mean anything or anybody from Europe, even later America.

Children rushed from all directions and offered the *Shahre-Farang* man their coins.

'Easy now! Four at a time!'

The first four tiny spectators would crouch and glue their eyes to the little windows that opened on to the magical world within, their hands cupped around the rims better to shut out light and reality. Presently the man would set his machine in motion turning a handle at the back, and a marvellous tapestry would unfold: Versailles, the Tuileries, Buckingham Palace, Windsor Castle ... Peacocks roamed amid luxuriant gardens, swans glided over glassy ponds, young lovers, princes and princesses one and all, resplendent in their fineries, strolled arm in arm towards bowers and woods. And, all the while, the man chanted a semi-rhymed commentary in a mesmeric voice. But just as you were completely transported into the exotic magical world he conjured, the image froze:

'End of your pennies!' he said cruelly. 'Next lot!'

It was all over in a second! But the seed of curiosity and desire had been planted: I longed to see those beautiful and exotic places, meet the strange people who lived beyond the Seven Mountains and the Seven Seas. It was the first stirring of an urge to move, search, perhaps in the end find a place where the soul would feel at home. Of such yearnings, exiles are made. *Le bonheur est ailleurs* – happiness is elsewhere ... The *Shahre-Farang* ignited a flame which nothing but time and experience could contain.

Autumn was the season of the quince and the pomegranate. The hard yellow quince, covered with gossamer-soft down, was transformed into delicious stews with meat or poultry, or made into jam and jelly. But the supreme pleasure of the season was the heavenly pomegranate, 'the fruit of the gods', so called for its beauty and health-giving properties. Its skin yielded a fast colour used in dyeing the wool for rugs and cloths; its juice 'broke down the bile' and cured liver ailments, and it looked so cheerful and decorative. Ali came from a pomegranate region and every autumn he went home for a holiday and brought back a ton of the most delicious variety – huge glowing red balloons with grains like liquid ruby. You could squeeze the skin gently until the grains crushed inside, then make a tiny incision with your teeth and suck the juice – ambrosia! More often, Nanny would grain the fruit and served it in a bowl, or give us glassfuls of juice. Pomegranate juice was sold at every street corner in autumn, and passers-by would stop to buy and drink a cup and hurry on.

Seasonal workers and odd-job men roamed the streets too:

woodcutters, coal-washers, pool-emptiers, quilt-makers ... In those days, there were no gas or electric cookers – cooking was done on charcoal braziers and log fires. The wood arrived in the form of large logs which had to be cut into smaller, more manageable pieces by a 'woodcutter'. Charcoal was delivered in bulk and had to be washed clean of impurities before being stored. Pools were emptied, refilled with clean water and covered with planks before the cold weather set in.

There was no central heating then. The traditional way of keeping warm in winter was by *korsi*: a low table covered with blankets and quilts under which a charcoal brazier burnt slowly, its embers covered with a thick layer of ashes to ensure an even distribution of heat and prevent burning. The *korsi* was similar to the Spanish *brasero* and functioned in the same way: you sat on mattresses around it with your hands and feet under the blankets, and leaned against cushions. At night you just stretched out sideways and slept, and at mealtimes you used the top as a table. In later years, *Korsi*s disappeared everywhere in our house and were replaced by oil stoves, but my father kept a tiny one in his study till the end. Much later, central heating was introduced into the country, but the majority of people to this day use the traditional *korsi* which is cheap, healthy and convivial.

One winter evening, we were sitting around the *korsi* in my mother's room having dinner, with Aunt Ashraf and a couple of cousins. It was an exceptionally cold night; earlier, an icy breeze had presaged snow, which was now falling silently in fine silky specks like white dust, covering the ground with a rapidly thickening blanket. Since dusk, no one had ventured out of doors and the streets were deserted as if by a curfew. Suddenly we heard a wailing voice, like a plaintive howl of a lonely roaming wolf: 'We empty your pool! ... We empty your pool!'

The pools had been emptied weeks before and were now frozen solid. We immediately understood that the man was crying for help. Conversation stopped; Father called Ali and asked him to take food and money to the poor wanderer whose melancholy singsong stopped at once. The party was resumed, but something had happened and the enchantment was broken, for we all felt that there but for the grace of God we would be, knee-deep in snow and begging for bread and shelter.

That kind of poverty disappeared, at least in cities, as the country prospered thanks to oil revenues and a new spirit of enterprise, but in those days beggars were a fact of life and you did what you could to help them.

At the end of winter when the *korsis* were put away, the quilt-maker was sent for. He sat in a back room and worked all day. He would undo the quilt and mattresses, take out the cotton which had gone flat and lumpy, and beat it into fluffy snow mounds. He would then refil the cases and sew them up again, using his fancy to produce elaborate arabesques and geometric designs for decorating the quilts. He had an instrument shaped like a harp, with a single string, and a wooden spatula with which he hit the string against the cotton, unravelling it bit by bit. It had a rhythmic, almost musical sound, and we used to sit and watch him work, mesmerised.

One day, when the snow had melted and preparations for *Norooz* had begun, an intinerant fortune-teller came through the streets: 'We tell your fortune! ... We read your stars! ... We see your future!' Mother was out *Norooz*-shopping, and as eligible young girls Zahra and Ozzie were keen to know what Fate had in store for them in the coming year. They called in the divine. He sat in the entrance and from his pocket took out an astrolabe and two sets of geomancy beads, all inscribed with Arabic words and engraved with abstract images. He threw the beads on the astrolabe and pondered for a while: 'I can see changes in the new year for you ... a short trip – perhaps a pilgrimage ... Several young men are after you, but only one is sincere ...' Nanny inadvertently fed him bits of information and helped him along with his innocuous predictions. The two girls drank in his words with rapt gullibility, thanked him profusely when he had finished, and offered him a cup of tea.

'I have more to say, if you can give me an extra two *qarans* [about twenty pence].' But the girls were satisfied with what they had heard and did not wish to pay the extra money.

The streets of our city were, above all, the playground of the poor. In the absence of parks, playing fields and nursery schools, those families who did not have anything but the tiniest courtyards sent their children to play outside as soon as they could walk. It was a male world, as female children remained at home with their mothers and became miniature women, wearing little *chadors* and playing with rag dolls. But the boys practically lived in the street, except when they were at school or sleeping. They would stretch a rope between two trees and play volley-ball, or put cardboard boxes at either end of the road as goals and play football; they would ride their bicycles, wrestle and box, watched by a circle of smaller, punier urchins. Sometimes their ball would fly over the wall and land in our garden; a few seconds later a knock would be heard on the front door and Ali would grumpily and grudgingly return it. Many a window-pane was shattered into smithereens by stray footballs.

As for us, we were lucky to have a large garden, large rooms and plenty of friends to play with. Still, boredom was a problem in those pre-television days. Later, in adolescence, we discovered books and music, parties and balls, not to mention romantic day-dreaming and exchange of confidences, and there was no time to get bored or think about the slow pace of life.

Neighbours

Our neighbourhood was a typical Persian town in miniature. It had a high street and a *bazaarcheh* – a tiny covered bazaar lined with shops – a bakery, a butcher's, a grocery and greengrocery, and a cooked-food shop which sold hot beetroots and porridge in winter, ice-cream and soft drinks in summer, and kebabs all year round. There was a little mosque at the entrance of the *bazaarcheh*

and a *hammam* (public baths) a few yards further in. It even had a caravanserai – a large courtyard surrounded with rooms which provided temporary accommodation for country people who came to town in search of work; for the rush to the city had already begun, long before the petrol boom of the 1960s and 1970s, when it gathered catastrophic speed and dimensions. The caravanserai was a kind of job centre for navvies and unskilled workers of all sorts, male and female. Many of its lodgers moved on after a short period for better, permanent homes near steady employments, others stayed for years and years, hoping that something would soon turn up.

The population of our district ranged over the whole social spectrum: shopkeepers lived above or behind their shops, workmen in the caravanserai or in shared homes, civil servants and teachers in small modern houses, and patrician families in large old houses with expansive gardens. But although people's social positions varied, there was a sense of community and of everyone performing his or her function within a structure that transcended class stratification. It was much later that the oil boom and new industries created a wealthy bourgeoisie and a new ruling class, whose members began to build themselves grand villas in new residential suburbs in the foothills north of the city: ghettoes of the rich and powerful, out of contact with the lives of ordinary people and without any community feeling, which became the first scenes of looting and carnage in 1979.

Among our immediate neighbours were some friends of my parents: a couple of Qajar princes, a university professor or two, a cabinet minister, some high-ranking civil servants and diplomats, an Army general, etc ... In the following decades, every one of these moved away, until in the end there were three old houses left, of which ours was one. It was a corner house at the junction of two streets. On the opposite corner lived Professor Bahram and his wife, in a large house with a very long garden. The Bahrams came from Kerman, a city in South East Persia famous for its rugs of which many fine specimens adorned their home, and spoke with a delicious regional accent. Like many of the University's dons, Professor Bahram had started life as a mullah. He had studied in a traditional *madrasah*, where he had specialised in Arabic grammar and literature, and had worn the traditional cloak-and-turban clerical costume. But, in 1930 when Reza Shah decreed that Western clothes – suit, tie and trilby – were *de rigueur* for all government employees including university staff, Professor Bahram had changed and defrocked himself like everyone else. My father was the only professor to be allowed, by a special dispensation from the Shah, to keep his costume.

Every morning at eight o'clock punctually, you heard the front door of Professor Bahram's house open and shut, and if you looked out of the window you saw him leave for the University: a tiny, trim figure in a dark suit, with a trilby, and in winter a black overcoat. He wore horn-rimmed glasses and carried an elegant ivory-topped walking-stick on his arm. He walked briskly, with short rapid steps, and never lifted his eyes from the ground in front of him. Occasionally he would touch his hat and bow slightly to acknowledge a passer-by's greetings.

The Bahrams had three sons, all of whom were studying in France at the time and were to return home several years later. Mrs Bahram missed them terribly and talked about them constantly – how clever and handsome they were, how well they were doing, what greatness they would surely achieve:

'Well this is a modern world and one has to bring up one's children accordingly,' she would sigh. 'Nowadays if you don't have a degree from a foreign university you have no hope of advancing in the world.'

When their sons were about to return to Persia, the Bahram's cut some trees at the end of their garden and had a modern bungalow built for their eldest to live in. They would have done better to keep the trees, for the ambitious young men married heiresses and moved up town as soon as they could. Mrs Bahram wanted one of them to marry my sister, but when she discovered that, contrary to appearances, my sister had no 'settlement', she gave up the idea and managed to find other brides who had.

I liked old Mrs Bahram who made delicious Kermani cakes and pastries and always gave me some when I visited her. On school holidays, I would sometimes knock on her door and go in to see her and listen to her tales about her sons in Europe. She described Paris in detail, as if she had been there, exaggerating its magnificent amenities to magical proportions. Her tales fired my own imagination and I dreamed about Paris as if it were the Promised Land. I could see myself sitting on a bench in the Jardin du Luxembourg, like Cosette in *Les Misérables*, or going for walks by the Seine in the company of a beautiful young man. I was about 10 or 11 then, and the likelihood of my going to Paris was as remote as my flying to the moon, yet I dreamed on.

One day, Mrs Bahram acquired a dog, Snowy, a pretty fluffy little white puppy which looked like a snowball as it ran around the garden yapping furiously as if pursued by a pack of wolves.

The acquisition of a dog was an unusual event, for although the Bahram's had adopted modern ways and sent their sons to Europe, they were still devout Muslims, and dogs are considered *najis* (impure) in Islam, allowed only as guards and sheepdogs, never as pets. The notion of keeping a dog purely for pleasure was a Western one, which over the years became a symbol of freedom from old-fashioned prohibitions.

In Persian folk-songs and tales, 'man's best friend' is not his dog but his horse, whose loyalty and affection is expressed in stories about great warrior heroes and saints, and sometimes contradicted:

> 'They say that a man's best friend is his horse,
> But I say it's his gun,
> For where would a horseman be without a gun?
> I had a silver-barrelled gun which I sold
> To buy a gown of golden brocade for my Beloved
> But she refused it, and now I have lost my gun
> And I have lost my heart ...'

So goes a folk-song from the tribal South.

Snowy had a wicked bite and tried it on the postman and the dustman, who had to be silenced with hefty tips, and thereafter she had to be chained to her kennel and let loose only at night, and when no visitors were expected. Mrs Bahram 'put a religious hat' on her dog-keeping by saying that Snowy was indeed a guardian, and a good one at that – you could ask the postman and the dustman if you didn't believe her! The religious interdict was based on health grounds – fear of rabies and other germ-induced diseases – but it was not a licence for cruelty. Yet in practice it was sometimes used as such. There were plenty of stray dogs roaming in the streets looking for food, or scavenging on garbage tips. They attacked wayward cats and fought with each other – more from hunger than malice – and were often found dead in wastelands, their putrefying mutilated corpses covered with flies and insects. Sometimes they would follow passers-by at a respectful distance to their doorsteps, hoping for food and shelter, only to be disappointed when doors were slammed shut. They were tormented and teased by street urchins who outnumbered them and were not that much better off themselves. People chased away stray dogs with stones which occasionally hit a spindly leg and cracked it. A howl of anguish would ensue, followed by pitiful yapping, and the poor animal would limp away on three legs for days, holding up the injured limb like a finger pointed at human cruelty. Things changed gradually over the years. Stray dogs disappeared or were collected by the municipality when the city became more affluent – at least in residential areas – and quite a few people adopted mongrels as pets.

Snowy was highly pampered, regularly washed and combed, and adorned with a red ribbon. It provoked one of Aunt Ashraf's philosophical extrapolations:

'Even animals are divided into two categories – the lucky and the unlucky. Look at Snowy, eating the best meat, living in a clean house, with his custom-made kennel; and look at a stray dog, born on a rubbish dump, hungry and kicked all its miserable life, paying for each morsel of food with humiliation and misery … Yes, even for animals, it's all written here …' And she ran her index finger over her forehead to show the exact location of fate's inexorable inscription.

Opposite the Bahrams lived the family of a well-known poet and landowner, Mr Javadi. He had three daughters, all clever and pretty, especially the eldest, Jaleh, who was a couple of years older than me but went to the same school and became my friend. Soon after the Javadis moved to our neighbourhood, Jaleh invited me to their house for tea, to meet her parents. Her mother was a tall, handsome woman, with reddish-brown wavy hair and beautiful sad eyes. But her father seemed prematurely aged: he was unusually thin and stooping; his skin was very dark, his cheeks sunken, and his eyes surrounded with a bluish shadow. Above all, his lips were black, and when he smiled his teeth were stained and unhealthy looking. Altogether, a gaunt, sickly man, but elegantly dressed and courteous. When he spoke, his voice was tremulous and had a nasal twang.

There was a peculiar smell in the house – a mixture of honey, charcoal and burnt flesh, sweet and sickly at once. Soon after tea, Mr Javadi disappeared, and presently the funny odour intensified.

'Let's go and play in your house now,' Jaleh suggested and, before I could say anthing, ushered me out of the house. I felt something was amiss but did not know what it was.

Eventually it transpired that the peculiar smell of the house was that of opium, and that Mr Javadi's appearance and nasal speech were tell-tale signs of his 'habit'. Mrs Javadi had hoped to keep it a secret in the neighbourhood, but soon everyone knew. One day, she called on my mother to make friends and after a while told us the story: her husband had inherited a vast estate in the North, with rice-fields, orange groves and woodlands. He was a young poet, handsome and rich, and much sought after by young girls – or rather their parents – but had chosen her:

'I was 17, and he 21. At first, all went well, but then he kept going out in the evenings and coming back looking tired and sleepy. One day I found a box of opium in his pocket and confronted him with it – he had to confess that he was an addict. But by then I was pregnant and there was nothing I could do.'

She had cried and made scenes and threatened suicide; she had even fled to her family for a while, but he had persuaded her to go back to him, promising to kick the habit. He never had. In the end, she had said to him:

'Alright, you needn't go out, you can smoke at home.'

I later discovered that this was the usual scenario: secret smoking followed by discovery and resignation on the part of relatives. Lower-class addicts ended up destitutes in dingy opium dens; the wealthy ones abdicated their responsibilities to other members of their families and lived to smoke. By the time they moved to our neighbourhood, Mr Javadi was on nearly one 'stick' a day, which is a great deal of opium, considering that each pipe used only a tiny piece, the size of half a finger-nail. He went out in the morning and occasionally in the early evenings, but the rest of the time he was reclining on a mattress, propped up against pillows, smoking. His visitors sat around him and his children went in and out of the room without taking any notice of what he was doing.

He would cut a little piece from the cigarette-shaped opium stick and press it to the round china bowl of his pipe beneath a little hole, then take an ember from the brazier with a pair of brass tongs, hold it over the opium and blow. The ember would glow red and the opium sizzle, and he would inhale the smoke in long, hissing draughts. When the piece of opium had burnt out he would rub the ember on the bowl to clean away the debris, poke the hole with a brass pin, and repeat the motions. After a few times he would lie back, close his eyes and enjoy 'the high'. If there were other smokers among his guests, he would pass the pipe round to them. When they were all 'high', they recited their poetry and drank wine accompanied by Mrs Javadi's delicious mezes.

For years now, Mr Javadi had done nothing but smoke and write poetry. His wife ran his estate, or what was left of it, and they lived off the proceeds. One day, I told my mother that Mr Javadi had guests and how several of them smoked opium and drank wine. She was horrified that I had witnessed such a scene and forbade me ever to go there again. But Jaleh and I walked home from school and she sometimes came and played with me, or we did our homework together, while Mrs Javadi visited my mother regularly 'to open her chest and empty her heart'.

Mr Javadi lived to a ripe old age, as smoked as a kipper. He left a couple of volumes of good lyrical poetry in classical style. Jaleh became a poet and lady of letters, and married another literary figure. I lost touch with them after a while, but that early experience of addiction produced a lasting horror of any form of dependence, indeed of anything that curtails human freedom and sovereignty, that is with me to this day. I saw how opium had destroyed Mr Javadi's will-power and made him a slave to his pipe. He was a good poet, a decent man and a fond father, but he had lost control over his life. I thought it a calamity and resolved that I would not allow anything like that ever happen to me.

Of all our immediate neighbours, the Ramy family were the closest to us. Their son, Jamsheed, was a playmate of my brothers and their daughter, Shireen, was my sister's age and her friend. The Ramys lived in a small, two-up-two-down house in a street parallel to ours, with a high wall between our garden and their courtyard. In summer, we could hear each other hoot, which was a signal to get together and play. Jamsheed played the penny-whistle quite well, and the strains of his doleful limited repertoire often wafted across the partition – a sign that the children were alone and wished to be invited over.

The Ramy family had fallen on hard times, hence the small dwelling and restricted living conditions. The father, old Mr Ramy, had been an official at the court of Ahamad Shah, the last Qajar king, who had abdicated in 1924, gone into exile in France and had been replaced by Reza Shah, the founder of the new Pahlavi dynasty and of modern Iran.

Like most courtiers of the *ancien régime* Mr Ramy had no skills or qualifications that would enable him to start a new profession. He had been His Excellency, the Honourable Master of the Royal Refectories, which simply meant he was responsible for the smooth running of the palace kitchens and the serving of refreshments. He had a host of valets and servants who worked under him, and by all accounts he discharged his duties reasonably well. The Qajar kings were in the habit of rewarding their employees with grandiloquent and bombastic titles totally out of proportion – or indeed any connection – to their functions: every man was *The Pillar of the Monarchy*, *The Grandeur of the Realm*, *The Pride of Kingdoms*; and every woman was *The Beauty of the Land*, *The Ornament of Princes*, *The Crown of Kings*, and so on. Reza Shah abolished all such titles and people became plain Mr, Mrs, or Miss, except in the case of blood princes, including his own children, who kept their titles.

His Excellency, the Honourable Master of the King's

Refectories had become plain Mr Ramy and pensioned off, but unable to adapt to his new circumstances he had taken to the bottle and gone to seed. As he was also an opium addict, his modest pension barely covered the cost of his dual dependence.

By contrast, his wife, Mrs Ramy, had taken advantage of women's emancipation and the possibility for women to earn their own living, and had found a job in the personnel department of a ministry. Over the years, she rose in rank to become Head of Personnel, but at that time her small salary was not enough to keep her family, and they had terrible money problems which they tried to conceal, in order to keep up appearances and save their *aberoo* (honour). They cut down on food to pay for decent clothes and entertainment; as a result, Shireen was as thin as a willow wand, had a sallow complexion, and was sluggish at school. Jamsheed too was a dunce, played truant and caused his mother despair, but he was shrewd, charming and very funny, with impeccable manners, so everyone said that he would be alright in the end, and he was: after a brief flirtation with the Army where the discipline was not at all to his taste he entered the Civil Service, through my father's string-pulling, where he continued to play truant. But nobody notices when a little dent is missing in the gigantic wheel of bureaucracy, and he got away with it. He charmed his superiors with his sense of humour and courtly manners, and they tolerated him. He climbed the Civil Service ladder without impediment and ended up as the director of a department, with a decent salary and a substantial status, without having to *do* anything much. But that was years later.

Old Mr Ramy was incarcerated in one of the two basement rooms adjoining their tiny kitchen where he lay on a mattress, wrapped in a tattered courtier's cape, in front of his charcoal brazier, with his opium pipe and his bottle of *araq* (Persian vodka), like some cannibal crouching in his den. At certain hours of the day, a sticky pungent smell drifted into the courtyard through the cracks of his closed door and pervaded the whole house – Mr Ramy was having 'his smoke'. No one remarked on the smell, as the children were embarrassed and pretended that nothing was untoward.

In the early days, Mr Ramy used to venture out sometimes,

just to buy his supply of *araq* and opium. You could see him walking briskly, a scruffy stooping figure, with his threadbare cape hanging askew over his shoulders, one corner dragging on the muddy ground, and his bottle of *araq* hidden under it. He wielded his walking-stick as a truncheon, as if he were still ordering about the Shah's kitchen staff or hitting a recalcitrant junior, muttering curses and threats. But after a few years he became a complete recluse and never went out. A relative brought him his *araq* and opium, and occasionally you heard him yell curses and swearwords at fate, the times, his wife and children.

Mrs Ramy hated her husband and despised him deeply, as she held him responsible for her family's plight. His children were ashamed of him, but they pitied him and were protective towards him. On the whole, everyone pretended he was not there.

And one day he was no longer there. It was a summer evening and we were sitting in the garden when we heard sounds of weeping and wailing coming from the Ramy's house. Presently a messenger came to announce that old Mr Ramy had died. We quickly dressed in black and went over to console the family and offer help. Mrs Ramy did her husband proud by giving him a decent funeral and fulfilling all the traditional rituals: She kept open house for three days, giving lavish hospitality and feeding the poor; she held prayer sessions and had obituaries published in the papers etc. .... The money for it all was of course borrowed, and it took her a long time to pay it off, but no other course of action would have been possible without loss of *aberoo*, and the risk of going down in the world.

After Mr Ramy's death, we became much closer to the family. The children were often with us, especially in summer when they were left alone in the house while their mother was at work. They did not belong to the same social circle as we did, rather they were like relatives, with easy access to our house and its informal hospitality. As Mrs Ramy's position improved, their lives became easier and they themselves much more sociable.

The Ramys were very modern. To start with, their mother *worked* which was still rare and meant that she went to the office every day bare-headed, wearing short-sleeved dresses and make-up, and mixed with men. Furthermore Mrs Ramy was more or less a free-thinker; she considered most religious observance nothing but 'superstition', did not perform the daily prayers nor fast during the Ramadan. She said she believed in God and the Day of Judgement but that she relied on her own conscience more than the fear of Hell. She was very liberal with her children, and Shireen was allowed all the things we were not: she wore short dresses, curled her hair and later on put on a little lipstick – though she denied doing so, maintaining that her lips were naturally redder than ours – and she went to parties where she danced with boys. The fact that she was bottom of her class at school and had fallen a couple of years behind by failing her exams did not matter to me two hoots, and I would have swapped my position at the top of the form and all my good marks for one of her dances any day!

When we were adolescents, Shireen and Jamsheed gave parties in their house, especially in summer, when they could arrange their courtyard by covering their little round pool with planks and rugs, turning it into a dance floor, with tables and chairs around it. Among others, they invited some of their cousins who were young cadets at the Officers' Academy. They wore elegant braided, brass-buttoned uniforms, looked dashing and confident, and danced all the fashionable dances of the day to perfection – the waltz, the tango, the rumba, the foxtrot ... We were always invited to these parties and allowed to go as long as we were accompanied by our older brothers and did not dance.

My parents negotiated a tricky course between moving with the times and staying with their traditional ways. They wanted us to enjoy the fruits of emancipation without 'going too far' and hurting the feelings of those who looked up to us as representatives of certain values. Moderation was the aim, but it was very hard to achieve and anyway we were too young to be philosophical – we just resented any infringement upon our freedom. Fortunately things were changing fast, and by the time we were adolescents we had a good deal more freedom than the generation before us, but we were always careful not to behave in ways that would be remotely considered 'loose' or 'common'. We were invited to parties and balls where there would be music and dancing, and returned the hospitality by giving parties in our beautiful garden. Only we could not have music, for, however progressive and enlightened, my father still wore the traditional priestly costume of cloak-and-turban, and the sound of dance music emanating from our house and filling the street would have shocked some of our neighbours deeply. Social change, like any movement, has a natural pace, a perfect tempo, which cannot be artificially accelerated or slackened with impunity. The precipitated rhythm of Westernisation in the 1960s and 1970s has been partly blamed for the explosion of 1979. At least it provided a powerful weapon for demogogues and reactionaries. But at the time we couldn't wait to throw away completely all the shackles of what we considered antiquated customs and prohibitions.

My mother deprived herself and economised on other things to buy us pretty dresses and ball gowns, made by Emily, her own and the town's best dressmaker, so that we would appear no less well-off and elegant than our friends, many of whom were much grander and wealthier than we were.

Meanwhile Shireen taught us the ways of the world. She made up for her lack of academic performance with expertise in *conquêterie*: she knew all about make-up, hair styles, the latest fashion from Paris, everything! Jamsheed had acquired an old His Master's Voice gramaphone with a huge brass funnel and some records, and during the holidays we spent entire days at their house playing them and learning to dance. By the time I was 13, I knew all the fashionable dances and practised them with school friends. I should add that I have not learnt anything newer than the tango and the waltz since! In the sixties I learnt, and for a while practised, the Twist, but soon its rhythmic monotony and jerky movements palled. Disco dancing in which the partners don't even touch each other seems pointless to me – not to say ungraceful. Luckily there are still old-fashioned waltzes and tangos at dances to set you dreaming ...

Shireen spent hours teaching my sister and me how to curl our hair with twisted bits of newspaper. We cut the strips of paper into five-inch pieces, wetted our hair, and rolled sections of it over them, then tied the two ends to keep them in place. We looked like roadside shrines covered with streelies. After waiting patiently for our hair to dry, we took out the paper rollers and combed out our hair into a style we had seen in a film or a foreign magazine. There were a few hair dressers who curled your hair with iron tongs heated on charcoal braziers, but you went to them on special occasions – weddings and balls and official receptions. It took a decade or so before high street hairdressers appeared everywhere and women availed themselves of their services on a regular basis. Later still, stylists trained by famous teachers in Paris and London opened glamorous salons in grand hotels and in private premises, and made fortunes from their trade.

Like everyone else, the Ramys eventually moved away to a more fashionable district. Their little house was bought and demolished, to be replaced with a modern four-storey building. Shireen enrolled at the new College of Nursing where the curriculum was less intellectually taxing than the baccalaureate. She fulfilled her dream of marrying a doctor and having several children. But Jamsheed never married – no girl lived up to his adolescent expectations. He was forever in love with a woman he could not have, either because she did not reciprocate his feelings or because she was already happily married. Meanwhile he had a string of mistresses whom he did not love or wish to marry because they were 'too loose'.

We had many neighbours, a little further away, who were friends and involved in our lives. One or two have stories of their own.

Prince Afsar

On the corner of the High Street, opposite the Swiss Embassy, was one of our city's few remaining nineteenth-century houses. It belonged to Prince Afsar, one of those noblemen of the *ancien régime* who had cooperated with Reza Shah and thereby retained their positions. Although Reza Shah had abolished all titles and honorifics bestowed by the Qajar sovereigns on their loyal subjects, people still used them in private, as a mark of respect, until the recipients grew old and died out. In public, Prince Afsar had become plain Mister, or at most His Excellency, but everyone knew him as 'the Prince'.

He was a landowner, with estates in the Eastern provinces, but he was also a poet and a Sufi, and he appeared to possess all the attributes of a true nobleman: he was a lover and patron of the arts and literature, kept open house and distributed largesse, and he was charming and courteous to everyone regardless of social distinctions.

On Thursday evenings – the eve of the Muslim sabbath – Prince Afsar held a literary salon in his house. He was a friend and admirer of my father's and insisted that he attend his soirées as the guest of honour, if not every week at least once in a while. His wife, the Princess, was a friend of my mother's, and often of a Thursday evening, while her husband entertained his literary and artistic guests, she received her friends in another room. My mother took me with her several times when she and my father went to the Prince's house, and although I was very small I have kept a vivid memory of our visits.

The Princess was a beautiful woman in old age; her hair had turned silky-white but her face had remained unwrinkled and her complexion rose-fresh. She had black eyes, lit with a humorous twinkle, and a slight charming regional accent. As for the Prince, he was a handsome and imposing figure in a black suit, with white hair, beard and drooping mustachios – like a photograph of Victor Hugo in old age. Was the resemblance cultivated? I doubt it, since I though of it twenty years later in

Paris, upon seeing the great French poet's picture, and was suddenly reminded of Prince Afsar, long since dead. Perhaps all grand old poets with white hair and a beard look alike in their photographs!

The Prince was very popular among his entourage on account of his exquisite manners, which combined traditional Persian courtesy with modern gallantry – he bowed and kissed women's hands, put his hand on his breast or touched his hat when greeting male friends, and dispensed the same attentive courtesy to everyone, regardless of social position.

The Afsars had one daughter whom they both adored. When she married another landowner and went to live near Meshad, the Princess pined for her constantly and spent months staying with her. During her long absences, the soirées were 'for men only'.

The Prince's house was a one-storey building with a large garden shaded by lines of tall ancient trees. The drawing-room opened by four full length glass-panelled doors on to a wide colonnaded veranda. On summer evenings, the veranda was spread with sumptuous rugs and lined with large brocade cushions to lean against, and the Prince held his literary salon there, while the Princess received her guests inside the drawing-room. The connecting doors were left open to allow the ladies to listen when poetry was recited or chanted, if they wished to.

In late afternoon, when the sun left the veranda, the gardeners watered the lawns and flowerbeds, freshened the air by splashing water on the paved paths, and even sprinkled the veranda to cool it. The parched stones absorbed the water at once, and for a moment you could see a light mist rising from them and felt the smell of earth fill the soft evening air. The servants brought out the samovar and the tea-set, jugs of soft drinks, trays of cakes and biscuits and fruit, which they placed at intervals on the carpeted floor. The *qalyan* (water-pipe) was made ready to be lit for the men.

At dusk, guests began to arrive and were welcomed by the Prince, who stood by the steps of the veranda and showed them to their places. After the guests of honour were seated, the Prince himself sat down and motioned the latecomers in with a bow and a slow, graceful movement of his hand. A good deal of *taarof* (ceremonial exchange of pleasantries) was dispensed on such occasions. The Prince insisted that my father sit at the very top, in the corner reserved normally for himself, which my father would refuse and ask him to sit there himself. Back and forth they would gesture at each other and eventually the Prince would prevail and Father would take the place of honour.

Such preoccupation with the *placement*, indicative of rank in a hierarchical society, was natural. Usually the guest of honour occupied the highest seat, furthest from the door, while others would be placed on his left and right according to their lineage, function or status. Hence the *taarof*, the minuet of generous concessions and polite refusals, as each insisted that the other be placed higher than himself.

There was a story that Aunt Ashraf once told us which illustrated this subtle hierarchical play. It was one of Mullah Nasroddin's stories. Mullah Nasroddin was a legendary character famous for his satirical and philosophical tales and sayings. This particular story was the following:

'One day, Mullah Nasroddin went to the Governor's house to attend a banquet to which he had been invited. He was wearing his ordinary, rather shabby clothes and the servants thought he was gatecrashing, but not wishing to appear inhospitable they let him in. He was placed at the humblest place, right by the door, and when the meal was served no one paid the slightest attention to him or tried to serve him. He managed to help himself to a little food and left as soon as he had finished. No one saw him out with even a 'God-protect-you'; on the contrary, everyone eyed him with contempt.

'The following Friday, he was again invited to the Governor's weekly lunch, but this time he went dressed like a grandest of the Grand Mullahs: he wore a gold and silver threaded gown, a silk shirt and a cloak made of the finest wool. The Governor's servants rushed forward to hold his stirrup as he dismounted his mule and led him in to the place of honour on the right of the host. When the meal was served, they pressed the choicest morsels on to his plate – the best part of the lamb, the most delicious rice and stew – and topped his cup of sherbet before he had put it down. So the mullah took the end of his sleeve and very loudly, so that everyone could hear, said, "Eat, sleeve! Eat, jacket! Eat, cloak! Eat, while you can." Everybody looked at him in embarrassed amazement, wondering whether he had not taken leave of his senses. Finally the Governor asked the mullah to explain what he meant by asking his clothes to eat instead of eating himself. "Well," said the cunning mullah, "last Friday, I came dressed in my humble everyday clothes and I was treated like a beggar. Today I borrowed these clothes and everybody is lavishing respect and attention on to me. Since I haven't changed and am still the same old Mullah Nasroddin, your humble servant, it must be my clothes that have made the difference. Therefore it's they who deserve to eat, not me!" At this the Governor apologised profusely and told his servants to treat the mullah with the respect he deserved, no matter how poorly he was dressed.'

At Prince Afsar's receptions, the servants kept serving drinks and tea while the assembly grew in number and animation. My father led the conversation, seasoning it with appropriate anecdotes and quotations, to which the guests listened with attention and responded with suitable exclamations. He had a deep, gentle voice and spoke an eloquent, pure Persian. He always spoke softly, so that one had to listen attentively to hear. This was an astute stratagem:

'In this way, if you are talking nonsense, people can stop listening to you! But, if they are interested in what you are saying, they will pay attention,' he once explained. Women were advised to speak softly at all times, 'since a loud voice can easily sound harsh and is unbecoming', my mother told us.

The *qalyan* was handed round to those who smoked; each had a few puffs before passing it on. They usually put some rose-petals in the water container so that when the smoker blew the pipe the water gurgled and bubbled and the rose-petals danced around in it. Unlike cigarettes and other intoxicants, the *qalyan* is not addictive and is used only occasionally, usually in social gatherings. You prepared it by putting a handful of wet tobacco in the bowl, covered with a few embers. These were taken from a charcoal brazier, if there was one ready, otherwise produced in a 'fire-turner' – a tiny wire-basket with a long flexible handle. A few pieces of charcoal were put in the 'fire-turner', ignited and turned round and round, like a ball attached to a string, until the coal glowed and became pure fire. Sometimes at night you could see a little ball of fire, sparkling and crackling and circling in the air while the wielder of the instrument remained hidden by darkness. You knew there were guests and a *qalyan* was being prepared for them. In memory I associate it with cosy evenings at home, with father and Aunt Ashraf and Grandma sharing it over a cup of tea, surrounded by the rest of us.

At Prince Afsar's, as the evening gathered momentum, poets began to recite their latest creations in passionate declamatory tones, to the delight of the audience who acknowledged their subtleties and eloquence with expressions of approval – 'lovely!' 'Well said!' 'Exquisite!' – thereby encouraging the poet to a paroxysm of excitement, when he let the dying strains of his verse fall upon a hushed and rapt assembly. Then the Prince would ask another of his young protégés to regale his guests.

Meanwhile, the women sat in the drawing-room, which was furnished with Louis XVI chairs and antique bibelots – Sèvres vases, Venetian crystal chandeliers, Bohemian glass lamps, beautiful rugs and hangings. But the room's unique feature was a fresco which covered an entire wall from the high ceiling to a couple of feet from the floor. It depicted an Edenic scene, where a silvery blue stream coiled down diagonally through the trees and spread into a basin in which nymphs frolicked or filled their jugs with the waters of Eternal Youth. Exotic birds and butterflies posed delicately on branches and flowers; Ruben-sesque houris lolled on the grass, clad in diaphanous pastel-coloured silk draperies; cherubs played together in one corner and angels conferred in another, while here and there a gazelle peeped through the thick foliage and in the foreground a few barefoot children played among lambs and chickens. An unknown artist in the previous century had painted it, leaving his illegible signature on the left-hand corner of the picture. He was clearly influenced by European artists, for the fresco was different from the Persian paintings of the period and the figures in it were clearly Western.

I used to gaze at the fresco for hours, mesmerised. Oblivious of the surroundings, my imagination soared towards those beautiful exotic regions, as desirable as out of reach, in the company of the humble artist who had put all his yearnings into this imagined paradise.

A few years later, Prince Afsar died. His wife sold their house and moved to Mashed, to be near her daughter. The new owners, whom we did not know, allowed the fresco to fall into disrepair and eventually covered it with a large piece of textile, as I was told years later. By then, most of the wealthier families had left our district and it was unlikely that anyone with sufficient taste to appreciate the architectural merits of the building, or with the sense of humour to relish the quaint charm of that fresco, would buy the house. But amazingly this did happen. A young doctor from a patrician family, who had originally owned the house, came back from England where he had been studying, married a beautiful girl, and took over the house.

On a visit to Persia some years later, I went to see them, as they were family friends. They had restored the house to its former splendour and furnished it in the same good taste as the Prince Afsars, harmonising comfortable European furniture with Persian rugs and antiques.

The fresco had been repaired too, which gave their drawing-room a unique atmosphere, and the garden had been rescued from years of neglect. The old pines, poplars and plane trees stood sentinel above lesser trees and saplings; the pool, relined with turquoise-blue tiles, reflected their swaying branches; the whole place seemed exactly as I remembered it. Only on the veranda things had changed: there were comfortable garden chairs and swinging sofas, parasols and tables, instead of the sumptuous carpets and brocade cushions of my memory. The guests of the past had nearly all died – the poets, philosophers and the philosopher-prince; the poetry-loving general and the enlightened young mullah who sang mystical chants so enchantingly ...

'You know that on the eve of sabbath,' Aunt Ashraf used to tell us, 'the souls of the departed come and sit on the eaves of the house in the shape of birds, begging for your prayers, which they take back with them to Heaven ...'

Perhaps the birds sitting on the eaves and trees, that last evening I saw the house, were the souls of Prince Afsar and his guests, in need of our prayers and remembrance ...

The young doctor and some of his colleagues set up a clinic uptown. He also worked in a hospital and taught at the University's Medical School. Eventually he became a cabinet minister in one of the late Shah's last governments. After the revolution of 1979, he and his family emigrated to America and their house was taken over by the mob. I do not know what has happened to it. I have heard that the fresco was destroyed straight away, with its cherubs and angels and blonde nymphs frolicking in the Fountain of Eternal Youth.

At Scheherazad's

❧❦

Scheherazad – The First Nursery School in Iran. This inscription was written in bold characters on a long board above the entrance door of an old two-storey town-house which had been converted into a nursery school. It was off Parliament Square, near the Ministry of Education, and was the creation of two Armenian sisters, the Misses Petrossian – Senior and Junior – whom the children called Madame Principal and Madame Supervisor. The older sister took care of administration and bookkeeping while the younger one looked after the children and the staff. The former never left her desk and her office, in contrast to the latter who hardly ever sat down, busy as she was in the playground, the refectory and the classrooms. There were three or four teachers, also Armenian, who were friends and relatives of the founders.

In the past, few children received formal schooling of any sort. Those who did stayed at home until they went to primary school at the age of 5 or 6. The country had an illiteracy rate of eighty to ninety per cent, but Reza Shah, who was himself almost unlettered, believed that the first step to modernisation was education and decreed that primary schooling be compulsory. He was a soldier, used to giving orders and having them carried out, but this task was not as simple as that, and no one dared tell him that it would take a very long time before literacy on a national scale could be achieved. Nevertheless, schools mushroomed all over the country, under the initiative of the Ministry of Education, at least in towns. With their traditional regard for learning, most Persians availed themselves of giving their children some education and thereby improving their chances of success in life, even if they themselves had never been to school. But the idea of play-school, or kindergarten as some called it, was entirely novel and imported from the West.

Soon it became fashionable among the élite to send their children to Scheherazad's, the new nursery school, and my mother decided that I should go too. So, one autumn morning, a droshky came to our door and took mother and me to Scheherazad's. We were met in the entrance hall by Miss Petrossian Junior and led upstairs to her sister's inner sanctum – a large airy room with a desk and a few chairs overlooking the courtyard. Madame Principal was a tall and fairly plump woman with a round pleasant face and a gentle smile. Her hair, streaked with silver threads, was held back in a Victorian bun with a coil in the middle, like a bird's nest. By contrast, her younger sister was tiny, wiry and nervous, not much bigger than the children in her charge. She had loosely permed dark hair and a face that was neatly divided in half from her forehead to the tip of her nose by the deep furrow of a permanent, intense frown.

After the usual exchange of pleasantries with my mother, the two sisters turned their attention to me:

'How old are you? ... I'm sure you're a good little girl and never disobedient or naughty!' They said that not only did I have to be good at school but also at home, and that otherwise a crow would report my bad behaviour to them and I would be severely punished. She went on to say that only that very morning a crow had reported to her that a naughty little girl had wetted her bed, that she had been duly punished and put to shame in front of her classmates, and that everybody had laughed at her and chanted, 'Bed-wetter! Bed-wetter!.'

I was terrified! There was a large population of crows in our garden, their nests perched high among the branches of the pine trees. Their noisy *va-et-vient* started at dawn and went on all day, only subsiding at sunset, when they returned home and settled down for the night. I wondered which one was Miss Petrossian Junior's spy. Since they all looked exactly the same I decided that the most cautious course of action was to consider them all spies! To this day the sight and sound of these harmless birds strike a chord of anxiety and revulsion in me.

The notion of childhood as a carefree, happy stage of life to be enjoyed for itself, before the responsibilities of adulthood began, was a novel one. As I recall, Scheherazad's was therefore more like a penitentiary for the under-aged, or it seemed so at the time.

A few minutes after the interview, my mother left, promising to send Ali to fetch me at noon. Miss Petrossian Junior took me by the hand and led me to a classroom full of boys and girls of the same age as myself, sitting at tables covered with bits of paper and coloured pencils.

'All stand up for Madame Supervisor,' said the teacher, and the children stood up and looked at the newcomer.

'I bring you a new friend today. Make sure you are nice to her and show her everything. OK?'

'Yes, Madame Supervisor,' came back in unison.

The two women conferred in Armenian for a few minutes, with occasional glances towards me, and then Miss Petrossian Junior left the room.

The teacher, Miss Dornushian, was a young attractive girl, with wavy brown hair down to her shoulders held off her face with a red ribbon that matched her lipstick and nail-varnish. She wore a tight short dress, with a slight cleavage in which nestled a gold cross. She looked in every way like a *Farangi*, such as you saw in fashion journals, quite different from most women around me, and I was immediately fascinated by her. But as soon as Miss Petrossian disappeared, the welcoming expression and sweet smile, that she had displayed to reassure me, vanished too.

'You'd better be good, or else! ...' she said sternly, fluttering her hands near my face, her long, painted nails flashing like the bloodstained claws of a bird of prey, as if to imply that they would dig my eyes out. She gave me a piece of thin cardboard with the outline of a bouquet drawn on it, some coloured pencils, and told me to fill in the flowers and leaves with whatever colours I liked. Then she ambled nonchalantly to her desk, sat down and buried her head in some magazine.

As a newcomer, I naturally provoked a certain amount of curiosity, a few furtive glances, a couple of enquiries as to where I lived, but at the slightest noise Miss Dornushian looked up and frowned: 'Hush! No noise! Do your work, or there will be severe punishment!'

I started painting the bouquet but it was no good – I missed home. I was frightened and shy, wanted my mother, Nanny, Zahra ... I thought that if I ever returned home I would never, never come back, and tears ran down my face.

'What do I hear?' asked Miss Dornushian, slowly and menacingly rising from her chair. 'A spoilt little girl whimpering for Mummy? Charming! Aren't you ashamed of yourself? Are your classmates crying? No! They're having fun, enjoying themselves. Now, you do the same!'

You bet! Twenty pairs of eyes darted towards me like a shower of arrows dipped in contempt and pity. In vain did I look for anything else – a wink of solidarity, a smile of understanding. I whimpered and went back to my painting, trying to distract myself. But tears kept running down my face. I must have learnt to weep silently then – it has stood me in good stead since.

Presently a gong resounded through the building and we were herded downstairs to the refectory for our snack, the *goûter* as Miss Dornushian called it to impress us with her knowledge of French. The refectory had long benches and tables laid with rose-patterned enamel plates and mugs, little knives and forks, and whatever we had brought with us to eat. Mine was a piece of cake and an apple. I picked the knife to peel and slice the apple when suddenly I heard a swish and felt a sizzling pain on my knuckles.

'This is your *left* hand!' admonished Miss Dornushian, towering over me. She grabbed the knife and put it in my right hand. I was left-handed and couldn't cut or peel with the right hand, but somehow managed to slice the apple roughly and swallow it with my anger. I have always had trouble telling left from right quickly, but for a long time whenever I hesitated the refectory scene came to my mind: the smitten hand was the left one.

Back in the classroom after the break, I was miserable and restless, but Miss Dornushian had devised a method of enforcing discipline which was as efficient as apparently harmless; she either twisted your ear-lobes until you screamed with pain, or brought down a long pencil on your knuckles which produced the same effect. Neither left any trace of physical injury. To be fair, she seldom resorted to such extreme measures; usually a frown of displeasure and a flutter of her claws were enough of a deterrent.

It was decreed that Ali should take me to Scheherazad's every morning and bring me back at noon, but the next day I declared that I did not wish to go:

'I want to stay here with you! I promise to be good!' I told my mother.

'Don't be silly,' she retorted. 'You may not like it there yet, but soon you'll make friends and love it. You don't want to stay here and be bored while everyone else is at school, do you?' I did, but Ali grabbed me and rushed out of the house. I cried and struggled and begged ... Nothing doing. Only when we had gone far enough did he put me down and pull me by the hand:

'Come along, young lady. I haven't got all day!'

And so it became a routine: every morning I woke up with a heavy heart and left the house in sorrow, crying and begging not to be sent away. The fear that the crow might have reported me to Miss Petrossian Junior for some misdemeanour was my main preoccupation, and indeed once or twice she told me that the crow had told her about my making a fuss before leaving for school.

Once there, I tried to make the best of the situation, got into the whirl of things, made friends and joined in games. Upon arrival, we would form into columns and march around the courtyard to the sound of Schubert's *Marche Militaire* and similar classical military tunes which emanated from an old hand-wound gramaphone with a brass funnel. On the front of the square box on which the turntable rotated was the picture of a dog sitting beside a similar gramophone and listening to the sound of His Master's Voice. We could not read the inscription, but we were fascinated by the machine. Sometimes as we marched we caught a glimpse of Miss Petrossian Senior, standing at the window of her office behind lace curtains, smiling like a benevolent ghost, even waving at times in the manner of royalty. We would smile and wave back.

After exercise, we would divide into several groups and go to our classrooms, where we painted and scribbled the alphabet and sang songs. Soon, I was singled out as the soloist and, being keen, learnt the tunes quickly. I was encouraged and held up as an example. My stock rose, and I became less unhappy.

The most memorable event of my year at Scheherazad's was our participation in the anniversary celebrations of the Women's Emancipation Day, on 8 January. Reza Shah had abolished the *chador* (veil) before I was born and proclaimed women's right to participate fully in the life of the nation. Women were to go to school and university, learn and practise professions, and help create a new, progressive Persia. More than any other measure, the abolition of the veil had met with opposition from certain mullahs and their followers in the Bazaar. Perhaps it was because, in the mind of ordinary people, the veil was bound up with the notions of honour, chastity, modesty, property and power, that it could be used by the less progressive clerics to regain some of the ground they had lost. To obviate such a reaction, some advocates of emancipation believed that it would be better to *educate* women out of the veil gradually, rather than force them. But how long would that take, went the counter-argument, and how could you educate them if they were swathed in yards of black cloth and shut up in their homes? No, it was better to make a clean break. The *chador* had always been a city phenomenon anyway: country and tribal women had their own costumes, with colourful headgear made of flimsy kerchiefs and ornate bonnets that protected them from the fierce sun without hampering their movements or covering their faces.

To set an example, Reza Shah had appeared in public and on photographs with his own unveiled wife and daughters, and the women of the ruling classes had immediately followed suit. It was in the more traditional religious families like ours that the unveiling of women created a conundrum: how to move with the times yet keep the basic religious precepts.

As is often the case, those whom the new law was designed to liberate resisted it most fiercely: some women simply refused to discard their *chador*s and drop their chains. So policemen were ordered to tear them off their heads in the streets if they defied the law. The women of our family consulted my father who, as a *Mujtahid*, could interpret the *Sharia* and pronounce judgements on such matters. He told them that the principle of the veil concerned women's honour and dignity but that it did not matter what shape it took, and that they could discard the *chador* if they wished. My mother and aunts had elegant loose coats made for them which they wore over their dresses, and covered their heads with silk scarfs. Soon everybody in the family discarded even these, and went out bareheaded like the majority of educated women. Only my mother kept her scarf and her traditional ways till the end.

Women of the younger generation took to their freedom as birds to the air. Indeed for us it was hard to imagine that women could *ever* have been wrapped up and shut away behind walls. At home, the *chador* survived in its lighter form, made of printed voile and worn over the shoulders like a shawl. When the law relaxed after the War, the *chador* reappeared in the streets, but in its lighter form and only among the poor, as a sort of *cache-misère*, to hide their old shabby clothes. But, as a symbol of subjugation and ignorance, the veil seemed to have gone for good! Why, half the country's doctors, dentists, teachers, lawyers and civil servants were soon women; how could it ever come back!

Then, suddenly in 1978, the *black* veil reappeared: there they were, women in their tens of thousands, wrapped in black, shaking their fists and shouting slogans, like an army of malignant crows in a nightmarish sequence of a science-fiction film, presaging doom and destruction.

'What has happened to the *women* of Persia?' they asked in the drawing-rooms of Paris, New York, London ... Who knows why and how a virus attacks the collective psyche of a nation? The evil mullahs may have been the agents who introduced it, but the infection swept across the country and the body politic because its immune system had been weakened by excess and injustice, by too much inequality, and above all by hubris. And now the disease has to run its devastating course and burn itself out before reconstruction can begin.

That year, Scheherazad's, as the first and only Western-style nursery school in Persia was to participate in the celebrations of Women's Emancipation Day by presenting a play based on Little Red Riding Hood. A boy with a big nose and a scar on his cheek – whose name I have forgotten – was to play the wolf; Miss Dornushian's favourite little girl, a pretty blonde whose mother was French, was to be the eponymous heroine, and I was to be her mother and sing a lullaby to her infant sister while waiting for her to come back from visiting her grandmother.

The play was to be staged appropriately at the Women's Teachers' Training College, which had a large amphitheatre used for lectures and ceremonies. Several of the Royal Princesses were to attend the show, together with the Prime Minister, members of the Cabinet, academics, Army officers, etc. ... My parents were invited but my father never went to such official gatherings, partly because of his costume and partly because he did not want to be in the world more than strictly necessary. But my mother was much younger than him and liked the excitement, the elegant clothes, the social whirlwind, and Uncle Alem usually escorted her.

Formal dress was *de rigueur*: tailcoat and top hat for men, hat and gloves for women. My mother had a special black silk suit made for the occasion by her dressmaker, Emily, and bought a matching black hat with a dotted *voilette*. She had a heavy corset full of whalebones and straps which Zahra used to help her put on:

'Pull! Pull hard! Harder, harder!' she would say, and Zahra would put her knee in the hollow of her back and pull the ribbons tight to make her waistline slimmer. Five childbirths and post-natal illness had taken their toll, and mother's figure 'was not what it used to be', to say the least!

We rehearsed the show endlessly and on the day of the performance were driven to the College in a private coach. Miss Petrossian Junior put one of her own dresses on me and held it up with a belt; she put a doll wrapped up in a shawl in my arms as a baby, and for the first time gave me a kiss before pushing me on to the stage. I dispatched my daughter, Little Red Riding Hood, with a basket of provisions for her grandmother, warning her of the Big Bad Wolf, and asking her not to take a short-cut through the forest. Then I sat down in a rocking-chair and sang my lullaby:

Lullaby and go to sleep, my Flower of the Tulip Tree,
The panther is prowling in the woods, looking for the one
    he loves,
Lullaby and go to sleep, my Flower of the Hazelnut Tree,
Your mother has gone to the chest of clothes to fetch you a
    pretty dress,
Lullaby and go to sleep, my   Flower of the Poppy,
Your father has gone away, may God protect him and bring
    him home soon ...

Applause. After the show, the 'actors' were introduced to the Royal Princesses, who kissed us and congratulated us on our performances. My stock rose at Scheherazad's even more, as well as at home and among friends. Miss Dornushian taught me songs in Armenian, French, English, which I learnt by rote without understanding the words and delivered on request.

In later years, nursery schools, private and public, appeared all over our town and many were bilingual in French or English. On a trip to Persia years later, I went on a sentimental journey to my old schools, which were all in the same area. The district had changed its physiognomy: the *Majlis* (Parliament) was there, so was the square in front of it, with flowerbeds and fountains and the statue of the Shah in the middle, but the buildings all round had been pulled down and replaced with new ones – office blocks and government premises. Amazingly the two-storey house of Scheherazad's was still there, now used as a depot. So was the board, weatherbeaten and crooked, its lettering faded to a mere outline, hanging limply on one side: *Scheherazads – The First Nursery School in Iran*. No one had bothered to remove it. I found out that Miss Dornushian had married a fellow Armenian and emigrated to America, and that the Petrossian sisters had got old, retired and eventually died. But I still remember them and their brain-child whenever I hear Schubert's *Marche Militaire*: the old gramophone with its glittering brass funnel, the lace curtains and, behind them, Miss Petrossian Senior, smiling at us and at her own contribution to progress and hope.

I have a picture of our year at Scheherazad's, with me standing in the back row and looking suspicious. I can't remember the names of any of the children except one: Roshan (Claire) who was my best friend and whom I never saw afterwards in Persia. But many years later I came across her in Paris: she had married a Polish engineer and gone to live in Warsaw, but now she and her husband were trying to emigrate back to Persia, and she was in Paris to work things out. I never saw her again. I wonder where she is now – in General Jaruzelski's Poland or in Khomeini's Persia. What a choice!

I recorded that lullaby on my first LP in London, which was a collection of Persian folk-songs and mystic chants. It became the signature tune of the Children's Hour on Persian Television and was played every evening for years, until the programme, the television and the whole country, went up in the conflagration of revolution.

The New Day

❦

> From the cradle to the grave, seek knowledge!
> Firdowsi

Norooz – Girls' Primary School Number Two, was one of the many state schools founded by the Ministry of Education. Its name means 'the New Day', which is also the name of the Persian New Year that occurs at the spring equinox on 21 March and whose origins go back to Zoroastrian times and beyond. This double meaning alluded to the dawn of a new era in Persian history with the advent of Reza Shah and his progressive plans, and was indicative of the country's confident, forward-looking mood.

An ornate tile surface beneath the signboard incorporated Firdowsi's injunction quoted above, which was the motto of the Ministry of Education and appeared on all their buildings and institutions, even on their headed paper. It was intended to assert the continuity of Persian history and its spiritual heritage, and the new dynasty's aspiration to an imperial pre-Islamic past as glorified by the poet's great epic *Shahnameh*, (*The Book of Kings*).

Norooz was in a little cul-de-sac off Parliament Square. All the main streets in the area had been surfaced, but it took the authorities years before they got round to asphalting the school alley, which became a pool of mud in winter and ruined our newly polished shoes.

The entrance door led to a covered hall and a large rectangular courtyard beyond, with a round pool in the middle. This was usually covered with planks to prevent children from falling into it while they played during breaks. A covered passage led to an adjoining, smaller courtyard which was used for sport and housed the refectory and some classrooms. The two houses had been the *andaroon* and the *birooni* of a grandee's residence in the past, now converted to a school. All round the big courtyard were classrooms, with doors and windows down to the ground, whence the children poured out, upon hearing the bell. There were several drinking-water barrels at the end of the courtyard, with taps and mugs chained to them, but the children rushed to drink directly from the taps by putting their mouths around them, with the result that any epidemic swept through the whole school like a forest fire.

The janitor and his wife lived in a room between the two courtyards, with one door opening on to the connecting passage and another on to the entrance hall. They guarded their privacy by keeping both doors firmly shut at all times and no one had ever seen the inside of their lodging. But the janitor's wife sat on a wooden stool outside their room in the covered passage, whence she monitored all the *va-et-vient*, issued endless orders to her husband, and showered admonitions and imprecations on the children: 'The-naughty-little-devils-may-God-burn-them-in-hell!'

'No one has ever heard her shut up!' her husband was overheard muttering.

The Principal's office, beside the entrance hall, rose above the one-storey edifice like a sentry's observation post, with a storage room beneath and a set of steps leading to it. From this ivory tower Madame Principal, as we called her, presided over the school, but she only appeared on special occasions, prize-givings and other such ceremonies, otherwise she would summon pupils to her inner sanctum and talk to them individually when the occasion arose. It was her formidable deputy, the Supervisor, appropriately called Miss Nazm (it means order, discipline), who ran the school, dealing with teachers and parents, and above all maintaining discipline.

Like the majority of teachers, Miss Order was a graduate of the Women's Teachers' Training College, and unmarried. It was still considered that only those girls who were too plain or too 'free' to 'catch a husband' went in for higher education and a career. The attractive, the rich and well-born were snapped up as soon as they left school, if not before. 'The rejects', 'the failures', the 'not-to-be-looked-at', were a few of the expressions used to describe women like Miss Order.

Things were changing though, and several of our teachers at

Norooz married during my six years there. But Miss Order did not: she was already 'old' – around 30 – and 'past it'. She was also much too plain. Tall and skinny, she had a gaunt face marked with several scars of childhood skin infections, a dark complexion and a severe expression. She hardly ever smiled, for fear of losing her authority, and always sported a long steel ruler with which she gently tapped her calf or the palm of her hand. The ruler was made of two thin, flexible strips of steel with layers of paper in between: its flexibility gave it the function of a whip which, when applied to the palm of your hand, produced a searing pain that shot right through your whole body, a punishment you could reasonably count on if you were cheeky, idle, or rowdy in class.

On the rare occasions that Miss Order did smile, her face opened and glowed, her eyes twinkled, as if a breeze had cleared away the cloud of frustration and unhappiness that surrounded her.

'She could be quite pretty you know, with a bit of make-up and a few more pounds of flesh,' my mother once said, but Miss Order had given up on life a long time ago. She had a little whistle which she wore on a ribbon round her neck and blew whenever things got out of hand in the playground, whereupon the scuffle would stop, the picture freeze into a *tableau*, and the culprit be found and punished.

In those days, Persia's system of education was modelled on the French: you spent six years at primary school at the end of which period you sat for an exam and, if successful, moved up to the *lycée* or high school. The curriculum and exam papers were set by the Ministry of Education to ensure the same standards everywhere.

It took us, my sister and me, twenty minutes to walk to *Norooz*. Ali accompanied us in the morning, brought our lunch in a three-tier container at noon and came to collect us at four o'clock. We would arrive at about eight in the morning, play around in the courtyard for half an hour and form into caterpillars outside our classrooms when the bell rang. Miss Order would stand in the middle by the pool and conduct us singing a couple of patriotic hymns followed by the National Anthem. When it was over, she would make a few announcements and say, 'Now it's time to punish the bad!' She would call out the names of the culprits, those who were guilty of disobedience, idleness, bad language, etc. ... and, one by one they would go forward and be reprimanded in front of the whole school and given several blows of the redoubtable steel ruler on the palm of their hands. Invariably they broke down and cried bitterly, more from shame than pain. I do not recall ever being called out, though I well remember the dread that made my entrails twist at every roll-call, for I was naughtier than most, I *knew*! Punishments over, we would file into our classrooms and begin the day.

Being left-handed, I started school-life on the wrong foot! One day at the beginning, I was practising the alphabet when the teacher walked to me and grabbed my hand; she put a pencil between my index and middle-finger and pressed so hard that I screamed and tears poured down my cheeks.

'This is *not* the hand you write with! This is your *left* hand!' she growled. Then she put the pencil in my right hand and guided it for a few lines: 'Now continue like that!'

I found it very awkward and uncomfortable, but she kept an eye on me and helped me the following days until I got used to writing with the 'correct' hand. As a result, I became ambidexterous, writing with the right hand and doing every-thing else with the left – sewing, cutting, cooking, etc.

I did not like school much, and would have preferred to stay at home; I often whimpered before leaving in the morning and developed mysterious aches and pains which were immediately diagnosed as malingering, stratagems for not going to school, and ignored. Gradually, I found consolation in learning to read and making friends. All those new children's books, full of pictures and stories by La Fontaine, Hans Christian Anderson, Grimm ... translated into Persian, which I used to beg my sister to read to me, were now within my reach. But, once I had grasped the lessons, I got bored in class and became restless. I moved about talking to my neighbours, and distracted everyone with my clowning. I was often reprimanded and put in a corner, my face turned to the wall, with the cardboard pinned to my back saying 'I am a naughty girl!' I did not mind much, as long as it did not say 'I'm a stupid girl and can't learn my lessons', which happened to several others. Once or twice I was summoned to the Principal's office and told off gently, after which I would be 'good' for a while until boredom got the better of me. But nothing gratifies a teacher more than a student's eagerness to learn, and since I was good at lessons my teachers tolerated me. But I did not become a 'model student' until the last years of the Lycée, when the subjects were more varied and the lessons much more taxing.

School became more enjoyable as we started artistic activities. Other than art and music lessons, we had theatre productions at the end of terms, competitions, singing sessions. The plays, usually written by Miss Order, were edifying tales about naughty, wicked children getting their come-uppance and being reformed into tidy, dutiful little ladies at the end. They had singing and dancing numbers inserted into them, and, of course, audience participation by other children. In one of them I played the lead, the dunce who starts life as a lazy no-good and ends up top-of-the-form. My mother came to the show and was quite proud of me, but I was not encouraged to sing and act, and no other member of the family ever came to see me.

The first blow at my extra-curricular activities came when our music teacher offered to teach me the violin free of charge if a little instrument could be procured for me. My mother did not mind my learning to play an instrument provided I did not do it in public. But when she broached the subject with my father, he frowned and simply said, 'What next?' and the matter was dropped. He knew that, if I had any talent and learnt to play, nothing would stop me doing it in public, and that was still not done. Years later in Paris, I rented a piano and exchanged music lessons for my rudimentary English. My piano teacher introduced me to a great opera singer, Mademoiselle Yvonne Galle, then a professor at the Paris Conservatoire, and I began training my voice. Yvonne Galle charged me very little, and I paid for the lessons by modelling and doing other holiday jobs.

That early deprivation taught me a lesson, and, in the sixties, I bought little violins for my sons when they were five years old and found them a good teacher. I knew they probably would not become professional musicians but at least they could play, would never be bored, and could not blame me for depriving them of the experience.

Despite my high-spirited, troublesome conduct, I loved all my teachers, though only a couple have remained vivid in my memory. My favourite was a Miss Najeeb (modest, virginal), the eldest daughter of a schoolteacher who had many children. The family lived in a small modern house not far from us and Miss Najeeb liked my mother and came to see her from time to time during the summer holidays. She too was a graduate of the Women's Teachers' Training College.

Miss Modest had huge dark-brown birthmarks which covered half her face and made her lower lip look tumescent on one side, as if stung by a bee or hit by a fist. The patches are called 'moon spots' in Persian, an allusion to the dark patches of the moon, since a pretty face is referred to as the moon by poets and minstrels; 'You look like the moon today!' you might say to a friend, which in English would be simply, 'How lovely you look', or 'How well you look'.

So prominent and large were Miss Modest's 'moon patches', that no one noticed her pretty blue eyes, her fair hair and lovely complexion 'on the other side'. On the contrary, her long face and ungainly figure won her the nickname of 'Horsey', and the street urchins teased her mercilessly as she went past, calling her 'Miss Patchy', 'Miss Striped', 'Miss Two-Flavours', etc. She would blush and quicken her pace, pretending that she had not heard or understood the allusion.

It was customary for eldest daughters to marry first, but Miss Modest's younger sisters had already married and left home, on the understanding that there was no point in ruining their chances by waiting for their eldest sister who was very probably destined for spinsterhood. There is a tacit scenario in every family, with each member being cast in a specific role. You either accept your allocated part and play it till the end – which is usually the case – or break away and mould your own destiny. Miss Modest was cast in the role of the Spinster-Elder-Daughter, the professional aunt to her nephews and nieces, the one who would look after her parents in their old age. But although she seemed on course to fulfil such expectations, in the end she broke away through sheer optimism and faith in life, and in her own good fortune. She believed that it was only a matter of time before the perfect husband would appear on the horizon and whisk her away to eternal bliss.

One day during the summer holidays, she came to visit my mother and recounted how on the previous evening she had been to a party, dressed in a red chiffon gown, her hair done up 'just so', her face made up by her sister, and how every man had asked her to dance and every women eyed her with envy. We suppressed our giggles of embarrassment, knowing that it was out of pity that the men had gallantly asked her to dance and that the women's interest had more to do with malice than envy. Yet Miss Modest was in seventh heaven, gliding on a cloud of happiness: she *knew* it would not be long before a Prince Charming would present himself at her door.

And, would you believe it, he did! Not on a white charger but in a large maroon Mercedes Benz. He had a niece at our school and had met Miss Modest at some function. Later his sister had invited her to lunch and he had seen her again, and he had simply fallen in love with her gaiety, cleverness and trust. He had proposed to her in preference to all the young, pretty, upper-class girls who had been pressed upon him. True to the spirit of fairy tales, Miss Modest and her husband lived happily ever after and had many children.

Madame Principal was a middle-aged, grey-haired plump woman with a benevolent smile, whom we loved as a grandmother. There was a deep sorrow in her life: her husband had died young and left her without any children. Thereafter she had devoted her life to the school. Further, her beloved only brother had gone 'cuckoo' and declared himself a prophet, sent by God to reform the country's religion. He had even gone so far as to change his name by deed poll to Mr Prophet. Muslims consider Mohammad the last link in the Chain of Prophesy, which starts with Abraham and runs through Moses and Jesus, and call him 'The Seal of Prophets'. Anyone who claims to be a

Messenger of God is, therefore, an impostor and a criminal, to be punished by death. In the past Mr Prophet would have been tried by a religious court, found guilty and hanged, but his neck was saved thanks to Reza Shah's abolition of religious courts and the prevalent atmosphere of religious tolerance. Mr Prophet was recognised as being 'off his rocker' and retired from his job in the Civil Service with a pension. His wife, a famous beauty, had run off with a rich industrialist and taken their two daughters with her, while Mr Prophet had moved in with his widowed sister and become a recluse, waiting 'for his time to come'.

His daughters, the Prophet sisters, Pari and Simeen (Fairy and Silvery Maid) came to *Norooz* and, being exactly the same age as my sister and me, became our friends. They came and stayed with us at weekends to the delight of the whole household, for they were ravishingly beautiful and had perfect manners. At the age of 10, my friend Simeen was already an accomplished proto-Lolita who cast her spell on everyone, male and female, young and old. It was she who taught me all about men and women and love and babies and movie-stars and 'abroad', meaning Europe.

Once or twice on Thursday afternoon (eve of sabbath and half-day holiday), I went to their house to play with her. It was a modern building in a newly developed residential district, furnished in Western style and adorned with a great many objects in crystal: chandeliers, birds, elephants and giraffes, vases and bowls, and so on. They were products of the industrialist stepfather's new crystal factory and very valuable. The house was run by Ebby, a congenital eunuch with a smooth beardless face like a baby's and a castrato's flutey voice. His devotion to the family knew no bounds and extended to the guests. But, above all, he loved 'his Lady' and, being a eunuch, was as close to her as a personal maid.

One Thursday afternoon, when we arrived at Simeen's house we found her mother in their drawing-room, reclining on a sofa reading a book. She was exquisitely beautiful, with auburn hair rippling down to her shoulders, green eyes shadowed by long dark eyelashes, a 'rose-bud' mouth and perfect bone-structure. She was wearing a silk negligee in *rose-antique*, which loosely covered her slightly plump figure; she had a wistful expression and a languid smile, as if she were posing for a photograph or in front of a cine camera.

'What are you reading, Mummy?' enquired Simeen as she bent down to kiss her.

'Oh, a French novel someone has translated, all about a woman who is deceived and abandoned by her lover. Ach Men! They say they love you, that they can't live without you, but once you have given yourself to them they get tired and move on! ... I tell you, little girls, never trust men, never!'

Ebby came in with a tray of tea and biscuits and fruit, and put it on the table in front of her.

'Now, Ebby is faithful! Oh yes, *he* loves me ...! Don't you, Ebby? He loves me very much, but he is a *eunuch*, not much good for anything! ...' She tossed her head back and laughed, while Ebby giggled and blushed and left the room. Mrs Prophet had run away with a young man, who was rich and handsome and had swept her off her feet, now she couldn't understand that his feelings had cooled somewhat.

We lost track of the Prophet sisters after primary school, but heard that they had married young, gone to Europe, divorced and remarried several times, as beautiful daughters of the new rich bourgeoisie were beginning to do. But they and other friends at *Norooz* opened a vista on to a world that was completely new to me – of wealthy industrialists, film-starish women in silk negligees, holidays abroad, and the pursuit of pleasure without religious restrictions. Their number grew fast in the decades that followed until it formed a substantial middle class. They were expected to stem the tide of revolution, instead they played into the hands of reactionary mullahs, on the one hand by their excesses, and on the other by their discontent.

Simeen and I were among the few pupils who stayed at school for lunch, our houses being too far to go back and forth. The janitor's wife warmed our food on a coal-stove in the little refectory and supervised us. Meanwhile her husband went around filling the stoves in the classrooms and the water-barrels in the courtyard. He was a tiny man with white hair and a beard that always seemed only three days long, just a white stubble. His grey uniform seemed several sizes too big for him, as if he floated in it. He always had a surly expression and shuffled around mumbling to himself. His wife was short and fat, shaped like a top. She had one blind eye and one bad leg which made her limp and waddle like a duck, swaying from side to side as if she were about to fall down. She wore a kerchief round her head and a flimsy *chador* tied round her waist, and she never stopped talking in a loud, husky voice, even when no one was paying the slightest attention to her.

At four o'clock, the school bell rang and children dispersed in all directions towards home. A few were collected in cars, some by servants already waiting outside the gate, but the majority walked away in small groups. Occasionally our escorts were late and we played while waiting for them. Sometimes we got so hot running and jumping and skipping that we discarded our gloves, scarves and jackets, then dashed away without picking them up when Ali arrived, only to remember when we had gone too far to return. The next day the janitor's wife would deny that she had found anything at all when cleaning the classrooms and the yards:

'You must have lost them in the street, because I never saw anything here,' she would say calmly. There was no way of proving that she had in fact purloined the clothes and stationery items that had been left behind. But she must have had a tidy little second-hand business on the side to supplement their meagre salary.

Every time I lost something, my mother scolded me, saying that I was the most scatter-brained child ever, that she was not made of money and her purse was not bottomless. My father would intervene, offering to replace the missing item and restore peace. Once I was given a very pretty white fur coat by a friend of my mother's who had brought it back from Europe. It was only rabbit-skin but very warm and chic – I loved it. One afternoon, Ali was late fetching me and I began to play in the courtyard with a couple of other girls who were also waiting. I took my fur coat off and put it on a step when I got too hot. Presently Ali arrived in a hurry saying we had guests at home and had to run back, so I forgot to pick up my coat. The next day the janitor's wife refused to give it back to me, saying that she had not seen it. I was panic-stricken: 'But you must have found it! I left it on the step, there! Please. Please, give it back!'

She was adamant: 'Are you accusing me of being a thief?' she asked indignantly. 'How do I know what you did with your coat!' As I insisted, she threw a tantrum and faked hysteria: 'Oh, people! Come and see how this little girl is accusing me of theft! Oh, people! Oh, Muslims! Is it fair, I ask you, me, a cripple, working my bones out for this school! I am dishonoured by calumny, oh, God's people! ...' She cried and screamed and her husband rushed to calm her down while she pretended to faint in his arms. Everyone looked at me as if I had committed murder.

'I call the Prophet as witness' she continued as she regained consciousness. 'Whoever is guilty of stealing this white rabbit coat will pay for it on the Day of Judgement!' I was very angry, and I did not give two hoots for what happened on the Day of Judgement – I wanted my pretty coat here and now! But there was nothing I could do, and finally gave up.

One day in my last year, I stayed alone in the classroom waiting for Ali after all the other children had left. Eventually I decided to walk and meet him on the way. When I came into the courtyard I realised that nobody knew I was still inside, for the gate was bolted. The janitor's door was for once ajar, and I looked in to ask if he could let me out. The room was dark and there were several people in it: a youngish woman, three children between the ages of 6 and 12, and, sitting in a corner, a thin, sickly young man. There was a small samovar before him, with some cups and saucers, and a little stove on which a pot was boiling.

It transpired that the janitor and his wife had one son who had become a cripple as a result of a 'fever' – it must have been polio – and that they did their best to help him and his family. So that was where all our coats, scarves, gloves, jackets, pens and pencils and rubbers went! To keep their *aberoo*, they never begged or complained, but everyone knew there was tragedy in their family. Everyone except the pupils, and I felt guilty about having made a fuss over my rabbit coat.

After I moved on to the *lycée*, I sometimes went to see the janitor and his wife, taking them money from my mother and hand-me-down clothes for their grandchildren. Then, one day, there was a new janitor: the old man had died, his wife had moved in with her son to look after his children while his wife went to work and earn a living for them all. No, no one knew their address and the new janitor's wife would love the clothes for her children and would pray for the young lady and ...

Mrs Principal retired shortly afterwards; Miss Order took over as the headmistress, and I never went back to *Norooz*.

The Princess

❧❧

The Princess was one of the three best *lycée*s for girls in the capital. It was at the end of a main road leading to Parliament Square, and whenever there was a demonstration in front of the *Majlis* we could hear the sound of the loudspeakers and the crowd. You entered the *lycée* at 12 or 13, spent five or six years there, and left with your baccalaureate, Part One and Part Two. The curriculum, like that of the French *lycée*s on which it was modelled, was varied and heavy, including the arts and the sciences. A number of pupils failed their exams at the end of each year and had to stay in the same class for a second year, and many more were refused their baccalaureate at the final examination. One older girl in my class had failed her finals four times and only managed to scrape through at the fifth attempt.

Upon entering the *lycée*, you chose a foreign language, either English or French. In the old days, most people preferred French – it was the language of the Court, of diplomacy and of Western culture – but since the War the trend had reversed, and most schoolchildren chose English. I had started learning English earlier, so I decided to continue. We had to learn the rudiments of Arabic as well. But, what with it being a very difficult language, having religious connotations which did not interest anyone, and being badly taught by teachers who did not know it themselves, it was every pupil's *bête noire* subject. However, I was interested in it because I loved Persian – language and literature – both of which were influenced by Arabic. You could trace the origin and ramifications of a word if you knew its Arabic root and thereby use it correctly. So Arabic was compulsory for the same reasons that Latin and Greek used to be in the West. Yet this analogy is not quite correct, since Arabic is a semitic language, while Persian is an Indo-European one, closer in structure and spirit to, say, English or German. Still, in Persia we had adopted and adapted the Arabic alphabet, after the Arab Conquest in the seventh century, and a good deal of our vocabulary was based on Arabic roots. My father was an Arabist and had written some of his philosophical books in Arabic, much as European scholars in the Middle Ages wrote in Latin. Our Arabic teacher at the *lycée* soon revealed himself as not knowing much, and I began to study it by myself, occasionally asking my father for help.

I was also keen on English. When still at primary school, I had asked my father to let me have private lessons with an American who had been sent to Persia in a cultural exchange programme, and was teaching some of my friends. My father had asked the advice of his colleague Olive Souratgar, an Englishwoman married to a Persian, who taught at the University, and she had kindly offered to teach me privately free of charge. So, twice a week, I went to her house after school for tea and lessons. Soon I was reading the English classics with her, and learning grammar and vocabulary as we went along. It was the beginning of a love affair that has lasted to this day but, unlike most passions, has not led to disillusion or a decline in enthusiasm.

Olive's husband, Dr Souratgar, was the Professor of English Literature at the University and a famous poet. A decade or so later he was elected 'the Prince of Poets' – the Poet Laureate – one of the rare prestigious appointments with which no one disagreed. He came from Shiraz, the 'city of poets', the cradle of the Persian language itself (*Farsi*, Persian, means 'from Fars', the region whose capital is Shiraz) and the birthplace of two of its greatest practitioners, Hafiz and Saadi, Persia's most popular classical poets. True to type, Dr Souratgar was a most romantic figure: tall, handsome, exceptionally attractive and charming, with a rare poetic gift that combined lofty eloquence with exquisite lyricism.

The Souratgars had one son, David (now a high-ranking banker in London), and their visits to our house were always keenly anticipated. Olive, who spoke perfect Persian, with a strong but attractive English accent, was a source of exotic wonder to us, and so was David who, although little like us, could speak English perfectly! As for Dr Souratgar himself, he had an inexhaustible flow of witty anecdotes, apposite poems, linguistic fireworks which he displayed with ease and grace. Listening to him and my father was akin to watching two lithe fencing champions compete, as they parried, teased, tackled, glided and lunged amid a shower of sparks. There was much laughter and expression of mutual appreciation, and we all enjoyed the spectacle.

Later I lost track of the Souratgars, except through my parents. After the revolution of 1979, Olive returned to England to be near her son and grandchildren, her husband having died some years earlier. She found my address and we met; she said she had felt lonely and a stranger in her own land, having spent all her adult life in Persia and all her friends being Persian. The England she had left behind was changed beyond recognition, and she was bewildered and did not enjoy living any more. She died a few years later and I went to her funeral. It was a forlorn occasion, with just a few of us sitting in the tiny chapel of the crematorium. Had she died in Persia in the old days, she would have had a grand funeral, with thousands of mourners. She had taught everyone, from the Royal Princes and Princesses to ordinary students of humble backgrounds, in a country where respect for learning and those who convey it was until recently very strong, and where the mixing of politics with teaching had not diminished the prestige of the latter.

Soon after her death, I received a letter from a cousin in which he said that he had recently visited Dr Souratgar's tomb in Shiraz, quoting a couplet from his epitaph:

'They say there is a place on the other side of the world
Where Grief and Sorrow have never walked ...'

An agnostic all his life and a sceptic in the mould of Omar Khayyam in his poetry, he had nonetheless expressed the hope that there might be a reality beyond death which would make sense of our tribulations in this world.

Thanks to Olive Souratgar, I was top of the form in English but came a cropper in everything else at the end of my first year at the *lycée* – I had not done a stroke of work! I had not realised that the heavy programme of the *lycée* was different from the simple fare of primary school, where I had sailed through exams nonchalantly and taken success for granted. I had to resit three subjects at the end of the summer holidays and move up if I passed. I was subjected to merciless teasing and sarcasm from my brothers and sister, gently reprimanded by my parents, and felt ashamed of by my teachers.

'How could a girl from your family behave like a dunce?' they inferred. I learnt my lesson – literally! From then on I worked; pranks and mischievous behaviour gradually gave way to 'seriousness', as the subjects became more complex and demanding. Self-doubt became a constant source of torment and has remained so to this day. I certainly never took successful exam results for granted but agonised with anxiety after every test. So I was utterly surprised when I came first in my baccalaureate.

The Princess was a two-storey building with classrooms on three sides. A huge wrought-iron gate led from the street to the rectangular courtyard. To prevent the girls from being seen from outside, a high concave brick wall was built in front of the gate, a couple of yards inside. There was no playground but the courtyard was laid out with white lines for games – volley-ball, basketball, etc. The janitor's room was near the gate but he did not live in it, rather used it as an office from which he supervised a team of cleaners and odd-job men who looked after the school. At the far end of the courtyard were the offices of the

Headmistress and her deputy, and the teacher's Common Room. We had a library/laboratory on the first floor and a conference hall on the ground floor for extra-curricular activities – lectures, theatricals, musical events, prize-givings, etc. The classrooms were light and airy, with high windows opening on to the vast courtyard. In winter they were heated by coal-stoves which were inadequate and diffused a certain amount of half-hearted warmth in the atmosphere. Sometimes, the janitor would try and cajole one of them into giving more heat, but it was a thankless task – the ceilings were too high, the windows too draughty, and the stoves old and tired.

Twice a week we had an hour of sport. We would don our black shorts and white tee-shirts, put on tennis shoes and white socks, and run out into the courtyard. The gym teacher was a young girl who could play all the ball games and perform 'Swedish exercises' beautifully. She had been to England and visited a skating-rink, then an unknown sport in Persia. She had a photograph in which she was wearing skating clothes and shoes and performing a complicated figure on one foot. It was her passport to fame; everybody had seen it or knew someone who had seen it, and we were all suitably awe-stricken by it.

Miss Sports – that is actually what we called her – would blow her whistle – and we would stand in a row in the courtyard; another whistle blow and we would break into groups of four and do our gymnastics under her instruction for about twenty minutes. The rest of the time was spent running, jumping, skipping or playing volley-ball, and basketball, etc. I loathed sport; perhaps because I was no good at it. In the last couple of years at the *lycée*, I took up ping-pong and learnt to play it adequately, but aerobics and running and ball-games were out of my ken and still are. So I always found an excuse not to do sport: I complained of tummy-ache, intimating that it was due to my 'period', and stayed inside the classroom hugging the hopeless stove and reading.

'How come you have your period every week,' Miss Sport once enquired, and we both laughed. A couple of times I ventured out and she was kind enough to put me in a volley-ball team, trying to engage my interest, but it was no good: the ball seemed to have a will of its own! In the end she gave up on me:

'I guess you're having your period again and don't want to come out, huh?' she would say through the window.

We had male and female teachers, all university graduates. Most of the women were spinsters, though a couple married later. The men were either old and married or so unprepossessing as to present no danger to nubile girls. All I remember of our chemistry teacher is his nose: it was so large as to constitute an independent entity, dangling and twitching and twisting, emitting a variety of noises. He was very shy and later married a beautiful girl from another *lycée*.

'It just shows, looks don't matter in a man,' Aunt Ashraf was sure, when I told her about it, 'they don't even matter in a girl, as long as she is lucky!'

I loved all my teachers: they taught me things and gave me what I did not receive at home – preferential treatment! But my favourite was our Persian teacher, Miss Heartless. Never was a name less appropriate, for she had a big and generous heart. She was not considered good-looking – her teeth were too large, her eyes not enough, her complexion far from rosy. But she was warm and witty and wise, with an infectious enthusiasm for classical poets and modern prose-writers. She gave us a solid foundation in Persian grammar and literature, and I owe her everything I know in that respect. If after all these years I still remember a fair number of poems, it is thanks to her.

Miss Heartless's best friend was our history teacher, a Miss Purity of the Aryans (I'm not making up these names, just translating them). She was permanently in a state of advanced pregnancy, it seemed, which elicited prurient comments from the more 'common' girls in the class. We were all afraid of her, for she used sarcasm and verbal bullying to keep us on our toes. If she found you had not done your homework, she poured such venom on you that no matter how strong, you would break down and cry – and next time you knew your lesson.

While the teachers exerted their authority in the classroom, outside discipline was imposed by the headmistress and her assistant, Miss Safa (Serenity) and Miss Barar (Concord). They were both confirmed spinsters, being in their early forties, and exuded sexual repression and frustration, which was still often the price of emancipation. They had been among Teheran University's first Ph.D. students and had obtained doctorates in Persian literature and history respectively. In the process they had abandoned any hope of matrimony they might have harboured. They wore no make-up, no fashionable clothes, possessed no sense of humour and showed no feminine softness, for fear of losing their authority. We were all afraid of them and avoided them as best we could. Once I fell foul of Miss Serenity's none-too-serene temper: I went to fetch a friend on my way to school and make the journey with her. She was late and delayed me as well. I did not notice the time until we arrived at school where, to my horror, I found the courtyard empty, the girls having already gone in, and the headmistress and her assistant pacing up and down and chatting. The former turned on me with a spontaneous rage and unleashed a torrent of abuse that left me totally speechless. I expected my friend to own up that she was responsible for our being late, but she was so glad to be off the hook that she forgot about honour! Before I could regain my balance or protest, still reeling under the blow, Miss Serenity turned on her heels and walked briskly towards her office, followed by a sheepish Miss Concord.

I was so shocked by the unfairness of it all, by the cowardice of my friend and the betrayal of Miss Concord – one of whose favourites I was – that I cried floods of tears and vowed never to allow anyone to make me late.

Miss Serenity rose in rank until she became one of the first women Members of Parliament, when in 1966 the late Shah reformed the electoral laws in favour of women, while Miss Concord became the headmistress of another famous girls' school.

Many of the girls at The Princess had 'crushes' on older girls or on the teachers. Miss Heartless had more than her share of admirers. She received billets-doux, flowers, poems ... She treated the whole thing as a joke and parried with dignity and kindness. It was a natural phase girls went through, and a harmless game at which, alas, once again I was no good. I loved my friends dearly and my teachers respectfully, but I had no 'crushes'. My pubescent infatuations from as far back as I can remember were with members of the opposite sex, 'The Other' *par excellence*, infinitely mysterious and incomprehensible, but utterly fascinating. My romantic dreams were usually focused – insofar as they ever were – on the star of the latest movie I had seen. Needless to say, with my background and upbringing, my feelings and fantasies were of utmost purity and grounded on steadfast chastity. Indeed so innocent – not to say naive – was I, that physical contact in my imagination was limited to what I saw in movies, which in those days was limited to at most the touching of lips.

At four o'clock the bell rang and we poured out into the courtyard and thence the road in twos and threes, arm in arm. After my first year at the *lycée*, my sister finished and left, but I was allowed to walk home with a couple of friends, which liberated Ali from making the journey twice a day. Outside, on the opposite side of the street, pupils from a boys' *lycée* stood to see their favourite girls come out and walk past. There were some ravishing beauties in the higher forms at The Princess – Heddy Lamars and Lana Turners and Ingrid Bergmans, etc. and the boys wanted to catch a glimpse of them.

Sometimes we would stop at Jasmin's on the Square, a new high-class café famous for its cream buns and snacks. It was beginning to be respectable for the sons of upper-class families to go into business and Jasmin's belonged to one of these. The Décor was elegant and discreet, the atmosphere cool and welcoming, above all the merchandise was of the highest quality. Soon people came from all over town to buy Jasmin's 'machine-made' ice-creams and cream cornets, nuts and home-made cakes, all beautifully packaged and gift-wrapped in boxes bearing the picture of a jasmine bush. In later years whenever I went back to Persia, Ali would buy me some cream cornets from Jasmin's, but the café itself had become seedy, the original owners having inevitably sold up and moved onto better things.

The years at the *lycée* were the time of awakening – emotional, artistic, political; of passionate friendship-ties I thought would last forever no matter what life might bring; of discovering literature, the cinema, the theatre, much of it new and imported from the West. My curiosity knew no bounds and my adolescent turmoils coincided with tremendous political upheavals in the country – which during this period was so galvanised by politics that schoolchildren from the age of 12 or 13 were politicised and turned into potential crowds. The major factions fought to capture our imaginations, and used our minds as their battle-grounds, with books and pamphlets and rallies and extravagant claims as weapons. Depending on background, temperament and circumstance we sympathised with different alignments.

It would be easy with hindsight to deride our gullibility as teenagers, but difficult to separate fun and games from serious political commitment. Our 'activities' were child's play compared to what is happening today, in the Third World in general and in the Middle East in particular, where ten-year-olds are brainwashed into joining wars, becoming 'martyrs', and playing at soldiers with real guns and bullets.

The main ideological currents were Nationalism and Cummunism. Both factions wooed my father, but he kept well clear of them. Perhaps with his far-seeing eyes he could envisage what would happen in the years to come. I used to argue with him.

'Nothing would ever change if people did not struggle, if there was no revolution – there would always be poverty and injustice and disease ...' But he argued that change could be achieved without violence and bloodshed. He told me the story of Socrates, how he had preferred to drink the hemlock and die rather than lead a rebellion against the State. Evolution and reform versus revolution – the perennial political divide. My own sympathies at the time were with the Communists because they were internationalists, on the side of progress, and sounded plausible. Above all, they had captured the media of the day. But I was a rebel, not a revolutionary, though it took me a long time to realise it. I was not prepared to accept that ends justify means, that the present must be sacrificed for the future, which by its nature is uncertain. I would never fit in with parties and clubs and cliques and factions, though I might sympathise with some of their aims at given moments.

Meanwhile we were discovering the cinema, the theatre, music, literature. Publishing firms had mushroomed with their teams of translators and every day there was a new book by a Russian, German, French, English or American writer to be acquired and read. We devoured them. I left a big library behind when I left for Europe – or it seemed big at the time.

A Little Night Music

> Music, moody food
> Of us that trade in love.
> Shakespeare, *Antony and Cleopatra*, II, v, 1

Despite Islam's ambivalent attitude towards music, the first sounds a Muslim child hears, outside its immediate surroundings, are musical: the chant of the muezzin calling the faithful to prayer from the minaret of the neighbourhood mosque, several times a day. How music came to be prohibited by the orthodox clergy is a long story, for nothing in the Qoran and the *hadiths* (sayings of the Prophet) warrants such an interdict. Among the Sufis and other mystically inclined sects, music has always been practised and is indeed part of the ritual – the *Sama*, chants and dances of the whirling dervishes are well-known even in the West. One verse in the Qoran, advising against 'games and distractions', clearly refers to gambling and other such habits, and it seems that a whole edifice of interdictions has been built on it by power-seeking mullahs, rather as Christ's 'I came not to send peace, but a sword' has been the justification of religious

147

wars and sectarian strifes among Christians for two thousand years. We know how wise advice can be misused by the ignorant or the greedy. Suffice it to say that there was no music in our house, though there was plenty of chanting, not only of the Qoran and prayers but also of mystic poetry, nursery rhymes and rhythmic limericks.

Persian classical music has miraculously survived and is said to be the basis of all music in the Middle East, from the Indian ragas to Arabic modal systems. Unacknowledged, even despised officially, Persian musicians have preserved their wonderful patrimony, and have developed and enriched it, taking sustenance from the appreciation of ordinary people and the patronage of the wealthy and unorthodox.

Folksingers have passed on their songs to successive generations, and itinerant instrumentalists and singers have earned their living by going from village to village, playing at weddings and other festivities. Travelling in Southern Persia in the seventies, I once heard the sound of music in a village nestled deep in the folds of the Alborz mountains.

'Music! Music!' chirped the children and rushed towards the village square, where the three itinerant musicians played and sang, surrounded by a motley crowd of villagers. Flute, *Kamancheh* (upright violin) and hand-drum were the instruments they carried, the fiddler doubling as a singer. When they had finished they passed their hats around and everyone contributed. Then they packed up their instruments and moved on. A noisy cortège of gleeful urchins and youngsters accompanied them to the edge of the village, until they had disappeared behind a mountain curve.

Of all musical instruments the human voice is the most beautiful, for it is made by God. My father had a beautiful voice, a deep, mellow baritone with an exceptionally rich and velvety timbre. As a child, I would sometimes wake up in the night and hear him chanting the Qoran and the midnight prayer in his study. There was a controlled pathos in his voice that informed every melodic strand, and which affected me deeply. In later years, I knew what it was, and I just listened and allowed it to transport me, but in those early years I sometimes cried, which brought Nanny or Zahra to my bedside with soothing words. It seems to me that I have searched for that enchantment in every beautiful voice ever since, and that my appreciation has been related to how close it gets to that original warm, gentle tone which had 'the quality of mercy', like spring rains.

'It is said that we should chant the Divine Words with pathos, for they have come with sorrow – the sorrow of God for the plight of man,' he once told me. Another *hadith* states:

'Two kinds of people should be particularly grateful to God, those with beautiful eyes and those with beautiful voices,' as they can affect the soul and ravish the heart. But, precisely because a beautiful singing voice can arouse feelings of love, women were doubly prohibited from singing and playing instruments:

'A woman who sings should have her tongue cut off,' was the other side of the coin. It is a measure of the changing times that, during my childhood, music gradually became respectable and musicians acquired a social status akin to poets and painters.

At sessions of *Rozeh-Khani* (commemoration of Imam Hossein's martyrdom) and during the Ramadan's midnight prayers, men with good voices gave free rein to their vocal prowess and sang to their hearts' delight: lyrical poems by the great Sufi poets, Rumi, Hafiz, Attar, etc. There is no poem that could not be fitted to one of the modal scales *(dastgah)* of Persian music, and my father's students used to sing their poems when they came to visit him. One of them, the son of a mullah who lived in our district, was endowed with the most exquisite, pure, crystalline and powerful tenor voice, and in command of every arabesque and modulation. Another was a bass-baritone with a magnificent timbre, and equally skillful. I can still see him close his eyes and sing, plunging down to the deepest and darkest recesses of the soul like a pearl diver reaching the bottom of the sea, only to ascend again and surface into light with the resolution of his cadenza:

Oh come, bearer of the Wine Cup, and pour forth,

For Love appeared easy at first, but became fraught with
   difficulties ...

You could hear the tenor for miles around as he intoned the first
verse of one of Hafiz's famous sonnets. His voice cut through the
silent night like a laser, illuminating those dark corners of the
psyche whence he drew his inspiration. Those two were our
favourites: they manipulated emotions like Samurais their
swords, leading their listeners where they wished. What Otellos,
Don Carloses, Don Giovannis, Figaros, etc. they could have
made!

As we grew up, we became acquainted with Western music, at
first through radio, and later records. Uncle Alem, ever alert to
the latest cultural imports, had bought a wireless and we listened
to it whenever we went to his house. Apart from Persian music,
the radio transmitted French *chansons*, Western dance tunes, and
sometimes classical music presented by an expert using imported
records. I was soon hooked: Tino Rossi, Bing Crosby, Frank
Sinatra, Danièle Darieux, Lucienne Boyer ... I loved them all,
and learnt their songs by rote, parrot-like, to sing them at school
and parties. Ever since nursery school, I had found singing a
powerful weapon, a means of propitiating hostility, and gaining
self-confidence and admiration. But after the age of 12, when I
went to the *lycée*, I was not allowed to appear in public, though
I could still sing in the privacy of friends' homes. Sadly I watched
others take the star roles I was offered in school musicals and
shows. I had to refuse for fear of provoking a scandal and
subjecting my parents to criticism. As a result, I developed a
mute hatred of religious bigotry and arbitrariness of any kind.
Luckily things were changing so fast that, within a decade, the
country would have a music *conservatoire*, a symphony orchestra,
a budding opera company, as well as many first-rate Persian
instrumentalists. But it was too late for me.

The young intelligentsia took to Western classical music
passionately. Gradually everyone acquired radios and record-
players, and young people gathered in each other's houses for
'concerts' – of imported records. I had a friend, Betty, whose

father was a British-educated mining engineer. She took lessons with an Armenian teacher in operatic singing and every week she taught me what she learnt. Mozart arias, Schubert *lieders*, Fauré *chansons* . . . I learnt them and sang them in several languages none of which I understood. An Armenian musician, a teacher at the new music *conservatoire*, went round the country and collected some traditional folk-songs, notated them in Western scales and arranged them for chorus. Through the radio, they were heard and learnt by everyone, and gave rise to a vogue for folk music. Soon the trickle of Western influence became a flood, and by the 1950s there was a flurry of intellectual and artistic activity unparalleled for decades.

As an art student, my brother Nasser was very much involved with the milieu of young progressive Westernised intellectuals. His friends were always in our house, and although we were not allowed to go out with them, in the privacy of our own home we mixed with them freely. They were all students at the University of Teheran. By then, a few other universities had been founded in other parts of the country, but the capital's was still the finest and most prestigious. Nasser and his friends spoke foreign languages – English, French, German and Russian – and translated the literature of these languages; they all wrote themselves, poetry and prose, and were published in literary magazines. Publishers had appeared on the scene who printed every manuscript they received, from the translations of European masterpieces to the emotional outpourings of local teenage poets. It mattered not how uneven the products were, there was ferment and creativity, and the artistic euphoria was all-pervasive.

Nasser was the ringleader of a group of young artists and writers, and the acknowledged star. He was the only one to become famous as a professional artist, while the others eventually gave in to necessity and, despite their high ideals, became diplomats, dons, civil servants, and settled down to family life. They all live in exile now, whether inside Persia or abroad.

The year before I left the country, I passed the first part of my baccalaureate and by some fluke came out first at the *lycée*. The

Ministry of Education gave me a prize: Rumi's *Mathnavi* and Attar's *The Conference of the Birds*. My parents gave me a prize too: permission to buy a record-player, provided it was never heard outside my room and did not distract my mother in her prayers. She generously cut down on everything to provide the necessary cash, and one day Nasser, my sister and I went to the Western Music Shop and bought the wonderous machine. It was one of those sophisticated gramaphones on which you could pile half-a-dozen 78 records which it then dealt out as it went along. Thus you could hear a whole symphony without having to get up and change the records every few minutes. We brought it home and Nasser mounted the pieces, but where to find records? Our friends rallied round and lent us some.

As befitted our ages and temperaments we favoured the Romantics: Beethoven, Brahms, Schumann, Schubert, Tchaikovsky, Rimsky Korsakov, Borodin, Mussorgsky ... lots of Russians, who seemed closer to us than other European composers. Bach, Handel, Haydn, not to mention the earlier composers, had to wait! From then on, I saved all my pocket-money and my clothes' allowance to buy records – and books. Often I had to borrow a dress from my sister for a party – by then I had reached her height – letting her listen to my records and borrow my books in exchange.

But what to buy? Mr Karim, the owner of the Western Music Shop became my guide. The first time I went to his shop with a school friend, he brought out a catalogue full of recordings by the world's greatest orchestras and soloists, and all I had was five shillings! Eventually on his recommendation I settled for a two-record piece by Mozart: *Eine Kleine Nachtmusik*, brought it home and played it over and over again. Thenceforth every time I managed to accumulate some money, back I went to Mr Karim. My collection grew, but not much, since my pocket-money was insubstantial and I left within a year. I gave my record-player to my sister and Nasser. When they too left the house and later the country, it was put in our closet to rust and be covered with dust, and eventually was thrown away.

But Mr Karim's story is worth telling, as it shows the change in social patterns and the development of a commercial bourgeoisie over the next two decades.

Mr Karim and his two younger brothers were the sons of a modest shopkeeper in Azarbayejan who had come to the capital after the War to seek work and adventure, with no baggage but their youth and energy. Noticing that classical music was becoming popular among the rapidly growing intelligentsia, they decided to try their luck in that field, so they started by selling a few 78 records from the sidewalk on Avenue Lalehzar (Tulips-field), then the fashionable shopping centre of town. It was not long before they became the focus of attention of all the young people who went to the cinemas in the area. Within a year Mr Karim and his brothers had acquired a shop in the same Avenue: The Western Music Shop. Soon they expanded and sold record-players as well. That was when I first went to their shop and bought mine.

When the fashionable centre of the capital moved northward and Avenue Tulips-field lost its prestige, they moved to much larger premises in Avenue Shah, which they called The Music Emporium. It had a section for popular music, another for Persian classical music, yet another for Western music. In an adjoining shop they sold radios, record-players, cassette-recorders, etc. Later still, they built a recording studio and started producing records with the most distinguished instrumentalists and singers in the country. They recorded several collections of folk-songs and regional music, of local orchestral offerings, and of show tunes.

And of course they became millionaires. Almost unlettered themselves, they sent their children to the best schools in Europe and America and covered their wives with expensive jewellery and furs; they drove large Mercedes cars and started a business in America. But they never lost their regional accent, which gave away their humble origins.

Many years later, I met Mr Karim and his brothers again: they imported my records from England and sold them at their shop. They were honourable in their dealings but could not sell many, because soon there were no less than three different bootleg cassette versions of my records in circulation. To be fair, the bootleggers had impeccable taste, for they had chosen the best songs of each record and made an anthology of fourteen songs for the cassettes. There were no copyright laws in Persia as yet (they were introduced in 1977) and everything was bootlegged – books, dictionaries, records. From Beethoven to the Beatles, everything was grabbed. Hardly had a Rolling Stones LP appeared than it was put on cassette and sold, even exported to other countries in the region. But not by the Karim brothers – they were rich enough doing business honestly.

The problem of copyright law was brought out and aired periodically. The argument against having one was that it would work one-way only: the only Persian books that were translated in the West were the classics, and already out of copyright.

'Well, the West has looted our natural resources for centuries, it won't do any harm if we get something free from them,' one official once told me. Unfortunately, innocent living artists were victimised in the process.

After 1979, there was no room for The Music Emporium in a fundamentalist Persia, and it was dismantled. Mr Karim and his brothers, far from being praised for their services to culture, were persecuted as 'corrupters of the land' and for having hobnobbed with the rich. They left the country. Most of the musicians they had recorded are either dead or in exile or living in obscurity, practising their art in private houses, if at all.

Whenever I listen to 'A Little Night Music', I remember the day I first heard it, in that tiny shop in Tulips-field Avenue, and the young Azarbayejani behind the counter saying:

'Tell you what, lady, why don't you buy this lovely two-record piece ...' All the hopes and yearnings of youth are locked forever in the notes.

The Hypochondriac

The advent of modern theatre in Persia was heralded by the production of Molière's *The Hypochondriac* by my father's half-brother, Uncle Emad. He was Haji Seyyed Mohammad's eldest son by his second wife, Amineh, and one of our favourite uncles. Although we did not see much of him on account of his busy life and his reluctance to leave his home, whenever we did visit him he displayed such dazzling charm, such sparkling wit and natural affection that we were spellbound for days after.

Amineh had married her two sons as soon as she had perceived 'the shadow of a down' on their upper lips, 'to keep them out of mischief'. Uncle Emad was 16 and his bride 14 when they married. She was a very pretty girl, with porcelain-white skin, deep blue eyes and long blonde hair, all rare and highly desirable attributes in a country of black-eyed women with complexions the colour of 'wheat and barley'. He had 'ravished her heart' straightaway, and soon charmed her into complete devotion and obedience. But when, after a while, she had become pregnant, he had left her in the *andaroon* with his mother Amineh and disappeared. When a week passed and there was no sign of him, his young bride had panicked, fearing that he might never return. She had cried and pined and prayed and made pilgrimages and sacrifices and tied streelies to shrines, but all to no avail. Periodically Emad had been sighted in the company of other women, or in some far-off city, but no one was sure if anybody had actually seen and spoken to him. Then, after a year, he had suddenly turned up, full of charm and loving care for his wife and new baby, as if nothing untoward had happened. He had covered her with kisses and vowed eternal love, got her pregnant again, and vanished once more. This pattern had continued for years, until he was about 30 and had six children, whereupon he had miraculously and drastically changed: he had settled down with his family in blissful harmony, produced two more children, and for the next twenty-odd years until his death at the age of 54 hardly ever left his house, indeed his room.

My mother always maintained that Uncle Emad's metamorphosis from adventurous rogue and Don Juan to model husband and paterfamilias was due to the love-potions of Mirza Saleem the Magician, but more likely he had finished sowing his wild oats, or was touched by his wife's patience and his children's needs. Perhaps he simply realised that his considerable talents could be put to better use than the trivial pursuit of pleasure.

During his long absences, his mother Amineh had kept his family together:

'He'll come back, you'll see,' she had reassured his wife, 'and he'll make you proud; he'll cover you with gold; just wait.' Not that Uncle Emad's wife had any choice: divorce would have been out of the question with several children, and she loved him.

'You go to your husband's house in your wedding dress and leave in your shroud,' was the saying, and women were enjoined to 'sit tight and bear it,' whatever 'it' turned out to be, if only for the sake of their children. (Such patience did not always pay off: my mother knew a woman whose husband had deserted her after the birth of her daughter and she was still praying for his return when that daughter was 25! But Uncle Emad's wife was more fortunate.)

In those early years, Uncle Emad had travelled a great deal, in Persia and Europe, had learnt French and Turkish, and collected a number of friends who would prove useful to him later in life. Yet no one knew where exactly he had been, nor to what extent his adventures were real or just fantasy. Some said that all those fantastic journeys in exotic lands, those dramatic encounters with beautiful women speaking foreign tongues, the brushes with death and last-minute reprieves, the prowesses of chivalry and displays of courage, had taken place in the confines of his neat little skull, that he had never set foot out of Teheran, let alone the country, and that he wove his tales like a spider its webs – to charm and captivate his human prey. Others maintained that what he recounted was but a fraction of his experiences, the tip of the iceberg, that he had been through the Underworld, Orpheus-like, and emerged unscathed. Well, almost, as he had acquired a taste for opium, and a 'weak heart', which eventually killed him.

Anyway, by the time I knew him, Uncle Emad was a happy successful man, surrounded by an adoring family and quite well-off. He had built a large house in one of the new residential districts, near the sports stadium, and he owned a car – still a rare privilege in those lean post-War days. It was a French model, with an outside hooter and running-boards, and whenever we visited him he insisted on driving us back home. We would squeeze in with several of his children who came for the ride, the older boys standing on the running-boards and hanging on to the windows. Festooned with the children of various ages, the car looked like a giant tortoise crawling.

Uncle Emad's chief occupation in those days was the editing of a weekly politico-literary satirical magazine called *Ashofteh*, which means 'Distracted', and which became very popular and influential. He got his famous friends to contribute the main articles in each issue, and filled the rest of the space with features written by himself in various styles and under a number of pseudonyms, some of which acquired considerable reputations. Similarly he signed his cartoons and satirical illustrations with different names.

He ran his life and his work from his 'office' – the largest room on the ground floor of his house, being also his reception room and his bedroom. He sat on a raised capacious mattress surrounded with papers and pens, inkpots and telephones. From dawn till late at night, a stream of visitors came to see him – printers, workmen, relatives and friends. Once a week, he held a politico-literary salon where his guests read their poetry and prose, some of which found its way on to the pages of *Ashofteh*. Twice a day, his opium pipe and charcoal brazier were brought to him and put near his dais: he would 'have a puff' while carrying on working, and pass the pipe round if anyone wanted it. At the end of the long day he would stretch out and go to sleep for a few hours. This routine went on till the end, and he succeeded in keeping his magazine alive during social and political turmoils which ground into oblivion most other such publications. *Ashofteh* died only when its progenitor did, sometime after I had left Persia.

To support his large family and his magazine, Uncle Emad wrote a novel in several volumes, a *roman-fleuve* as well as *à clef*, called *The Honourable Ones*. It was a moral tale about the venality and corruption of politicians and public men, the ruthlessness and greed of the new bourgeoisie, the lust and social-climbing of young *arrivistes*, the vulnerability and fickleness of women, etc., told with tremendous verve and humour. It was serialised in *Ashofteh* and became a best-seller. Some critics hailed it as the Persian *Les Liaisons Dangereuses*, especially since for the first time fairly explicit scenes of seduction and sexual fencing were strewn along the narrative. By today's standards these were extremely tame, all innuendos and elisions, but in those days they seemed explosive. The novel's notoriety contributed to a certain coolness between my father and his half-brother, although it was never openly expressed, and my mother kept the relationship between the two households going until the dust settled and the incident was forgotten – as indeed was the novel.

It was alleged that *The Honourable Ones* was autobiographical and that many of its incidents were based on Uncle Emad's own adventures, notably his seduction of married women. Perhaps it was true, for he believed that there was no such thing as a virtuous woman, and that any woman, however pious and faithful, could eventually be seduced. All you needed was determination and patience.

'Women are much too tender-hearted and good not to succumb!' he would say. He was worried about his own daughters' innocence and married them off as soon as they left school at 16. It was a sign of the changing times that, unlike his father, Haji Seyyed Mohammad, he chose suitable young men of means and breeding, and sought the girls' consent.

As for his sons, all but one joined the Army. 'You are not academic enough to go to the University,' he told them, 'the clergy is discredited and unworthy, you don't have enough capital to start a business, which leaves you the Army. You are just clever enough to get into the Military Academy and do well.' They followed his advice and rose in rank in due course. Only one of his five sons, the youngest but one, was exceptionally intelligent and gifted. He became his father's assistant from the age of 10 and ended up editing the magazine at the age of 18, when his father's health had deteriorated. Every day he would come home from the *lycée* and work with his father till late at night. He even slept in the same room, spreading his mattress at the foot of his father's dais.

One night, Uncle Emad went to sleep and never woke up – the young son found him dead in the morning. Ever since he could remember he had been his father's constant companion, amanuensis, beloved friend, and now his entire life had lost its meaning. Cleverer and more sensitive than his brothers, who had inevitably somewhat coarsened in the Army, he felt isolated and lost, and he went mad with grief. Three weeks later, he committed suicide. *Ashofteh* just ceased to appear on news-stands.

Many years before his death, when we were still children, Uncle Emad had translated into Persian Molière's *The Hypochondriac* which he staged at the city's first modern theatre, in Avenue Lalehzar. He himself played the lead, while his children performed all the other roles. The play ran for three nights and was seen by *le tout Teheran* – politicians, members of the intelligentsia, everybody who was anybody rushed to see it and be seen at it. The event was widely reported by the media of the day and its most important consequence was that it conferred dignity upon theatrical enterprise: if a well-known editor and writer, who happened to be the son of a *Mujtahid* (a Grand Mullah) could produce and act in a play without attracting opprobrium, then anybody could! It gave the green light to others who, in later years, started theatre companies and staged European classics in Persian translation, as well as new, home-grown plays. Uncle Emad's *The Hypochondriac* made a profound impression on me, and I have loved the theatre ever since.

Before this event, Persia had its own indigenous dramas, both sacred and profane. The former, called *Tazieh*, is the Islamic equivalent of European medieval Passion plays. It depicts the martyrdom of various Imams, in particular that of Imam Hossein, grandson of the Prophet Mohammad and the Third of the Duodecimal Imams of Shiism. The *Tazieh* actors were always amateurs – artisans, shopkeepers and labourers – who came together for the purpose of the show and dispersed afterwards. The texts were usually in rhymed verse and transmitted orally from one generation to the next, since most of the *Tazieh* actors were illiterate.

Some *Taziehs* had been written down and compiled into volumes; there were often different versions of each, written by mostly unknown authors in various eras. A *Tazieh* could be a simple affair with just two or three 'actors' playing all the various parts, or a grand spectacle including horses and camels, extras, battle-scenes and prisoners in chains, all accompanied by drums and Persian bugles – *sorna*. It could be staged in the village square or in a side-street by itinerant players, or in a vast open arena accommodating thousands of spectators. Such huge theatres-in-the-round were known as *Takieh*, and came into being when needed. In the nineteenth century, even the Shah and his Vizier attended the *Tazieh* in the Capital's big *Takieh*. The historical basis of Imam Hossein's *Tazieh* is as follows:

In AD 661, urged by a large section of the Islamic community, Imam Hossein claimed the *Khalifat* – leadership of the Islamic world – from the Umayad Khalif Yazid. The resultant conflict led to war, and the final battle took place at Karbala, in present day Iraq, where the Imam, deserted by all those who had pledged him allegiance save for a handful of relatives and disciples, fought on valiantly against hopeless odds, and lost. He and his companions were ruthlessly massacred and their women taken prisoner. The great battle leading to the Imam's martyrdom had taken place on the 10th of Moharram – the first month of the Islamic lunar calendar – and ever since this has been a month of mourning for the Shiites. During Moharram, devout women like my mother would wear black and refrain from celebrations; there were no weddings, no large parties and no music on the radio. Instead, there were commemorative ceremonies, including processions in the streets with penitents singing dirges and indulging in self-flagellation, which reached a paroxysm of collective sorrow on *Tasua* and *Ashura*, the days when the Imam and his companions had fought and been killed.

As with Christ's Passion, Imam Hossein's martyrdom today forms the basis of a vast and complex religio-philosophical edifice that extends far beyond its merely historical dimension, and which combines strands of Zoroastrianism, Christianity and Judaism, and has influenced the development of the Persian psyche at a deep unconscious level. It raises questions of the legitimacy of government, the separation of temporal and eternal power, the absolute and the contingent in human affairs; and there are other ramifications far beyond the scope of my story. Suffice it to say that some of the horrors perpetrated in Iran today, and the virulence of Shia fundamentalism in the Middle East generally, can be traced back to this historical incident, which to the unbeliever was just a political and military conflict between two Arab factions – just as the Crucifixion, to an agnostic, is merely an incident in one rebellious corner of the Roman Empire. But today children are sent to war to be 'martyred' and gain paradise, and youngsters are killed because they question the legitimacy of the present 'Imam's' power; terror is spread by those who claim the mantle of the Prophet, and so on.

When Reza Shah came to power in the mid-twenties, he tried his best to rid religion of its superstitious elements and to curb the power of the more obscurantist clergy – progressive mullahs who did not oppose his programme of reforms were left alone. *Tazieh* went underground and eventually disappeared; the *Takiehs* were dismantled, Moharram commemorative ceremonies and processions were forbidden. After World War Two, the new Shah relaxed all these interdictions, but *Tazieh* never came back – at least not in big cities – the world had moved on. I certainly saw none, but I heard about it from older people. Perhaps because by then the radio, the cinema, and modern theatre had replaced *Tazieh* as mass entertainment.

In the artistic revival of the sixties and the seventies, modern theatre groups appeared all over the country, and young dramatists and actors began to look for their own, indigenous dramatic roots. They sought out *Tazieh* performers in remote towns and villages. Finally a grand and beautiful *Tazieh* was performed at the Shiraz Arts Festival and was seen by visitors from all over the world. Its influence was absorbed by Western directors who saw it, including Peter Brook, who that year staged his *Orgast* at nearby Persepolis. Later, certain aspects of *Tazieh* were incorporated in various productions in the West, notably Peter Brook's famous *Midsummer Night's Dream* at the Royal Shakespeare Theatre.

In contrast to the sacred drama of *Tazieh*, Persia's popular theatre was the *Roo-Hosy* – On-the-pool – so called because it was usually staged over the pool, in the garden, which was covered with planks and rugs, with spectators sitting all around it.

The *Roo-Hosy* was usually performed by itinerant groups of professional showmen and women, including dancers, musicians and singers, each playing a variety of roles. They were invited for weddings, circumcisions, celebrations of all kinds. In the old days, wedding parties were segregated: men were invited to dinner on the wedding night, when the bride would be arriving at her new home, and women the next day in the afternoon. The *Roo-Hosy* took place after dinner on the wedding night and went on till the small hours of the morning. Close female relatives and members of the household watched it from the windows or the roof.

By the time I was growing up this two-parties system had disappeared from our social circle; the more educated, Westernised families gave one mixed party, either at home or in the ballroom of one of the new grand hotels. There would be a dance band playing European and South American tunes and couples would dance the fashionable dances of the day. In summer, the party would be in the garden, whether at home or at an hotel, and the dance-floor would be the covered pool.

However, a cousin of my father's had married a Bazaar merchant, and her son's wedding party was an 'old-fashioned' affair, with men and women invited separately. She asked us to go on the wedding night when there was to be a *Roo-Hosy* show, which enabled me to see one. After dinner we climbed on to the roof to watch the play. Rugs and mattresses were spread near the edge, and we sat in a row, in the dark, watching the men's party below in the illuminated garden. Anyone who looked up would see our dark silouettes against the starry sky, like the children of the gods mesmerised by the drama.

As with *commedia dell'arte*, or Punch and Judy shows, all *Roo-Hosy* plays had the same basic plots and characters. In the one we saw, they were as follows: a young prince, heir to his father's throne in a rich and powerful country, is visited by a wandering dervish who shows him the portrait of a princess from a foreign country on the other side of the world. She is ravishingly, irresistibly beautiful and the prince falls head over heels in love with her there and then. He takes the portrait from the dervish, and sets out on a long journey to find the princess wherever she may be and marry her. He is accompanied by his black slave, who is his Fool and confidant, and provides the comic relief to the story. Their journey is fraught with endless obstacles and hazards, but nothing can weaken the prince's resolve. They cross the Seven Mountains and Seven Seas, kill dragons and beasts and poisonous snakes, until they reach the princess's country. Meanwhile several hours have elapsed and the audience has been treated to the Fool's jokes and satirical sketches, the prince's love-songs and lyrical effusion, the princess's solo dances, laments and worries. For while the prince has been looking for her, she has been shown *his* portrait by the same wandering dervish – clearly Cupid and the agent of Fate – and has fallen desperately in love with him. At the end of the play, the two young people marry and the prince becomes King at his father's death.

By then, the sky had turned pearly grey and the muezzin could be heard calling the faithful to prayer from the minaret of the Shah's mosque in the Bazaar.

At the women's party the next afternoon, a couple of hundred women of all ages sat around the garden at tables laden with cakes and fruit. Presently the little band played the Persian wedding tune and the bride came in, to the applause and ululation of the assembly, on her husband's arm. The couple went round the garden greeting everybody and receiving congratulations, then sat down at a table specially decorated for them, with ribbons and lights and cornucopias of sweets and fruit. The bride was very beautiful in a classical Persian way: dark eyes and milky skin and 'rose-bud' mouth and straight nose, and wore a very open silk taffeta dress. I remember some guests exchanging looks and winks, suppressing giggles or whispering to their neighbours: the bride's arms and chest and neck were covered in love-bites, patches of blue fading into the peachy complexion, as if she had been thoroughly knocked about. Apparently the husband was desperately in love with her and had to wait six months between the marriage ceremony and the wedding, hence the overflow of unbridled passion, now that the girl was at last his! When afterwards they talked about it, Mother thought it was barbaric, others said it was normal. The bride herself looked perfectly serene, but I remember thinking that, if that was marriage, I would never get married!

The groom being the only man among hundreds of women, sitting bolt upright and listening to music, got bored pretty quickly and left, leaving his wife to enjoy herself with her friends. I never saw that couple again, but I heard from relatives that they remained most loving and devoted to one another, had six children, all of whom emigrated to America, and are having an even more contented and amorous middle-age together.

Two itinerant *Roo-Hosy* groups settled down in the forties and early fifties in a couple of modern theatres in Teheran. They drew their audiences from the working people – labourers, shopkeepers, mechanics, and showed similarly simple plays based on old legends or comedies of manners. Ali went to one of these theatres once, and told us what happened afterwards: the legendary hero, Rostam (Persia's Achilles and, like him, invulnerable) meets his companions to discuss plans for a battle against a foreign enemy. Later, they set off for the battlefield on the eastern frontier. On the way, they have to cross treacherous rivers and deep gorges and bug-infested terrain – all mimed action and flimsy papier-maché decor. At one point, Rostam has to shift a huge rock weighing tons – and without the slightest effort he picks it up and holds it above his head for a second before hurling it down the abyss, somewhere off-stage. At this point, the audience is supposed to burst into applause, as an appreciation of his physical strength, but on this occasion they did not:

'Heavy rock my arse!' someone shouted from the balcony. 'It's cardboard!' Everyone guffawed.

'He can't even pretend it's heavy! You want a hand with it?' More guffaws. The entire auditorium laughed and tittered; sarcastic comments flew towards the stage like lethal projectiles, whereupon Rostam advanced to the footlights and addressed the public:

'Who's the son-of-a-whore who is making fun of me? What do you expect? That I give myself a hernia by lifting a *real* stone? Just for your lousy two *Qarans* [about 20 pence]? Anyone who interrupts again is a son of a whore and a pimp!'

'He's right! He's right!' several voices were heard, and Rostam went quietly back to the rock, rolled it over to the side and shouted to his companions, 'Advance!' Everyone applauded and the play continued without further trouble.

Gradually, better, much more sophisticated theatre companies appeared on the cultural scene, created by actors and producers who had worked in Europe. But the *Roo-Hosy* continued to exist among the more old-fashioned sections of the population and in provincial towns. Again in the sixties, attempts were made to revive it, and many visiting avant-garde producers were inspired by its style and technique, and later used some of its characteristics in their own productions.

Soon there were drama schools, theatres, television dramas and films in Teheran and other major cities. Acting became a respectable profession amd moved up on the social ladder. But this whole young and fragile edifice has now collapsed and many actors have retired or gone into exile.

As for the cinema, well that's another story.

Blame it on the Movies

Cinema had come to Persia long before my time, and had immediately become one of the most popular forms of entertainment. At first it was patronised by male audiences only, and the auditoriums were in the southern, poorer parts of town. Later, classier cinemas opened in the new commercial areas in the centre, notably a couple in Avenue Lalehzar. These had plush seats and private boxes at the back and sides, and were frequented by the more educated and Westernised sections of the population. The boxes were expensive, but afforded privacy, and were usually booked by courting couples and their chaperones.

Downtown cinemas showed mostly Egyptian and Indian films. The former were the most popular – usually musical weepies with happy endings starring Egypt's two top singing stars, Abdol Wahab and Umm Kolthum. Such cinemas were crowded, dirty, noisy, male enclaves where the air was thick with the stench of urine, sweat and *araq* (local vodka), the ground covered with husks of watermelon seeds and nuts, the atmosphere explosive with suppressed passion. Audience participation was as noisy as at a children's pantomime show. There were lascivious remarks and noises during the seduction scenes, fighters were egged on, winners cheered, while everyone talked to his neighbour as well:

'Close that f— door!' some would shout if anybody opened a door and let in the light.

'Shut your trap, you pimp!' another would respond. Occasionally fights would break out, whereupon everybody would forget the movie and watch the live show in the auditorium.

I heard all this from Ali who had been to a cinema near Execution Square, called Cinema Execution. Not that public hangings took place in the Square at the time, but in the past they had, and the name had stuck. The cinema's management could cope with everything except stopping the 'patrons' from urinating on the floor; for rather than leave the auditorium and miss part of the action, some men preferred to relieve themselves on the spot. In desperation, the management projected a plea on the screen before each showing:

'Gentlemen are requested to kindly refrain from relieving themselves inside this cinema,' or simply, 'Please do not urinate here but use lavatories outside.'

When polite language failed to produce the expected result, harsher words were used:

'God's curse on the son-of-a-whore who pisses in this cinema!' or, 'Whoever pisses in this place is the son and brother and husband of whores! He himself is a bugger!' No good. Finally, it was thought that the image would succeed where words had proved ineffectual – a drawing of a huge equine penis was projected with the caption:

'This will bugger any son of a whore who dares to piss here, and will then take care of his wife, mother and sister as well!' The audience just laughed, and turned the insult back on to the management by drawing similar niceties on the walls of the cinema. Eventually a solution was found: a little ditch was dug all around the auditorium which carried away any liquid from the floor to the sewers.

I was told this story years later in Paris, by someone who had heard it from someone else. Perhaps it had undergone the usual overstatement and exaggeration accumulated over a long time; Persian humour is self-deprecatory and often class-based, and in later years educated Persians liked telling jokes that illustrated how benighted and ignorant they had formerly been, as if uncivilised behaviour were limited to them.

Gradually, things changed; cinemas acquired moquettes and plush seats, ashtrays and decent lavatories, and people began behaving impeccably. By the time I went to the cinema, it had become an entertainment for the intelligentsia, the new bourgeoisie and the upper classes.

For a long time cinema presented a language problem as well. It was years before local studios made films in Persian for popular consumption and there were at first no dubbing facilities in the country. Silent films were easy but the 'talkies' required a translator, who sat in the front row and spoke a running commentary into a microphone, keeping it down to a bare minimum. These 'translators' were usually *lycée* students and knew very little French or English, so they used their imaginations and invented the dialogue. Often they just described what was shown on the screen, but said absolutely nothing when the actors had a conversation:

'Now the hero is getting angry and exchanging harsh words with his rival . . . Now the rival is getting up and walking towards the hero in a threatening manner . . . Now they have come to blows and the hero's nose is bleeding . . .'

All the while, no one knew what the bone of contention was. Sometimes the interpreter knew a bit of English but no French, or vice versa, and had been hired for the wrong language. Rather than lose the job, he would let fly his own fantasy and effuse lyrically:

'Oh Pierre, I love you!', 'Oh Jacqueline, I love you too! Your eyes are like two sparkling diamonds that dispel the darkness of my heart!', and so on . . .

Later, when dubbing came, it was often so out of sync as to be useless: two people would meet, shake hands, have a conversation and go their separate ways. At that point, you would hear their greetings: 'How do you do, Michael?' In the better cinemas, important parts of the dialogue were projected on to the screen in Persian at intervals, which broke the continuity, but the spell of the image was so deep that we did not mind.

My brothers went to the cinema often and told us about the films they saw. They entertained us with Chaplin's comedies, Laurel and Hardy gags, Abbott and Costello jokes. They knew English and French, which enhanced their enjoyment, and vicariously ours. My sister and I being girls and younger were not allowed to go to the cinema till much later.

One day, Uncle Alem arrived at our house saying, 'I'm going to take the girls to see a film – the droshky is waiting outside.' My mother, who never dared to contradict her brother, had to acquiesce. We were beyond ourselves with excitement, and dressed very quickly to go, before mother changed her mind and withdrew her permission. The cinema was the latest and chic-est in Avenue Lalehzar, and the film starred Charles Boyer and Greta Garbo as Napoleon and his Polish mistress, Marie Walewska. I have forgotten the story but remember Garbo's sad face and tearful eyes as she bade her illustrious lover goodbye, and the tears of sympathy that ran down my own cheeks. When the lights came on, Uncle Alem noticed I had been crying: 'I shan't take you again if you're going to be so upset. It's just a story, all made up – none of it is true!' True or false, I was hooked, and have been a movie-buff to this day.

From then on, there was no stopping us. We two girls wanted to go to the cinema all the time, and were eventually allowed to, as teenagers, if accompanied by our brothers and cousins, or at least Ali. At the *lycée*, we went with our friends, chaperoned by a servant who had gone ahead and bought our tickets so as to spare us having to queue and mingle with the crowd. For a week after each film, we were spellbound: 'Do you remember the scene when he says ... ? Do you remember when she ... ?' And we relived the experience over and over again. If the story had been particularly poignant, I would hide behind the hedges in the garden and cry for days afterwards, giving my sister the opportunity to tease me about being 'soppy'. And of course I identified with all the stars and fell hopelessly in love with their male partners.

In those days, films reached us a long time after their release in the West – it was some time before the latest products of Hollywood and European studios were shown simultaneously in Western capitals and Teheran. At school, we collected photographs of film stars, male and female, in ornate albums. We gave them to each other as presents, with elaborate dedications written on the back. We compared our collections and vied with each other in their variety and richness. We each had our favourite stars and argued endlessly as to their respective merits, their beauty and skill. We emulated their hair-styles, their clothes, their expressions. Any resemblance to a filmstar, however remote and nebulous was assiduously cultivated, and secured the reputation of the lucky girl – or boy. Gradually and insidiously, the cinema changed the criteria of beauty: a girl was no longer considered beautiful because she conformed to the ideal depicted by poets, the Persian miniatures, the friezes of Persepolis, but because she looked – oh ever so slightly! – like Hedy Lamarr or Danièle Darieux or Ingrid Bergman.

More than any other product, cinema introduced Western liberal ideas and values. One of its major effects was that girls were no longer willing to put up with arranged marriages. What with emancipation and a degree of freedom, Persian girls wished to choose their own husbands on the basis of mutual attraction and romantic love. Endowed as they often were with passionate romantic temperaments, they associated love with youth and beauty, and were no longer content with someone who would be 'suitable' in every way but totally unappetising. This caused endless dramas in more traditional families, as in the case of my cousin, Zabiheh.

Zabiheh was the only daughter of Uncle Wild, my father's youngest half-brother. Wild was not his real name but his pen-name, chosen when, as a young man, he had started writing poetry. The poetic vein had dried up very quickly indeed, but the pen-name remained. After he stopped writing, 'because it wasn't good enough', he devoted his poetic energy to learning other, better poets' verses. He knew an infinite number of poems – good, bad, indifferent – often by obscure poets whose names he did not know, which he recited at the slightest provocation.

Uncle Wild's mother, Amineh, had secured him a wife when he was 15 – a distant cousin who was only 12. For the first few years, he and his wife had slept on either side of this mother in the same room. During the day they fought, as children of their age would, and Amineh separated them with words of wisdom, but it was no good.

'I don't like her! Send her away!' he had said repeatedly. But after a few years when Uncle Wild was about 17 and his wife 14, Amineh decided to make a pilgrimage to the holy city of Meshad and left the young couple alone in her bedroom. Nine months later, their only daughter was born. From then on, Uncle Wild and his wife seemed a perfectly harmonious couple.

When I was a child, Uncle Wild was still fairly young and

darkly handsome. He sported a rosary of ambergris beads and wore tinted glasses, and he smoked heavily. In his youth, he had been a terrific womaniser, but now he was a kind and affectionate paterfamilias, albeit somewhat stern and autocratic. His wife, Zakieh (the Pure One) was a model of patience and loyalty; all those years when he had 'slept out' and 'played at women', she had turned a blind eye as if nothing was untoward, and cultivated her own gifts. She was a first-class chef, an adroit dressmaker, a sophisticated embroiderer, and adept at other such general feminine crafts. She did not use any of it professionally, but for the benefit of her family and friends.

Uncle Wild's hospitality was lavish; family gatherings at their house were culinary feasts enhanced by his entertaining panache of verses, jokes, ad lib repartees, etc. He would welcome the guests with extravagant terms of endearment and cover them with kisses.

'I'm *Wild* about you! Welcome to my humble abode! Light of my eyes, cooler of my fiery heart!' ... His pockets were always full of sweets and shelled pistachio nuts for children. He would hold a nut between his thumb and index finger and when I stretched my hand to take it he would let it drop into the palm of his hand and seemingly disappear. This trick was repeated several times and just at the moment when frustration took over from excitement he would let me have it. No one had ever seen him angry, but they said that, because he was so good-humoured and jolly, whenever he did get angry, woe betide the person who had provoked him. Certainly his wife and daughter were afraid of him, as were his servants.

Having been 'naughty' himself, he jealously guarded his wife and daughter's virtues, and did not allow them to go out uncovered – they wore elegant silk scarves instead of the discarded *chador*. Not that he had anything to fear from either, because both were supremely modest, but his daughter, Zabiheh, being a post-Emancipation child, had dreams, and there was the rub. She had the gentle disposition of her name (the sacrificial lamb), but had been kept down and crushed by her father to such an extent that her meekness had given way to lethargy. She had been educated at home and learnt all the domestic arts from her mother. She and her mother adored each other and, being so close in age, they were like devoted friends. Both were very plump, to say the least, which did not matter in the case of the older woman but was a source of misery for her daughter. In the past, Persian women went to any length to make themselves fat. They rubbed themselves with all sorts of concoctions and consumed quantities of chicken fat to 'add a layer of flesh'. But now the ideals and norms of beauty had changed: you could not wear all those lovely Western clothes, nor acquire the allure of film stars, if you were shaped like a balloon.

After several attempts at dieting, Cousin Zabiheh had given up and became sad and languorous. Yet she had a pretty face with dark wistful eyes and a sweet smile, so everyone knew she would find a husband sooner or later.

'All this business of being thin is a *Farangi* craze,' Aunt Ashraf would say encouragingly. 'Men *like* plump women, even if they pretend otherwise. Who wants to fondle and squeeze a bag of bones!'

But Cousin Zabiheh would not be consoled. She knew that her weight was a handicap, especially since most of the extra pounds were up top.

'Her legs and arms are alright, it's just her breasts ... they're like a couple of watermelons!' people commented. Nowadays a simple operation would have solved her problem, but then there was nothing anyone could do.

By the time she was 18, even Uncle Wild began to worry, and to look around for a suitable husband. He was so charming and generous that it seemed any man would wish to marry her just to have him as father-in-law, yet no one suitable came forward. He set about cultivating a cousin who was in the Civil Service and presentable.

'My house is yours,' he would say to him, and invite him to meals several times a week. After a while, the whole family took it for granted that a marriage was imminent, but the cousin in question thought that all the hospitality and affection lavished on him was for his *beaux yeux*! Eventually his own father broached the subject:

'Well, when do you want us to go and talk to Uncle Wild about Zabiheh?'

'Talk about Zabiheh? What do you mean?'

'Everyone knows you are interested in her; you're always going to their house, sometimes staying for several days, and ...'

'I have no intention of marrying her! I go to their house when Uncle Wild invites me, and mostly when there are other guests as well. It never occurred to me that ... It never crossed my mind even!'

News reached Uncle Wild that Cousin Samad had baulked. He behaved with flawless dignity and pretended that indeed the thought had never crossed *his* mind either!

'Banish the thought! They're like brother-and-sister, how could they marry?' he said, when some indiscreet relative made an allusion. Later, Cousin Samad married a girl of his choice – slim, modern, educated and gay – while Uncle Wild started finding someone else for his daughter.

Time passed.

One day, when everyone had more or less despaired about Zabiheh's chances of not staying on the shelf, a friend of a friend of a friend came forward with a firm proposal. He too was a civil servant, from a good family, and with a decent salary. The only reservation was that, at 40 he was nearly twice her age, and not very prepossessing. He was almost bald, wore glasses and was as thin as a scarecrow. On the other hand, he was infinitely gentle and kind, and 'you can't have everything'. By then, even the most traditional families allowed their daughters 'to-see-and-like' their prospective husbands before a final decision was reached by the parents. So, when Uncle Wild had in principle accepted the proposal, he invited his future son-in-law and his brother to dinner (his parents being dead). He also asked my mother and Aunt Ashraf and a few other elders of the family. After dinner, Zabiheh was called in, but she was much too shy to lift her eyes and look at her betrothed. Only at the end, just before leaving the room, she threw a furtive glance towards the two strangers: one bald and middle-aged, the other youngish and handsome. She thought her fiancé was the latter, and her heart leapt with joy. Afterwards when Uncle Wild asked her, 'Well? What do you think?', she tried not to appear unduly eager, and said, 'Your wish is my command, sir.'

But later, when her mother explained that the husband-to-be was 'the other one', she burst into tears.

'Oh, no! He is so old and plain! I can't possibly marry him, Mother. Please stop the whole thing before it's too late! Please!'

Uncle Wild's reaction to his wife's tentative expression of doubt was as violent as it was predictable:

'Whaaaat?' he roared. 'Who asked her opinion? I've given my word and can't retract it. Besides, who else is there? They're not exactly queueing outside, are they?'

'She finds him old and awfully plain ...'

'Who does she think she is, Hedy Lamarr?'

'?'

Uncle Wild's wife had not heard of Hedy Lamarr, but, alas, Zabiheh had: she had been to the cinema once, with us, and seen a film in which Hedy Lamarr starred opposite, I think, Robert Taylor. Her father's sarcasm pierced her bleeding heart like a dagger and she stopped crying – anger and despair took over from panic.

'Don't worry,' her mother tried to comfort her. 'You'll be your own mistress in your own house. You'll get used to him and grow fond of him – he seems so kind ... You'll be able to wear make-up and pretty clothes. It'll all work out, you'll see.'

Meanwhile Uncle Wild had calmed down. 'Your mother and I didn't like each other at first either, but look at us now – two love-birds!' He tried to make Zabiheh giggle, but she thought: 'Look at you, indeed! Master and slave! But at least you are almost the same age and good-looking, not a bald dry stick!' She did not say any of this, just started crying again.

I remember her wedding on a late spring evening – her beautiful white organza dress made by her mother, the sumptuous banquet, the elegant guests, the decorated limousines ... Zabiheh did her best to appear cheerful – after all *any* husband was better than none – but anyone perceptive could detect the anguish behind her wistful smile. After dinner, the cars took the immediate family to Zabiheh's new home, furnished entirely with her trousseau. The bridal car, bedecked with white flowers and ribbons, contained the married couple and the best man – the handsome younger brother who looked like Robert Taylor – oh, ever so slightly! – with a thin mustachio and wavy hair. Zabiheh sat between the two men and waved at the applauding well-wishers as the car pulled away.

'Pity she didn't marry the younger brother,' some tactless guest remarked *sotto voce*. 'Of course, she should've married someone younger – he's as old as her father!' whispered another. But the bridal car was receding.

Zabiheh means Sacrificial Lamb. She was given the name because she had been born on the Day of Sacrifice, when pilgrims to Mecca kill a lamb and distribute it to the poor at the completion of haj. It could not have been more apt. But she was not the only such – in my own family, there were many.

Much was done to change women's lot in the following decades, but the changes affected only those with access to education. They did not penetrate deep enough to resist the complete reversal that has occurred since 1979.

Zabiheh produced two sons, but never got used to her husband. She just tolerated him, and soon after the birth of her second son arranged a separate bedroom for him. She developed migraines and a host of other ailments, which kept her often in bed, with the curtains drawn. Uncle Wild blamed it all on the cinema:

'It's all these movies! Before, girls accepted anybody their parents chose for them. Now they go to the cinema and get ideas! They fall for these pimps and gigolos and pansies you call film stars, and no one else can find favour with them! I blame it all on the movies, I tell you ...'

But we were singing, 'Put the blame on men, boys! Put the blame on men!', the song Rita Hayworth sang in *Gilda*!

Aroos, the Bride of Brides

❧

There were several *hammam*s (public baths, known in the West as Turkish baths) in our district. The one we used was conveniently near our house, at the entrance of the *bazaarcheh*, and was considered the best on account of its high-class clients. Standing on high ground in a Persian village, you could always tell a *hammam* from the shape of its roof as, unlike residential houses which had flat roofs, it had several little domes with glass portholes at the apex, to let the daylight into the windowless baths below. From dawn till early morning, and after sunset till late at night, the *hammam* was reserved for men, the rest of the day for women, on the assumption that men used them on their way to or from work, while women had the whole day at their disposal.

For humble folk, the weekly, fortnightly, or even monthly visit to the baths (depending on their means) was a break from routine, a holiday and an outing combined. They went there with their children, and spent the whole day in the hot, steamy atmosphere, soaking, scrubbing, massaging and washing away grime and fatigue from their work-weary, care-worn bodies till their skins became raw. They took their lunch with them – meatballs, mashed chickpeas, cheese and seasonal fruit – and passed the time of day gossiping, confiding, exchanging useful tips. Wealthier women spent much less time at the *hammam*, since their visits were more frequent and they kept clean in their own houses in between.

As with other aspects of life in those days, the *hammam* ritual denoted social and economic distinctions: ordinary people wrapped their towels and clean clothes in a bundle which they carried themselves, while women of the upper class sent their bath paraphernalia ahead by a servant. It consisted of a *soozani* (a light brocade spread, covered with an ornately embroidered linen cloth) on which to sit when dressing after the bath, a couple of large towels, a linen headscarf, a loincloth, some silver-plated copper bowls for pouring water, and a round tray on which to sit without touching the hot and none-too-clean bath floor.

Our *hammam* had an old wooden entrance door embossed with brass studs and a heavy knocker, beyond which a short passage led to a thick curtain and the dressing area. This was a large hexagonal room with a high, domed ceiling and a circular blue-tiled shallow pool in the middle. White, yellow and red rose-petals waltzed around in the cold limpid water to the gurgling of the little central fountain, and, around the pool, stone platforms covered with rugs provided space for dressing and undressing.

Upon arrival, you gave your clothes to the attendant, who put them away in individual compartments at the back, then you wrapped your loincloth around your body and entered the bath. The public area was a vast steamy room with hot and cold water taps along the walls, a foot or so above the gutter that ran all round carrying away waste water. Higher up, the walls were dotted with little niches which used to contain oil-lamps, but now lodged naked electric bulbs. At the far end was a pool – more like a large water tank since you had to climb several high steps to get into it – in which you immersed, after you had washed and rinsed yourself, in order to perform your Grand Ablutions.

On one side of this public area were a series of private 'bathrooms' – small cubicles which were a good deal more expensive than the fixed entrance fee and could be reserved in advance. These private baths had showers, which enabled you to dispense with immersion in the common pool. Showers were then a novelty, and available only at the best establishments. Their arrival had provoked the usual religious controversies which greeted every new import from the West: was a shower as 'cleansing' as the pool? The big mullahs in Qom had decreed that it was, since running water is the ideal purifying substance, provided that it runs in sufficient quantity over the body. It was at a time when the mullahs were fairly progressive and got along with the government instead of seizing every opportunity to create mischief and cause trouble. Nonetheless, old habits die hard and the pools – called reservoirs – continued to exist for a long time in traditional *hammam*s, and many women preferred immersion to showering. Some baths had a cold pool as well, in which children played and taught themselves to swim. That is where my father had taught my brothers, most proficiently I may add, but our *hammam* did not have any, and my sister and I did not learn to swim until much later.

Ritual cleansing and ablutions are the first stage of daily prayers, although the concept of 'purity' (*taharat*) refers to the state of the mind and the heart much more than to the body. Sometimes this preoccupation with physical cleanliness degenerates into neurosis, even mania, especially in women. My mother suffered from a touch of this affliction, though by no means as badly as some of her friends. One of these, a grand old lady of saintly disposition and deep culture, used to break several inches of ice in the heart of winter and immerse herself in her pool every day before dawn, without doing which she did not believe herself 'cleansed' and her prayers worthy of acceptance! Another, an otherwise highly Westernised woman, was in the habit of washing her hands constantly, Lady Macbeth-like, and wore gloves night and day for fear of touching anything impure. Yet another friend, now living in exile in California, refuses to accept that washing-machines 'cleanse' her clothes properly. Luckily, there is a jacuzzi pool in her building, and every so often she gets up in the middle of the night while other occupants of the building are asleep, and takes her bedclothes and garments to immerse in it undetected. What her neighbours would think, if one night they caught her in the act of Jacuzziing the laundry, is hard to imagine!

My mother considered all of us *najis* (impure) since we had all become *Farangi* and were not meticulous enough in our rituals, and she forbade us to touch her towels, rosary, prayer book and other religious paraphernalia. Even then, the reasoning of such an authority as my father was of no avail – the matter did not belong to the realm of reason.

As a small child, I was carried by mother to the pool in the *hammam* and immersed three times in quick succession in accordance with religious rites. Breathless and terrified, I protested and cried, but in vain – I had to be 'purified'! In later years, when bathrooms were built in our house, we gave up going to the *hammam* at all, and then my mother used to stand for what seemed like hours under the shower, and in the end be still doubtful as to her 'cleanliness'. Once, staying with me in London, she stood so long under the shower that it ran out of hot water. I lost patience and gently suggested that enough water had run over her to 'purify' a regiment.

'You really think so?' she wondered. 'Well, if my prayers are not accepted you'll have to answer for me Up There!'

I promised to take all her sins upon myself and burn in hell forever if need be, so long as she got out of the bathroom! I did not have the heart to horrify her by saying that in the West we sometimes washed in the tub, *without* a shower afterwards!

On bath-days, Ali would gather up all our '*hammam* trousseau', take it round in the morning and reserve our private cubicle. My mother would arrive in the early afternoon, and my sister and I would join her on our way from school. We would be received by the attendant with a good deal of *taarof*, she would help us undress and then lead us inside. The public area we had to enter before reaching our private bath was filled with women of all ages, whose naked outlines – ranging from Rubensesque to Giacometti-thin – could be discerned through a dense white fog of steam striped with shafts of light from the glass portholes on the ceiling, like sirens beached on a tropical shore. Small children milled around playing with water; their gleeful sounds were mixed with their mothers' loud voices and magnified tenfold in the enclosed space. The whole scene was like a dream sequence filmed by some erotomane, all slow motion and echo. To me, as a child, it was simply awesome and slightly frightening.

Presently we were inside the cubicle where my mother was being massaged and washed by Aroos, our personal *dallak* (cleaner). Every *hammam* had a number of professional cleaners who were hired for a small sum that varied according to their reputation and seniority, and each had her own clients with whom, over the years, she established a kind of intimacy and trust. As we grew older, my mother did not accompany us to the *hammam* but entrusted us to Aroos's care. She would wash our hair and body, rinse and shower us thoroughly, dry and dress us, and hand us over to Ali or Nanny when they came to collect us. There were no hair-driers in those days and Aroos did her best with towels. She would wrap our head in large linen kerchiefs to protect us against the cold in winter. I had long thick plaits which hung down my back and froze solid in the icy air.

'You know, Aroos, by the time I get home, my plaits are frozen stiff, and there are lots of icicles at the ends, like diamonds', I told her.

'Like frozen tear-drops,', she ventured.

Aroos's life had not been easy. Aroos means both *bride* and *daughter-in-law* and she was given this nickname because when she had first arrived at the *hammam*, years before, she had been a newly-married girl. She and her husband had left their village and come to town in search of work. They had taken temporary lodgings at the caravanserai in the *bazaarcheh*, where their first and only son was born, and her husband had found work as a navvy. But, soon after her baby's birth, her husband had died in a typhoid epidemic, and she had become a *dallak* to earn her living. There she still was, although her son was now married and had a family of his own. He had offered to support her and have her live with him, but Aroos was a proud, independent soul and did not wish to be a burden on him.

'Times have changed; sons have enough trouble earning a living for themselves, and wives are not willing to be saddled with their in-laws. I shall work as long as I can, and when I no longer am able to, I shall drop dead!'

And that is what she did.

The *hammam* was at the core of community life – a job-centre coupled with a free information service. If you needed a maid, a carpenter, a snow-sweeper or an odd-job man, you asked the attendant of your local *hammam*, and soon one would be found. The *hammam* was also the place where all local gossip was circulated and processed, confidences exchanged, tips offered. Above all, the *dallak*s often acted as marriage-brokers and go-betweens by talking about the young girls they knew to women who had elligible sons. Many a marriage in the district had been arranged through the good offices of Aroos, whose good-nature, experience and discretion could be relied upon. If a marriage took place as a result of the recommendation of a *dallak*, she was rewarded by being invited to the wedding, given money, food and clothes, and she would remain connected to the family for ever after.

Among many marriages in which Aroos had played a part was that of our neighbour, Professor Bahram's eldest son, Mohsen, with a young heiress from Shiraz. Shortly before her son came back from Europe, Mrs Bahram began to shop around for suitable brides for him and asked Aroos if she knew any girl who fitted the bill: she had to be beautiful, well-born, and *najeeb* (modest). As it happened, Aroos knew just the right girl, the daughter of a landowner who had recently moved to a grand house nearby, and she promised to let Mrs Bahram know next time the young lady was visiting the *hammam*.

A few days later, a messenger arrived from Aroos advising Mrs Bahram that 'the Gazelle was approaching the snare'. The heiress was already there when Mrs Bahram arrived at the *hammam* and Aroos took her to her cubicle saying that, since it was an exceptionally crowded day and all other private baths were occupied, she was sure the young lady would not mind sharing hers with the distinguished Professor's wife. The girl graciously conceded that it would indeed be an honour. In the hour that followed, Mrs Bahram managed to extract all the information she needed from the innocent girl without appearing unduly inquisitive: She averred that her mother had died giving birth to her, that her disconsolate father had vowed never to remarry but devote his life to his only daughter, which promise he had gallantly kept despite frequent temptations and a number of seductive offers, but that lately she had persuaded him to marry one of her own best friends who, although twenty-five years younger than him, was 'perfect' and 'a joy to have around the house'.

Mrs Bahram was much taken by the girl's simplicity and delicate manners, her lovely face and delicious Shirazi accent – not to mention all those villages her father owned in one of the most fertile parts of the country – and praised her sky-high to her son when she returned home. In the usual circuitous way, through intermediaries and friends, words passed between the two families that they were in principle interested in a match. A sumptuous tea-party was arranged at the landowner's house where the two young people could see each other – a concession to Mohsen's sojourn at a French university – and their engagement was announced. We heard that the bride's father had agreed to give his daughter one of his villages, complete with *rayat*s (peasants, virtually serfs), fields, orchards, woodlands and waterways, by way of a wedding-present.

'Just in time!' Aunt Ashraf commented. 'Her stepmother will soon produce sons and her father will have his affection divided; she might not get anything!'

Several sons were indeed born to the wealthy feudal chieftain and his young wife, and had he not already parted with her share, his daughter would have received only a fraction of his wealth after his death.

Mohsen's wedding was the most magical I had ever seen. The Bahram's garden was decorated like a fairyland: colourful lanterns hung from the trees, candles illuminated the pathways and flowerbeds, tables overflowed with cornucopias of fruit and sweetmeats, liveried waiters milled around filling the glasses and the plates ... The festivities went on for two days. The first day was for family and friends of all ages, with a traditional orchestra playing classical Persian music, and the next evening was a party '*pour la jeunesse*', for the bride and the bridegroom's young friends and relations. A jazz band played Western dance tunes while couples whirled around in each other's arms on the covered pool. My mother was to be invited the first day and, although my sister and I were too young to be invited the next day, Mrs Bahram liked us and insisted that we go. We sat in a corner and watched, entranced by the beauty and novelty of it all.

Aroos was there too, on both days, wearing a light flowery *chador* Mrs Bahram had brought her. She sat inside a room by the open window and surveyed the scene, delighted to have been instrumental in the marriage. She muttered prayers for the young couple's happiness and fertility, and as far as I know they were answered – the marriage proved durable and fruitful.

By the time I was at the *lycée*, several baths had opened in our district which were much more modern and had no public rooms, only well-equipped, luxurious individual shower rooms with connecting dressing cubicles. One of these was called Brilliant Baths and was on our way to school. We went there with our friends, dispensing with the services of a *dallak*, washing our own hair with shampoo – a recent product which made life much easier than the old soap. Later, bathrooms were built in our house, but by then we children had dispersed to various parts of the world. Aroos came to wash my mother at home.

Years later, in the early 1970s, I went to Southern Persia to make a film on the migration of the Bakhtiari tribes. At the end of the six-week trek through the mountains, during which I had bathed only in ice-cold streams of melted snow, I asked if there was a *hammam* in the village at journey's end and could I go there for a hot bath. There was, and I went with my hostess, a tribal chieftain's daughter. This village *hammam* had no private cubicles and only a single shower, but the hot steamy chamber, with a lone naked electric bulb hanging from the ceiling, was filled with tribeswomen scrubbing weeks of grime from their travel-weary bodies. As a mark of friendship, my hostess insisted on playing the *dallak* and rubbing me with a special loofah. I had forgotten how delicious it was! Even though her touch was less professional than Aroos's! I had forgotten the conviviality of the atmosphere, the natural intimacy the women evidently enjoyed.

Even now, sometimes lying in the bath I remember the old *hammam*, the cubicle where in later years we went with our friends and talked and laughed while Aroos rubbed us clean; Aroos rinsing my feet in a little pool full of rose-petals: Aroos combing and plaiting my hair ... Would that she were still there, soothing away Time and Memory with her delicate hands.

Ramadan

Ramadan is the seventh month of the lunar calendar and the Muslim equivalent of Lent. For thirty days, Muslims must fast from sunrise to sunset, which means total abstinence not only from food and drink but also from smoking and sexual intercourse. As the lunar calendar, based on the rotation of the moon round the earth, is ten days or so shorter than the solar year, the date of Ramadan varies accordingly. When it occurs in winter, when the days are short, fasting is fairly easy, but in summer when a long fifteen-hour day stretches between the 'dawn-meal' and the 'break-fast' dinner at sunset, hunger and thirst – particularly the latter – are very hard to bear. Yet fasting, like the daily prayers, is one of the major duties of a Muslim. Only on health grounds can it be abandoned, as the care and preservation of the body are paramount duties too. Women must stop fasting during menstruation and childbirth, which gives them a few days of respite in the month. But, for whatever reason the Ramadan has been interrupted, the number of lost fasting days have to be compensated for sometime in the course of the year, otherwise 'fasting debts' accumulate and will be counted against one on Judgement Day. My mother often fasted in winter: 'I have a lot of debts,' she would say, making up for the days she had been ill or 'indisposed'.

Rich men who died without having performed all the fasting days of their lives allocated a portion of their estate to the 'purchase of prayers and fasts', usually performed by impoverished theology students in *madrasahs* who supplemented their inadequate grants by fasting all winter and praying all day.

In those days of religious tolerance and social ferment, not everyone observed Ramadan: agonstics, the weak-willed, the underaged and religious minorities disregarded it, but no Muslim adult would flaunt his fast-breaking. Public places, cafés and restaurants, were less crowded during the day, while the mosques were fuller at noon for the midday prayer and the sermon that followed, Ramadan being the month of abstinence and prayer, of meditation and repentance. People who were lax in their duties all year round tried to make up for it during this period.

In our house, the daily routine changed completely during Ramadan. A few hours before dawn, Nanny and Ali would wake up and start preparing the 'dawn meal', which had to be substantial enough to sustain us through the day: rice and stew, salad, cheese, yoghurt, cold soft drinks and plenty of tea. When the meal was ready, an hour or so before dawn, Ali went round the house and woke up everybody else. Oh, the agony of being dragged out of a deep sleep! Eyes refused to open, feet were numb and hands hardly capable of grasping the spoon . . .

In winter, the tablecloth was spread over my mother's large *korsi* and the aromatic food displayed upon it. But we were so sleepy that we would have gladly relinquished caviar and champagne for permission to go back to bed. To be fair, we were never coerced into keeping religious observances; rather we were prompted by our own faith, and by the sense of participation in the collective life with its special ritual and social activities. So Ramadan had an element of fun in it. When, in later years, some of us wavered and gave up the more exacting religious duties such as fasting, my mother's anguish was painful to watch. She was certain we would go straight to Hell and, worse still, be separated from her! She did not try to force or admonish us, but she pleaded. When it proved ineffective, she turned to my father:

'Won't *you* tell them something?' But he knew it would be no use, that preaching and bullying would be counter-productive and only fuel the adolescent rebelliousness. You could only set an example with your own conduct and hope for the best. Faith had to come from within, and if we had lost it, for the time being, there was nothing anyone could do. And, of course, he was right: one by one, and by different paths, we returned to some form of spiritual discipline later in life, though they were no longer alive to witness and rejoice.

In the summer, the table was set in the garden. Father presided over the meal which was swallowed reluctantly in silence. Only the purring of the samovar and the click of the ice-cubes in the water jug provided a soft accompaniment to the nocturnal rites. Over the walls, we could see lights in the neighbouring houses, and occasionally hear the faint clutter of crockery and glass as other families consumed their meal as silently and sleepily as we. All the garden insects gathered around the table, attracted by the pool of light. One night, we saw a large, yellow scorpion fixed on the wall behind my mother. Aunt Ashraf took off her slipper and banged it hard against the wall, without saying anything so as not to cause panic. The frightful creature fell on the ground and was killed. 'Those little yellow ones are deadly,' she said.

The next day she told us how, in Kashan, a town famous for its fine rugs and lethal scorpions, people placed the feet of their beds in bowls of water to stop them climbing into their beds; nonetheless casualties were reported every year.

> 'The sting of a scorpion does not come from malice
> But from its nature.'

She quoted the poet, and told us the following story: A frog was passing a river when he saw a scorpion struggling in the water and shouting for help: 'I can't swim, save me!' it begged. The good-natured frog offered to carry it to the other side on its back. When they reached the middle of the stream the scorpion stang its benefactor. 'What did you do that for?' asked the frog. 'Now we will both die!' 'I can't help it – it's my nature,' answered the scorpion, apologetically.

'The moral of the story is that you must not offer lifts to scorpions!' we ventured.

'No, the moral is that you must try and save the scorpion, but *expect* it to sting you for your pain and take precautions!'

Sometimes we would hear the voice of a cantor chanting *Monajat* – a special Ramadan prayer compounded of poetry and improvisation, a kind of supplication addressed to God, which sounds more like a lyrical outpouring of a lover to the object of his affection. In summer, those who had beautiful voices climbed on to their roofs and sang to their hearts' content. When there was more than one in the neighbourhood, a chorus of vocal arabesques and modulations wafted through the night air and imbued the atmosphere with a wistful, spiritual harmony.

Presently the black sky turned pigeon-breast, the stars faded, and the call of the muezzin was heard. We rushed to do our dawn prayers before the sun rose on the horizon, then went back to bed. Everyone slept late, even such early risers as Nanny and Zahra, as there was to be no preparation of lunch. Too small to fast, I was given a midday meal from the night's leftovers. Even in later years, I never managed more than a few days fasting in the middle of the month – it interfered with school work, and I was not strong enough to sustain the physical strain.

At noon, Nanny sometimes went to the local mosque to pray and hear the sermon. She would come back relaxed and smiling.

'Ah, the mullah talked so well today, it gladdened my heart!'

'What did he say, Nanny?' we would ask.

'I haven't got a clue, but it was very good!'

'How do you know it was good, if you didn't know what he said?'

'I haven't been to school like you! Don't ask me clever questions! All I can tell you is that he spoke well and made sense!'

There was a famous preacher on the radio too, and occasionally we listened to him, but *he* didn't say anything in particular either, although he sounded eloquent. He had a mellifluous voice which he used like a musical instrument to convey all the crescendos and diminuendos of his rhetoric. I had made up a comedy number about a very eloquent-sounding sermon which was complete gibberish and regaled our friends with it.

'A bunch of narrow-minded parasitic charlatans all these mullahs!', we all thought, 'but quite harmless.' Would that it had been true!

The hardest time of the day was the last couple of hours before sunset. My father would walk round and round the garden murmuring prayers as the last rays of the sun left the top of the trees and shadows lengthened on the lawn. Ali laid the table and brought out the samovar. The smell of Nanny's cooking floated through the kitchen windows and made us dizzy. As a child, I used to sit on a stool and watch while she cooked in front of an open fire, frying cutlets and aubergines and courgettes, sweat pouring down her face. 'It's not hunger that's killing me, it's thirst!' she would say.

I felt sorry for her and guilty that I could drink as much as I wanted. Worse still was the plight of workers on building sites and on the roads. You could see them struggling, weakened by hunger and parched with thirst, to finish the day's work. 'My tongue is like a stick rattling against my palate,' Ali once remarked, which summed up the state of all those who worked in the torrid sun of the summer midday, when temperatures reached a hundred in the shade. Yet they carried on, upheld by a faith that was stronger than the dictates of their bodies. It gave them satisfaction and informed their lives with meaning. That such sincerity and trust could be ruthlessly exploited by power-maniacs and demagogues has become evident now.

At last, the cry of the muezzin would announce the breaking of the fast and we would all sit round the table to eat. The impulse was to go for the glass of iced water, but it was unhealthy and spoiled the appetite, so we were urged to refrain until some food had been consumed first. Unlike the dawn meal, the 'break-fast' was a cheerful affair. We always had guests – cousins and aunts and uncles and friends. Others would often join us after dinner and we would spend the evening having a party, consuming quantities of nuts and seeds and fruit, until late into the night.

There was an extra dimension to the month of fasting for the Shiites: the anniversary of the martyrdom, on the 21st day of the month, of Imam Ali, son-in-law of the Prophet and the first of the twelve Imams of the Shia sect. The account of his martyrdom at the hands of a terrorist, one of his disaffected political disciples, can be read in history books; suffice it to say that it gave rise later to the first schism in Islam. Since then, the majority of Muslims throughout the world belong to the Sunni (Orthodox) sect, except in Persia where an overwhelming majority is Shiite, and Shiism has been the state religion of the country since the end of the sixteenth century.

Imam Ali is the patron saint of the Sufis and dervishes. One Sufi sect even believes in his divinity, and all others, even Sunni mystics, regard him as the greatest saint and statesman in all Islamic history. He represents the Perfect Man, of which the first example is the Prophet himself, an embodiment of all virtues – valour, fortitude, justice, tolerance, wisdom, etc.

The date of Imam Ali's martyrdom coincides with the Night of Atonement – evidently a variation on the Jewish Day of Atonement – during which everyone's fate for the coming year is decided by Providence and written in his/her ledger by the angels.

For three days and nights there were lamentations and prayers of propitiation, all-night vigils and sermons at the mosques. We never went to the night sessions, ever-wary of mixing with crowds, but prayed at home. Once my sister and I begged to be allowed to go with some friends and Nanny, and were granted permission.

The local mosque was packed to the rafters and the crowd overflowed into the street. Loudspeakers relayed the mullah's sermon, which was based on the goodness and greatness of the First Imam, who was bound to be interceding on this Night of Atonement for his followers. At the end of his speech, he burst into chant, lamenting the Imam's martyrdom, to which the crowd responded with cries of supplication and invocations. When it was all over, the congregation dispersed. Only with hindsight can one see how dangerous such manipulation of popular emotions can be. Would that we had perceived it at the time, and taken the necessary measures to avert the catastrophe which hit the country several decades later!

After the three days of mourning for the Imam, the back of Ramadan was broken. There was only a week or so left before the new moon would mark the end of the month.

The last days of Ramadan were the hardest. After close to thirty days of fasting, bodies were weakened, nerves stretched, will-power overtaxed. But there was also a feeling of exhilaration and achievement for carrying through an act of will and an exercise in self-discipline.

No one was sure when exactly Ramadan ended, as it depended on the sighting of the new moon and could be a day sooner or later than the date indicated by the calendar. Never was 'the bride of the sky' more closely and longingly observed as it changed its shape from a luminous crescent to a golden disc and back to a thin pale thread through the month! On the last evening, people climbed on to their roofs at sunset to find the new moon before it disappeared. It was not easy, as it rose early and vanished soon after in the milky light diffused by the setting sun.

'I see it! I see it!'

'Where? Where? I can't see ...'

'Over there, to the left, above the poplars ...'

Everybody was cheering and pointing to a spot on the eastern horizon. Then a cannon ball was heard, announcing the sighting of the new moon and the end of Ramadan.

In later years, this pattern broke up in our house. My eldest brother left for Europe on his first diplomatic posting. We younger children had lost faith and were much more interested in new ideologies. We thought religion was obsolete, a leftover from the dark, superstitious past, and that it would disappear completely when everyone received the education we were privileged to have. Ali had moved out, so had Nanny, and the new Ali was not given to rigid observance of Ramadan. Something was lost, to which we already looked back with nostalgia. But from the 19th to the 23rd day of the month my mother would still hold ceremonies of commemoration for the Imam's martyrdom. Many friends came and took part, and when the cathartic lamentation was over, the gathering would naturally develop into a party. Once in later years, I was in Persia with my small sons. They were astonished at the whole ceremony and its development from mourning to feast in the space of a couple of hours! On our return, I heard them relate the experience to their father:

'You know Persians are funny people! They get together and sit around while a mullah comes and sings something sad and makes them all cry. Then they have a party and eat lots of cakes and fruit!'

In the end, hardly anyone fasted. 'The world is changing,'

Mother once said. 'People are becoming Godless. What will happen to the world when no one prays and god forgets humanity?' To which father answered: 'Don't worry, there will always be some beacon of faith burning in the depth of darkness. God will never abandon humanity completely.'

I wonder!

The end of Ramadan is marked by a holiday – the most popular in the Islamic calendar all over the world. But in Persia in those days it was just one closing day among others, without special ceremonies. For Persians have preserved their ancient, Zoroastrian customs of seasonal feasts and celebrations, often adapting them to Islamic landmarks, which they observe more fully. The greatest of these is the New Year, *Norooz* (New Day), which occurs at the spring equinox on 21 March. It goes back to the rites of the spring in Zoroastrian times, and corresponds to Easter in Christianity and the Passover in Judaism. But that is another story.

Norooz – *the New Year*

The origins of *Norooz* are lost in the mists of antiquity. We know that the ancient Persians celebrated the end of winter and the arrival of a new season of fertility and abundance. They called this spring festival '*Norooz*', which means 'the New Day', and made it the beginning of their solar calendar. When the Arabs conquered Persia in the seventh century and the Persians gradually converted to Islam, they kept *Norooz* and the rites, but started a new era from the date of the Prophet's *Hejira*, in 621, while all other conquered territories adopted the Arab lunar calendar. So *Norooz* celebrations and rituals have remained unchanged from time immemorial, although the exact symbolic meanings of its varied customs are no longer known by the average Persian.

In our house, preparations for *Norooz* started weeks before it arrived. Sometimes winter lingered and delayed things, with snowfalls as late as the beginning of March. But usually, at the approach of *Norooz*, spring was in the air. There was a change in the quality of light; buds appeared on the bare branches, and sudden downpours of warm rain left everything glistening in the soft sun. Then the swallows began to return from the South to their nests in our eaves – there was one immediately above my window, and as soon as I heard rustling in it, I knew it was refurbishing its home with fresh twigs and feathers, and that winter was gone for good.

My mother would have the house springcleaned from top to bottom, the *korsis* were dismantled and stored away, the paraffin stoves washed and made ready in case the weather took a turn for the worse. Money was always a problem, considering the size of our household and our social obligations, and my mother had to juggle and fret and find enough to satisfy everyone's needs and expectations while keeping our *aberoo* (honour) safe. Everyone had to have new clothes, servants had to be given extra money for their own New Year expenses, quantities of silver and gold coins had to be bought for 'New Year tips' – people always tipped each other's servants when they went visiting – and for children, and so on ... She managed somehow, appearing better off and behaving more open-handedly than many a rich chatelaine, but with much worrying and flustering. '*L'honneur est sauf!*' she would say, and as long as that was true she was content.

My brothers would have suits, shirts and shoes made by Uncle Alem's taylor and shoemaker, and my mother would take my sister and me *Norooz*-shopping in Lalehzar – Westernised people no longer bought their materials in the Bazaar but from the new expensive stores that imported silks from France and woollen cloths from England, all of which were around the centre of town. She would spend a long time looking, comparing, discussing matters with shopkeepers, before deciding on what she wanted for our new dresses and light, *demi-saison* coats. In later years, she would let us choose ourselves, as by our teens we knew exactly what we liked, and she was there only to pay for it. From Lalehzar we would go to her dressmaker's, Emily's house nearby, to have the cloths made up into outfits. We would spend hours drinking tea and socialising with her other clients, who were often acquaintances, while looking at the latest Parisian fashion journals. Some of the pictures showed mothers with their children, wearing dresses made of the same material but in more suitable designs. The children looked so different from us: they were usually blond, with little *retroussé* noses, softly curled hair and blue eyes, while we were dark, with straight hair and black eyes ... We found their exotic looks most alluring, and envied their elegance and air of self-confidence. One model, I recall, had a little girl on one side and a little boy on the other, and I thought the boy looked adorable, with short wavy hair, a tiny nose, and a bright cheeky smile.

'Wouldn't you like to have children like that one day when you grow up?' I asked my sister.

'Ours would look different, darker, but just as pretty,' she said realistically. It did not occur to me then that one day I would indeed produce little boys like the one in that picture – that it was 'written on my brow'!

My mother, who never usually cooked, made all the pastries and sweetmeats and sugar almonds and marzipan fruit and endless other goodies for *Norooz* herself. They were too delicate and complicated to be tackled by any but the most competent pastry-cook, which she had taught herself to be. As there were no gas and electric ovens in those days, she had procured a primitive, makeshift charcoal variety, with which she made do. The oven was rather temperamental, and subject to extremes of temperature for no apparent reason. Yet she got the better of it and seldom burnt anything. Hundreds of visitors came to the house during the New Year celebrations, which lasted thirteen days, and tons of sweetmeats and pastries were needed if each took the tiniest piece. So Mother spent weeks making abundant quantities of each variety, arranged them in airtight tins and stored them in a cool larder.

She would make dough with different flours – wheat, rice,

chick-pea – butter and sugar; then roll it out thin and, with the help of tiny metal moulds, cut it into hearts, circles, crescents, stars, clovers ... This was part of the process to which we all contributed with tremendous excitement. We would sit around her *korsi* in the evenings and press the moulds on to the flat dough, then arrange the pieces on oven trays ready to be cooked, while Aunt Ashraf entertained us with stories and anecdotes of past *Noroozes* in her father's *andaroon*, at her in-laws, or on pilgrimage.

A couple of weeks before *Norooz*, Mother began preparing the *Haft-Seen* – a collection of seven items whose names start with the letter 'S' in Persian, like grass, apple, certain spices and berries, each item symbolising fertility in a different area of life. First she planted the *sabzi* (grass), soaking a cup of wheat grains or green lentils in water for three days, then, when it began to sprout, taking the grains out of water and spreading them on a plate, which she covered with a damp cloth. Over the next few days, the sprouts would grow and green blades appear. Every day she would sprinkle the grass a little, until by New Year's Eve it had grown a couple of inches tall – the symbol of new growth.

The *Haft-Seen* varies in size, and can be modest enough to be contained on one tray, or large enough to spread over a whole table, depending on the size and inclination of the family. Ours was a rich decorative affair, with coloured eggs, a goldfish in a glass container (fertility at sea), an orange with stem and leaf in a bowl of water (a metaphor for the earth turning in the atmosphere), candles, a mirror, platefuls of sweetmeats and marzipan mulberries, etc ...

Excitement gathered as New Year's Day approached. On the last Wednesday before *Norooz*, there was the public Feast of Fire, a custom that has survived from Zoroastrian times. Peasants brought cart-loads of thorn-bushes to the city and hawked them through the streets. Everybody bought some to burn on Fire Wednesday. For a short while at dusk, the streets were aflame with burning thorn-bushes, over which children and youngsters jumped saying, 'Fire! Fire! Give me your glowing cheeks and take away my sallow complexion!' From the air, the town must have looked strewn with stars, all bright and twinkling. The dry bushes blazed quickly and lusciously and died without leaving any debris. We did not join the street celebrations, but Ali bought some thorn-bushes so that we could light fires on the paved paths in the garden, and jump over them with our friends.

While the fire died out, you could make a wish and then stand on a dark street corner, listen to what people said as they went past, and interpret their words as an oracle. Young girls like Ozzie and Zahra, keen to know if marriage was in the stars for them, spent the early evening of Fire Wednesday eavesdropping. It was always a cheering experience, as in the atmosphere of general excitement and good will you could interpret everything to fit your wishes.

On New Year's Eve, Nanny would always produce the traditional dinner of rice and spring herbs, usually served with fish and a herb omelette. Walking in the streets, you could smell the aroma of wild garlic and saffron, of fried fish and fresh bread, emanating from people's kitchens. Herbs, rice and fish were not cheap, as fishmongers and hawkers always increased their prices in accordance with the surge in public demand. The poor could not afford it, but everyone sent platefuls to those they knew to be needy yet too proud to show their poverty. We had two families in the neighbourhood to whom my mother sent food and sweetmeats at *Norooz*. Both improved their conditions in later years with the economic boom, through their children who grew up and 'made good'. One son became a car salesman and a millionaire. But in those days they were grateful for the discreet help they received.

Unlike the Christian New Year which is fixed at midnight, *Norooz* varies according to the exact moment when the sun reaches the equinox. The first day of the year depends on whether this happens before or after midday. Unless the new year arrived in the middle of the night while we were asleep, we used to sit around the *Haft-Seen* table and wait impatiently. They said that when the earth turns and enters the new year, the orange in the bowl of water rotates as well. As children we believed this and fixed our eyes on the orange to catch its movement. If the orange moved for some natural reason we would all clap and hoot and cheer. Presently we would hear the cannon detonate in Army Square at the centre of town, and the radio would wish everyone a happy *Norooz*. Kisses and hugs all round, then the tasting of sweetmeats 'to sweeten the new year' and the handing out of presents by Father.

'Who will go out and come in first?' Mother would ask, as the first person who crossed the threshold would bring good or bad fortune to the house. It was usually my sister who performed this little ritual – she had a 'lucky foot', they said. At other times it was Nanny whose piety and goodness ensured similar blessings.

Hardly had we risen from the table than a flood of visitors would start. According to a strict hierarchical gradation you visited your relatives first, then friends – age, social position, authority, everything fitted into the traditional order of things. My mother's brothers and sisters arrived before anyone else, as she was the eldest sister and my father the head of the family, then our paternal relatives, much more numerous, streamed in soon after. For the next few days the door remained open, the samovar purred from dawn to midnight, and extra staff came to cope with serving several sets of guests in different rooms. Mother received our female relatives and her own friends in the drawing-room, while my father saw the male relations, his students, University colleagues and friends in his study. He often moved from one room to another to greet the guests who were with Mother.

So strict were the rules of etiquette and so time-hallowed that everyone obeyed them even when they blatantly defied rationality. For example, time had to be found somehow on the first day for us to visit my grandmother and my father's two older brothers because of their seniority, even though the stream of visitors never let up and juggling with minutes was frustrating and unnecessary. But 'that is how things had always been and would always be'.

After the first few days, my Mother started 'returning the calls' with my sister and me: a dozen calls in the space of half a day, staying a few minutes at each house, enough time for kisses and expressions of affection. One tiny sweetmeat taken with a minute glass of tea in each place and you were replete by the time you reached home. It was bliss when we were children, but in adolescence we were always on a diet to keep skinny, and suffered agonies by trying not to give in to temptation.

In later years, *Norooz* obligations became so heavy, with endless visiting and return-visiting and tipping and leaving cards and making sure that no one was left out or offended, that those who could afford it went away to Europe or to their country houses by the Caspian Sea, to escape from it all. But as children we loved the razzmatazz – the new clothes, the visitors – some of whom were distant cousins we never saw during the year – the succulent dishes and sweets.

Norooz festivities lasted thirteen days, during which schools and offices were closed and everything stood at a standstill. It was the time of renewing bonds of friendship and good neighbourliness, of gifts and forgiveness.

On the thirteenth day after *Norooz*, everyone who could would leave the city for a picnic in the country, to throw away their plate of *sabzi* and with it the cares and worries of the old year. As usual, the whole extended family took part in the outing – grandparents, parents, children, servants ... Everyone took basketfuls of food and soft drinks, even samovars, and rugs to spread on the ground. Ordinary folk had to rely on public transport, and piled into buses so crowded as to be festooned with people hanging on the outside. Pandemonium reigned in the streets from dawn till the end of the exodus around noon, and again from sunset to midnight when people returned to town. A monorail train linked the capital to Rey, some twenty kilometres to the south. It was the first train in Persia, built at the beginning of the century, as a pilot scheme for a network that would eventually cover the whole country, and was popularly called 'the smoke machine'. On the thirteenth day of *Norooz*, it carried ten times its capacity, with people standing on the steps and lying on the roof as it puffed along like a tired dragon heading for Hades. Humble folk liked it for its cheapness and used the fields around the Shrine of Hazrat Abdul-Aziz for their picnics. But better-off people went north, to Shemiran and the villages in surrounding mountains. Those who had country houses hired private coaches to take family and friends with them.

Our family hardly ever went on such collective expeditions – keeping away from the crowds was one of our first principles of conduct. But once or twice friends brought cars to the door and took us with them, despite refusals and protestations on the part of my mother. Of course, we children wanted to go very badly, but she was reluctant, while my father was glad to be left alone in his study for a day.

Once outside the city, every patch of grass was covered with picnicking families, every green valley alive with the sound of music – from live performers as well as radios and hand-wound gramophones. Feathers of smoke from little samovars and makeshift charcoal braziers curled up in the air and drifted with the breeze: the smell of grilled meats and stews saturated the atmosphere.

In adolescence, we used to join a group of our own friends, hire a large coach, and go to a country house in the mountains near the city which belonged to a brother and sister, heirs to a wealthy landowner. The sister, a plump girl of 18, had a special talent for organising parties and was forever giving dances and dinners and lunches. It was the last couple of years of my life in Persia and, although I was younger than the others, my brothers and sister took me so that I did not feel left out. And of course I could sing and entertain everybody if the opportunity arose.

We took quantities of food, cooked by Nanny and packed by Ali. The staff at our arrival would unpack the baskets and prepare lunch while we roamed in the orchards and fields. By the beginning of April, the short spring was at its height: the orchards, running down as far as the eye could see, were a riot of pink and white blossoms, the mountain slopes, still streaked with snow on high ground, carpeted with wild flowers – tulips, crocuses, irises, narcissi – the limpid air filled with their heady scent. We would run down the paths and disperse in the gardens and orchards, go through a wooden door that opened on to the woods, and disappear in small groups of twos and threes. Peasants gathering mushrooms and wild herbs would smile and offer us their pickings. The soft dewy undergrowth shimmered blue with forget-me-nots, wild violets and, hiding in the darker patches, asphodels. The whole scene was so idyllic, so conducive to romance, that we could feel the sap rising in us as surely as in the surrounding vegetation. You felt Cupid's wings fluttering frenetically amongst young girls and boys, though everyone pretended to ignore it: we were all chaperoned! But love affairs flourished despite – or perhaps because – of restrictions, which inevitably led to marriages: 'honest' girls would not 'give themselves' to anyone before wedlock! I heard about the various couplings and weddings from my sister after I had left the country, until one day she announced her own engagement to one of her young admirers, a law graduate who had just entered the Foreign Office.

At the end of the day, you threw away your *sabzi* as far as you could, and returned home. For weeks after *Norooz*, if you drove to the country, you saw bunches of drying, rotting *sabzis* strewn in the fields, until the new corn hid them from sight. After the picnic of the Thirteenth Day, *Norooz* was over. We went back to school wearing our new shoes and coats, and telling each other about all that we had done.

Every year in spring, I think of those old New Year festivities: the table laid with a colourful *Haft-Seen*, the cornucopias of fruit and sweets, the porcelain and crystal containers brimming with Mother's sweet-bakhlavas, marzipan mulberries, sugar almonds – the atmosphere of warmth and affection. My heart bleeds for those who have died, those who have gone into exile, those who have been killed in revolution and war, above all for Persia herself, humiliated and torn to pieces. But I soon cheer up: a nation that can invent and produce food as delicate, as sophisticated and aesthetically pleasing as those tiny sweetmeats in the shape of hearts, crescents, stars, flowers, will survive temporary set-backs. For, long after the memory of fundamentalism is but a nightmare, and Khomeini and his minions forgotten, save as a sad footnote in history books, Persia will celebrate the arrival of the spring with the ancient rites and timeless memories that belong to her only, and that no one can ever take away.

Doctor Hypocrates' Cabinet

After Dr Amran's death, we had no particular family doctor. Among my father's acquaintances and colleagues there were a few reputable physicians, upon whom we called whenever necessary – in particular three elderly brothers, who had been among the first students to be sent to France at the turn of the century, to study at the Sorbonne. On their return to Persia, they had been appointed Court doctors, and married into the old aristocracy. They had treated the last two Qajar Shahs, who had rewarded them with land and lofty honorific titles related to their profession: one was called The Hypocrates of the Age, the second The Healer of the Realm, and the third The Physician of Kings. They were supposed to combine the best of modern Western medical knowledge with traditional native know-how, the use of new chemical medicines with age-old herbal treatments. Once or twice, my mother took me to see Dr Hypocrates of the Age, but on the whole we did what people had done through the centuries, and what most people were still doing in the country and among the tribes, which was to rely on folk-medicine and traditional treatments.

With its reliance on the diet and on natural substances, as well as the body's own immune system, folk-medicine was quite efficient in normal circumstances. As in medieval Europe, every village had an apothecary, with an array of leaves, berries, roots, powders and ointments, stored in sacs and pots and jars, whose properties and usages he knew. His knowledge was transmitted orally, from father to son, from generation to generation, and this was based on the belief that all substances are either 'hot' or 'cold', roughly the equivalent of the Chinese concepts of Yin and Yang, or Vitamins C and B today. You just learnt about it as you grew up and you tried to balance the two elements in your diet. Citrus fruit, yoghurt, certain herbs and green vegetables were 'cold', while chocolate, fried food and nuts were 'hot', and so on.

At the first sign of a cold, my mother would have oranges and sweet lemons squeezed for us 'to prevent the temperature from rising and producing convulsions'; at the same time, she would prepare and give us a herbal medicine. Meanwhile, chicken broth was *de rigueur*, 'to build you up'.

Apart from the usual herbs, flowers and berries, the district apothecary stocked some very *recherché* medicines for certain conditions, for example 'she-donkey-droppings', recommended for laringitis and chest congestion. Why it had to be the stools of a *she*-donkey and not her male companion, or indeed how you could tell the difference, was never explained. You bought a few of the dried round brown droppings, boiled them for a few minutes and let it brew like tea before sieving and drinking it. A few thimblefuls of this foul black nauseous 'tea' would soon cure the most persistent cough and tenacious bronchial congestion – or so we were told. Yet so repulsive was the thought of such a beverage that it was always the last resort, otherwise people preferred to be patient and put up with their ailments the whole winter rather than swallow she-donkey-dropping brew.

Once my mother had laryngitis and lost her voice completely. Syrups, pills, even antibiotics were tried and found wanting. 'You know what you have to do, don't you?' Aunt Ashraf ventured gently. 'You've been trying to avoid it, haven't you? Well, you must face up to it now – she-donkey-dropping is the answer.'

After much protestation, my mother was persuaded to take the treatment. Aunt Ashraf prepared the 'tea' herself. 'Close your eyes, hold your nose and swallow it in one draught.' My mother obeyed. Whether the illness had run its course or the jolt to the system was sufficient to dislodge it, her laryngitis improved overnight and disappeared altogether within a couple of days.

In a recent biography of Queen Victoria, I read that Prince Albert had died from the after-effects of a cold, or so it seemed. His doctors had prescribed a little brandy every day and assured the Queen that he would soon recover, while every day his condition deteriorated. Now alcohol is considered *the* 'hottest' element as any old Persian peasant would tell you – why, it even burns if you put a match to it! It is therefore the worst possible prescription for colds and flus, which should be treated with 'cold' substances such as citrus fruit and yoghurt. In fact, Prince Albert's doctors were giving him a daily dose of poison which finally killed him. Had they consulted an old Persian apothecary at the time, his life might have been spared and the course of history altered! Prince Albert's brandy was like 'Cleopatra's nose', which had it been shorter, Pascal suggested, would have changed the history of the world!

Parallel to folk-medicine, prayers, vows, alms, streelies and exorcism were used in dealing with illness. The most common form of exorcism was 'breaking the Evil Eye'. If you praised a baby's chubbiness or a young man's handsome figure, you had to say, 'Praise be to God,' otherwise you might inadvertently cast them the evil-eye. Sometimes the evil-eye was indeed cast out of malice or envy, but whatever the reason the spell had to be broken. As there was no possibility of breaking the eye itself, even if you knew whose it was, you broke an egg instead, in a special ritual.

Once, my sister developed a patch of eczema on her back. It watered and itched and looked raw, and she suffered agonies of discomfort. Nothing could cure her, though several doctors had been consulted and some old-wives' ointments tried as well. It was thought that, as a pretty nubile girl, she might have been the subject of an evil-eye. In desperation, my mother sent for an 'egg-breaker', a stout, heavily perspiring middle-aged widow who lived near the Southern Gate of the city and wheezed every time she opened her mouth to utter a word. She sat on the floor cross-legged near my sister's bed and we all gathered around to watch her perform the exorcism. A small basin, an egg, two coins and a piece of charcoal were provided for her; she held the egg between the two coins in one hand and with the charcoal in the other drew tiny circles on it as my mother mentioned the names of all the people who had come into contact with the patient and might have cast her the evil-eye. As the exorcist drew the little circles on the egg, she gently pressed it with the coins, until finally it broke and dropped into the basin. The person whose name had caused the crack was the culprit. In this case it was Nanny, which meant that there had been no malice in it, just simple affectionate admiration. The spell was broken and the patient would soon recover – the 'egg-breaker' was certain. It was a safe bet, since at the same time all sorts of medications were applied which eventually cured her eczema.

By then, we all mocked these old superstitions, while my father tolerated them and said nothing, as long as they were harmless, for the psychological effect they might have. He himself had studied traditional medicine and indeed was considered the foremost authority on Avicenna's medical treatise, *Healing*. He was wary of doctors and avoided them as far as possible, believing that moderation and a balanced diet, combined with sufficient exercise constituted the best preventive medicine. He consumed very little food, walked a great deal and was never ill. He often recommended unheard-of remedies which proved efficacious. Once, my brother Nasser developed a skin disease similar to eczema which made his hands scaly and red, like the skin of dried fish. He had consulted several specialists in Paris but none of their remedies had worked. As he was a painter, it was thought that he might be allergic to the paints he used, but tests had proved negative. Stoically he just put up with the discomfort and unpleasantness without complaint. On a trip to Persia, he showed his hands to my father who examined them and prescribed an ointment made of henna and his own urine. It was not an agreeable treatment, but he tried it by putting it on at night and wearing gloves. After a week the scales vanished, and his hands looked normal again, and the disease was gone never to return.

On another occasion we were in the country for the summer, miles away from doctors. One of our house-guests developed a sudden toothache. It got worse and worse and eventually became unbearable. Father looked at her teeth and prescribed saffron, brewed like tea and drunk in small quantities, and the pain abated within a few minutes.

'Why saffron?' we asked.

'There is no sign of cavity or decay, no abscess or lesion, therefore it must be just nerves, perhaps caused by some worry or anxiety, and saffron is, among other things, a tranquiliser.'

These are very old anecdotes, for, with the spread of modern medicine, apothecaries gradually disappeared and were replaced by chemists, at least in towns. Some greengrocers continued to stock some of the most popular medicinal herbs and berries, but only the older people used them. The younger generation lost faith in the 'hot' and 'cold' division, and the notion of dieting and abstinence.

'Why put up with illness and deprive yourself of good food for weeks when a few antibiotics can get rid of it within a couple of days?' they reasoned. Ironically, while Westernised Persians were throwing away hundreds of years of knowledge on the principle that everything Western was good and everything native obsolete, the West had come full circle and was looking into traditional remedies – alternative medicine, herbal treatment, homoeopathy, etc. . . . In Marxist-Leninist China (and you can't get more Western than that!), they were using acupuncture and other old methods again, while in Japan, which has the highest rate of longevity in the world, both types of medicine were practised. Unfortunately, once a tradition is lost it has gone forever, especially when it has been transmitted orally and there is no written knowledge of it.

When it came to serious illness, then Dr Hypocrates of the Age or his brother The Healer of the Realm, or some other high medical personage was called in. Dr Hypocrates was famous for his unfailingly accurate diagnosis: 'He only has to look at a patient to know exactly what's wrong with him, or her, and what should be done about it,' everyone knew. As wrong diagnosis and the consequent erroneous prescription were the cause of most deaths from otherwise curable illnesses, his skill as diagnostician was much appreciated. For example, he had never been known to confuse malaria with typhoid, two common illnesses with almost identical symptoms but requiring opposite treatments. Unfortunately, Dr Hypocrates was often called in too late, when another doctor had already nearly killed the patient.

Dr Hypocrates was a tiny figure in a grey suit which seemed several sizes too big for him. His white hair had thinned to a few unruly wisps which either stood on end, or fell in every direction except the one intended by the comb – on the rare occasions that this was applied. He wore steel-rimmed glasses which he prevented from slipping off by screwing up his nose. This created a permanent scowl which, combined with his quick temper and inability to suffer fools gladly, gave him a reputation for ill-humour, even rudeness. But underneath the gruff appearance he was a kind, generous man and a vocational doctor who often treated his poor patients free of charge and even paid for their prescriptions himself. His knack for correct diagnosis was all the more remarkable as he had a soft spot for *araq* (Persian vodka), and was permanently in a state of mild inebriation. His breath reeked of garlic, which he took with his meze, and he had a tendency to shout. A stethoscope hung from his neck, but he seldom used it, preferring his delicate, tobacco-stained fingers for osculation. By a process of osmosis over forty years, his elderly valet looked and behaved exactly like him; he bossed the patients around but was attentive to the needy, whom he often allowed to jump the queue.

One morning, I caught my index finger in a door and hurt it badly. The pain was excruciating and shot through my whole body. I was small and writhed in agony for what seemed an eternity, but gradually the pain abated leaving only a throbbing, feverish sensation. My mother, fearing that an infection might develop, followed by gangrene, amputation, etc. . . . , took me to Dr Hypocrates' cabinet in Electricity Avenue. The good doctor lived in an old house with two buildings, the *andaroon* and the *birooni*, with a large garden in between. His waiting-room and surgery overlooked the garden, and as it was summer the windows were open. Through them you could see old trees rising up to a cloudless sky, lawns and flowerbeds full of birds and butterflies.

The waiting-room was full, save for a seat next to a woman with a sick child, which my mother occupied, with me on her lap. The woman wore a flimsy sleeveless dress and no stockings; her face was pale and drawn, her brown hair gathered roughly in a bun had clearly not been brushed for some time. She had a distracted, helpless expression and kept looking at the doctor's door as though begging it to open. With one hand she help up the head of her child which lay on her lap and with the other fanned him gently. It was hard to say how old the child was – a year, two years – so emaciated were his limbs, so ravaged his face. His large black eyes looked at his mother beseechingly while his twiggy legs jerked from time to time and his mouth, half-opened in the shape of a moan, uttered faint whimpers.

'He has had diarrhoea for a week, but since yesterday he has been really bad. He can't keep anything down, even water passes right through him ...' the woman volunteered to my mother.

Gastroenteritis was one of the major causes of infant mortality in those days, for which the traditional remedy was boiled rice and yoghurt: the rice to contract the muscles, and the yoghurt to kill the germs. But the woman was Armenian, judging by her accent and her clothes – it was still unusual for a woman to be so uncovered in a public place – so perhaps she did not know.

My mother had sent in her name and presently Dr Hypocrates came out to greet her and take us in himself. But she motioned to the woman with the sick child, asking the good doctor to see her first.

Dr Hypocrates' eyes swivelled to the woman and her baby, and immediately he began to shout: '*Now* you bring him to me! When it's too late! What you need now is the Exterminating Angel Izrail, not a doctor!'

At the allusion to death, the woman uttered a short sob, like a muffled explosion, and a flood of tears rushed down her face. Dr Hypocrates softened at once, returned to his cabinet and a minute later brought out a prescription which he handed to his valet, urging him to be 'as quick as the wind'. Meanwhile he had a look at my finger, assured my mother that it was nothing, and asked me to be careful with it for a couple of days. In truth I was so overcome with pity for the little boy that I had completely forgotten about my finger. We left. But I could not keep the scene out of my mind and asked my mother if there was nothing we could do to make him better.

'Just pray for him,' she said, and gave me some coins to give to beggars on the way home on behalf of the boy. Perhaps Dr Hypocrates did save him or perhaps he died soon after, as thousands of children did every summer in those pre-filtered water days, and still do all over the Third World.

After I left Persia, Dr Hypocrates and his two brothers died of old age and I forgot about this episode. Then, in the early seventies, I went to join the Bakhtiari tribes on their spring migrations from the plains of Khuzistan in the south, by the Persian Gulf, to their summer pastures in the Zagros mountains near Isfahan. Since the purpose of the migration is to find food for the flocks when the plains become parched and every blade of grass withers to dust, even those who have nothing but a couple of goats undertake the arduous journey. Only those few tribespeople who have no livestock whatever and therefore no reason to move, nor any money for the trek, stay on in the winter quarters, while the temperature soars to 120 degrees in the shade and the deserted village turns into an inferno of heat and dust.

I was doing a reportage on the tribes and wished to see all aspects of their lives, so I sought out these few 'strayers', as they were called – the truly destitute whose *raison d'être* was in jeopardy. I found a few in the shell of an old, ruined building on the edge of the village. In one corner sat a young woman, with a baby on her lap, its head held up with one hand as the other fanned him with a little straw fan ... I had a feeling of *déjà vu*; the scene was a *tableau vivant* I had seen before, a long time ago ... I remembered Dr Hypocrates' cabinet, the Armenian woman and her dying child ... But this was a quarter of a century later, the country was in the middle of an unprecedented economic boom, 'the streets were paved with black gold'; what is more that 'black gold' came from the ground on which this woman and her sick child were squatting, watching their better-off neighbours leave with longing and despair. During that quarter of a century, hospitals and clinics had been built all over the country; tens of thousands of doctors had been trained in Persia and abroad, many of whom were supposed to spend their National Service in remote areas and look after the poor and the disenfranchised. Yet there was none in that little tribal market village, they were all in Teheran or other major cities, where the streets were bedecked with doctors' notice-boards, and expensive private clinics provided the best medical care for those who could afford it. Something was amiss, but in the meantime what to do for the dying child?

I sent for a doctor from the nearest town, offered to pay for his services myself, and threatened to report the situation to the Shah on my return if something was not done to save the little creature. The tribesmen spoke in their local dialect which I could not understand, but from their expressions I could see that they were mocking me.

'There is not just one like him, there are thousands,' my host, a tribal chief, told me. 'You're here this year, but what about next year and the year after? Let's go, *Khanoom* (Lady)!' We left the next day at dawn, and I never found out what happened to that woman and her child.

On my return to Teheran, I went to see the Shah and interview him on the subject of the tribes for my story. His Chamberlain came in to greet me and turned out to be Dr Hypocrates' son, a career diplomat now attached to the Court. We sat and reminisced about his father, the old valet, the house and garden. Then I was summoned in.

Since the revolution of 1979 I have often thought of the tribes, and wondered what has happened to the ones I got to know well and make friends with. It seems that, far from making their condition better, the revolution has made it worse. Now 'the black gold' that runs under their ground is spent on buying arms with which to kill their children in war or in prisons.

Sometimes when modern medicine failed, even the most Westernised Persians turned to traditional remedies as a last resort. Once my mother's ankle swelled for no apparent reason, causing her great pain. A doctor was consulted and various ointments applied, without much success.

'You should try leeches,' Aunt Ashraf suggested.

There was a 'leech man' in the *bazaarcheh*, a greengrocer whose hobby was the application of leeches. He was summoned to the house and brought a tin in which dozens of the little black horrors wriggled lazily. He took a few out with a small pair of tongs and applied them on Mother's swollen ankle. Some fell off and had to be put on again until eventually quite a few 'took' and stuck to the flesh. Over the next few minutes they grew to several times their original sizes, until, replete with blood, they looked like large black slugs, and finally fell on to the plate of ashes on which the foot was placed, to be disposed of. They were supposed to have extracted whatever poison was causing the tumescence and pain. Once again they seemed to have worked. The swelling and the pain disappeared after a couple of days.

Another time, a woman was called in to apply cupping-glasses to Aunt Ashraf's back. She made some incisions at the nape of her neck and stuck the glasses over them. Slowly blood filled the glasses, thick and blackish, and was emptied into a bowl. About half a pint of blood was extracted from her. It was not a sight for a squeamish nine-year-old.

'Don't make such funny faces as if I was being murdered!' she said, noticing my discomfort. 'It's good for me. When the blood thickens, the pressure goes up and you have a heart attack. This way you clean your blood and avoid dropping dead.'

A week earlier, coming home from school, we had seen a woman stretched out in the street, her face covered with a handkerchief, surrounded by a crowd of children and adults. Presently a policeman and a doctor arrived; the latter examined the woman whose face was as red as a beetroot, and pronounced her dead.

'The heart,' he simply said. We had been shocked and told Aunt Ashraf about it, hence her prophylactic bloodletting, after which she told us a story.

'Once in ancient times, a man had a heart attack and fell on the ground. He was pronounced dead, put on a bier and was being taken to the cemetery, when the great philosopher Avicenna saw the cortège. He ordered the bier to be put down, moved the man's limbs, and incised them to let out his blood. Gradually the man came back to life. When asked how he had known that the man was not dead, Avicenna said that he had noticed his feet were upright, instead of limp and flopped to the side, as a dead man's would. So you see, a little bloodletting in time can do wonders!'

I don't know if that story is true, but it fits in with Avicenna's reputation as 'the greatest doctor that ever lived'.

One day, when I was about 11 or 12, the telephone rang and I ran to answer it. I caught my leg in the carpet and fell down the stairs, landing on my wrist. It looked broken, hurt badly, and swelled immediately. Ali was sent to bring a droshky and my mother took me to the bazaar to see Mashdi Habib, the bone-setter. He had a pottery shop in the potters' section where he sold ceramics from his native Hamadan, in the north-west of Persia: bowls, jugs, plates, pitchers, tiles, crockery of all sorts, in earthenware or glazed with ornamental patterns, above all in the famous turquoise-blue of his region. Bone-setting was his hobby, and he was so skilled that his reputation had spread far beyond the confines of the Bazaar. They said that even when a bone was broken into smithereens he could make it whole again. He practised his craft on broken pottery. He was said to break a pitcher into a dozen pieces, put them in a sack, and from the outside manipulate the pieces into place like a jigsaw puzzle! Whether this was true or a poetic exaggeration no one knew, for reputations spread in the Bazaar like ivy on a stone wall. 'Give the *Bazaaris* a molehill and they will turn it not just into a mountain, but into a whole range of mountains!' Aunt Ashraf would say. But one thing was certain – that Mashdi Habib was very good indeed, for had he crippled even one client by setting his bones wrong, everybody would have known and he would have been ruined.

Mashdi Habib had once set my brother Nasser's arm. Nasser was so naughty and had such reserves of irrepressible energy that he often got into scrapes – his knees were permanently gashed from falls, his clothes were torn by branches of the trees he climbed, his hands were always covered with cuts. On this occasion he had been doing acrobatics with his bicycle when another had run into him and thrown him down on his arm. Mashdi Habib had set this bone and urged him to give up mischief for a while. But no sooner was his arm out of the sling than he had gone and done it again, this time breaking the bone in several places. Mashdi Habib had dealt with the situation and the arm had mended perfectly.

Mashdi Habib was sitting on a stool outside his shop when we arrived. Upon seeing us, he got up, bowed courteously and motioned us inside. With infinite gentleness he manipulated my wrist and said that it was not broken but only slightly cracked, and that he could soon put it right. He took some warm ashes from the brazier and poured them into a calico bag, then wrapped the bag around my wrist. (If the bone had been broken he would have kept it motionless by putting it between two strips of wood, after manipulating it into place, and covered it with hot ashes). He then tore a piece of rag from a sheet and made me a sling, saying: 'Keep it still for a couple of days – in a week your wrist will be as good as new!'

A whole chapter could be written on the use of ashes in Persia's traditional folk-medicine: they are the antiseptic of the poor even today. Before penicillin was easily available, ashes were used to staunch cuts, sterilise wounds, assuage rheumatic pains, absorb blood, and much more. Nor should one forget their symbolic and mystical connotations of humility and submission, or metaphorical ones for denoting martyrdom and life's transience.

Alas, Mashdi Habib and the other bone-setters all eventually beat a retreat before the onslaught of modern methods of surgery and plaster casting in dealing with broken bones. But sometimes a damaged limb would emerge from the plaster crooked, and have to be broken and set again! This indeed happened to one of our cousins, who had rejected the services of Mashdi Habib in favour of a doctor freshly back from America.

'What do you expect from these new-fangled doctors?' Aunt Ashraf wished to know. 'These *Farangi*s don't know anything except what they read in books! Mashdi Habib can't even read, but he has never messed up anybody's bones! He would have been lynched if he had ever made a mistake! But these new doctors get away with murder, just because they have a diploma from some fancy foreign university!'

Mashdi Habib disappeared like his beautiful blue pots and pitchers – colourful plastic ones were so much cheaper and more practical, people thought. When Persian pottery became fashionable again, from the 1960s onwards, workshops were set up in Hamadan and other traditional centres of faience to revive the old crafts and meet the increasing demand. But the secret of the dye that for centuries had produced the luminous, opalescent turquoise-blue of the old faience was lost, as surely as Mashdi Habib's bone-setting skill. The blue of the new potters is tarnished, no longer translucent *abi* – 'water blue', the loveliest and most evocative colour in a land of rocks and thorns.

The Society of Friends

Moons and stars, nay the whole firmament,
have no will of their own
'Tis the Friend who determines their course.

Hafiz of Shiraz

The verb 'to love' in Persian is 'to have as a friend'. 'I love you' translated literally is 'I have you as a friend', and 'I don't like you' simply means 'I don't have you as a friend'. Such emotional variations and nuances of feeling as tenderness, sympathy, passion, ecstasy, etc. ... are expressed by countless other words and phrases, but the essential, generic verb 'to love' is 'to have as a friend'.

Sufism which found its most profound and tender expression in Persian poetry, is centred around this concept: the Sufi poet longs for the Friend, aspires to union with the Friend, laments separation from the Friend, goes through the various stations of trying to reach the Friend. The Friend is the Beloved, the Centre and the Goal.

Perhaps the cult of friendship in Persia is an emanation on the earthly plane of this transcendental aspiration, for it is believed that often the human friend acts as the catalyst who opens the doors of perception; the guide on the soul's pilgrimage towards the celestial Friend.

In the old days, the cult of friendship ran through all the layers of society, forming the basis of every social intercourse. Even practical relationships such as contact at work or business negotiations were influenced and dignified by it. Persians' famous hospitality stemmed from it: the best food was always reserved for friends, the prettiest room in the house, the loveliest presents.

My parents had a wide circle of friends and acquaintances. Their social life was very busy and in those days still segregated into male and female circles. In his relationship with others, my father was all gift and no request: he was always available for those who needed him. He often saw his students at home, between the dawn prayer and when he had to leave for the University, or early in the evening, for extra tutorials if they requested any; he had callers at all hours of the day. Ali was the hatchet man whose task was politely to turn away the importunates and the bores: he would ask their names and say, 'I'll see if the Master is in.' Then he would go to the study and give the name to father who would indicate to him if he wished to see the caller or not. If not, Ali would return to the door and say, 'I'm sorry the Master is out; is there a message?' He performed the same routine with telephone calls, saying: 'If the Master received all those who importune him and answered all his phone calls he would have no time to work.'

But no one who had come for a purpose was turned away. Nor was Father ever surprised when the man, who had lavished the most effusive promises of eternal devotion when he had brought a petition, disappeared without trace once the right strings had been pulled and his problem solved. He knew the world and how to handle it, but did not give a fig for it. He had the true Sufi's detachment and prescience, and often when his behaviour seemed out of character or baffling the reason for it would become apparent later. Once, Prince Ali-Reza, the late Shah's eldest brother, expressed a desire to see him. Father was reluctant and kept stalling. Of Reza Shah's seven sons, Prince Ali-Reza was the most like him: tall and handsome, he had his father's sharp mind and physical courage, and certainly in his later years he was the most spiritually inclined of his children. He had read the great Sufi poets and become interested in mysticism, and having heard about Father he wished to see him.

'Why don't you want to meet him, sir?' we asked. 'You never refuse to see anyone or do a favour, why not him?'

'It's not that I don't wish to see him – he sounds a sincere and charming young man – but not just now ...'

A couple of months later, Prince Ali-Reza died in an air crash: he was piloting his own airplane over the mountains from the Caspian Sea, trying to bring a sick retainer to hospital in Teheran. The weather was bad but the man's condition was critical and he defied the storm; he got lost and hit the hillside.

'Now you see why I was reluctant to see him,' said Father. 'If I had and he had become a friend I would now be heartbroken, instead of just sad for his youth and potential.'

One of my father's best friends was a Sufi poet and a famous literary figure who was among the greatest contemporary authorities on Rumi. He was the son of a *Sheikh* (Sufi Master) but like everyone else had changed into modern Western clothes to work for the government as a high-ranking official at the Ministry of Culture – he once became the Minister of Culture for a while but soon resigned, as it meant giving up all his other activities. His wife and sisters were close friends of my mother's, and our families had been connected for a long time. He adored my father, and all of us for being related to him, and we called him Uncle Hadi in response.

Uncle Hadi lived in a house which consisted of two buildings, *andaroon* and *birooni*, long after such luxuries had disappeared. His wife held court in one house and he in the other, while their children and servants milled around between the two. When his wife died and his children grew up and left, he kept the huge house out of reluctance to change, but neglected it completely. The servants were too old to deal with it and soon it became a repository of dust and cobwebs, haunted by bats and ghosts; the flowerbeds withered, the trees languished, and the garden sank into permanent autumnal desolation; but his literary salon went on once a week and he kept open house the rest of the time.

I visited him whenever I went to Persia, usually in his study which looked as if burglars had just ransacked it – books and papers strewn everywhere, overflowing wastepaper baskets, haphazard objects and furniture, all covered in inches of dust. He would pick up a book to read me a passage or check some date, and just blow on it to remove the dust, which would rise in a dense cloud, hover a while, and settle down again, without his paying the slightest attention.

Uncle Hadi came to visit my father often, to the delight of the whole household. He was in every way larger than life and highly eccentric. Tall and heavy, he had white hair and drooping mustachios, an aquiline nose and black piercing eyes. His loud, sonorous, basso-profundo voice resounded through the house as soon as he entered, and sent everyone scurrying. Ali would rush to bring ashtrays and soft drinks, we would come down from our rooms to gather round him, usually in my mother's drawing-room, and Father would join us too. He would entertain us with a pyrotechnic display of puns in several languages, anecdotes, verses, ad lib poems which gushed forth from the rich treasury of his uncanny memory. He knew Rumi's entire output by heart, tens of thousands of lines of verse, and much more; he used poetry to back logic: every argument was clinched with an apposite quotation.

When my father died a few years before the revolution of 1979, Uncle Hadi was disconsolate and wrote a beautiful elegy which was engraved on his tombstone, and which I copied the first time I visited his grave on my last trip to Persia. Having been told that Uncle Hadi was ill in hospital, with a broken hip and other ailments, I went to see him. All his life he had chain-smoked with the result that a few years earlier he had developed cancer of the throat. The tumour had been removed, but his doctor had warned him of a recurrence in the lungs if he did not stop smoking.

'Imbecile!' he had roared. 'I want my lungs to smoke with, not to live in order to preserve my lungs!' Now the disease had returned. I found him in bed with his leg up in a contraption attached to the ceiling; his face was emaciated and pallid, his nose almost transparent; he was evidently in great pain and discomfort. With his fiery eyes and sunken cheeks, his white hair and beard, he looked like a wounded eagle. As soon as he saw me, he tried to sit up and engulfed me in a whirlwind of loud extravagant versified greetings and endearments:

'From the rosewater comes the fragrance of the Rose,' he quoted by reference to my father. 'The light of my eyes! My heart, my dear child.'

'How are you, dear Uncle?' I enquired, after the flood of affection had subsided.

'*I* am very well. How would a dervish feel but well? It's my *leg* that's hurting!'

He then proceeded to entertain me with an assortment of puns, limericks, poems ... Soon we were laughing as if he had no pain and not a care in the world. Finally I said that I had been to see my father's grave and how moved I was by his wonderful poem. At this, his expression changed, a veil of sadness came over his eyes, his nostrils quivered, and tears poured down his corrugated cheek.

'Alas! That my dear friend should be dead and I still alive! I hope it won't be for long now; what is the use of living when you have lost such a friend?'

I went to see him once more before returning to England.

'I shall not see you again in this world my dear child, but it will be wonderful to join your father!'

Sometime later I heard that he had died. I would like to think of them together, sitting on a rug in the shade of a tree, in the Garden of Eden, chatting and laughing ...

Another old friend and frequent visitor of my father's was a cousin of Uncle Hadi's. He was a *Sheikh*, the son of an Ayatollah, and the only member of their large family to have kept his mullah's attire of 'cloak-and-turban'. Yet he was not a professional cleric but a landowner. He was exceptionally progressive and enlightened for a mullah, endorsed the country's modernisation programme and sent his children to Europe for higher education – including his daughters, a very rare thing in those days. He had read much modern European literature, especially Anatole France for whom he professed a great admiration. We called him Diogenes because, just as his ancient Greek homonym had spurned Alexander the Great's offer of help, so he had turned down Reza Shah's. The story behind his nickname was also the reason for his being allowed to keep his mullah's costume at a time when it was forbidden for anyone except a few professional *Mujtahids* in Qom.

Diogenes' estate was in Arak, a province in South-East Persia. Long before Reza Shah became King, when he was an officer in a Cossack battalion, he was sent on a mission to Arak. On the eve of sabbath, Thursday, he asked his companions what they did by way of amusement. They told him that the local landowner, who was a *Sheikh*, held a reception where all the notables of the town assembled and spent the evening in pleasant, interesting company. Having nothing better to do, Reza Shah (then plain Reza Khan) agreed to accompany them. When they arrived, the room was already full of guests and they found somewhere near the door – a humble position far from the host and guests of honour at the other end. Not much notice was taken of them and towards the end of the evening they rose to leave. Diogenes saw the officers going and motioned to Reza Khan to stay a while. He told him that, although he was just a simple soldier now, he would go far and some day be a colonel, even a general, adding, 'Mark my word, eventually you will even become the Shah.' The object of this extravagant prediction laughed, as did his companions, and they left.

Years passed.

One Thursday evening, Reza Khan, by now a colonel in the Army, went on a pilgrimage to the shrine of Hazrat Abdul-Azim in Rey, near Teheran. Inside the mausoleum, he saw a *Sheikh* whom he did not recognise, but who accosted him, saying, 'Don't you remember me? You came to my house in Arak once, years ago. I told you then you would go far and become a colonel, didn't I? Soon you'll be a general, and one day you'll be the Shah!'

Reza Khan laughed again, chatted for a while and left.

Many years passed and Reza Khan did become Chief of Staff, Prime Minister and finally Shah. This time he remembered the oracular *Sheikh* and sent for him. 'Ask for anything you wish and you shall have it,' he told him.

But, true to his Greek predecessor, Diogenes answered: I want nothing. I already have all I need – a clear conscience and a free spirit, and I wish you the same. Just don't force me to change my clothes, not because clothes are important but because I'm used to mine!'

Nonetheless Reza Shah sent him a large packet containing money. How much was in it? We do not know, for Diogenes sent it back without opening it, just jotting on the back a poem which I used to know but have now forgotten, save for the first line which said: 'We cannot dishonour Poverty and Contentment . . . by accepting your gift.' So it was that our Diogenes kept his 'cloak-and-turban' and acquired his nickname. All other members of his family gave up their clerical garb and rose in the administration to positions of power and renown, as did his children.

My mother's social life was different from my father's: she went out a great deal and gave frequent lunch, dinner and tea parties. She had a vast circle of friends with a few close ones whom she adored and depended on. She was often 'out to tea' when we came back from school at 4.30, and we knew it at once – the house seemed forlorn, empty and silent. Zahra or Nanny would give us our tea and we would do our homework. By the time Mother came back for dinner, we were ready for bed. I did not like it, and many years later I contrived, as far as my work allowed me, to be at home when my own two children returned from school – all the more since they had no Zahra or Nanny to greet them with warmth and a good meal.

Sometimes we came home and found a tea party in full swing, with the sound of laughter and conversation reaching the front door and beyond. Persian tea parties have a certain fixed pattern – at least they did then. On arrival, the guests were refreshed with a glass of sherbet, then tea was served in small glasses with ornate silver and enamel holders, with pastries and cream cakes. Assorted biscuits were offered with the second cup of tea, after which great quantities of nuts and watermelon seeds were consumed, while the conversation gathered momentum. After a while, a large bowl of the season's fruit would be brought in and served. Finally in winter something hot, and in summer ice-cream, would seal the party. How anyone could contemplate dinner after such a tea defied understanding – no wonder most better-off women beyond a certain age were 'plump', to put it mildly. But the young and fashionable had discovered dieting, ate nothing and kept their figures.

For lunch and dinner parties my mother supervised the cooking, which included such luxury items as chicken, duck, and fresh roasts as well as traditional Persian dishes of pilau and stews. Everything was laid out before guests were summoned to the table, which was designed to be as colourful and aesthetically pleasing as it was aromatic and delicious. After the guests had eaten, the rest of the household would sit down to a meal. Nanny used to give me the giblets on a tiny plate in the kitchen when I was too small to join the grown-ups.

At such gatherings, several generations mixed, as grand-mothers, mothers and daughters of various ages were invited together. Among the older women, conversational topics ranged from problems of daily life to plans for pilgrimages and weddings, the efficacy of certain prayers and vows, the competence of medical specialists, the changing times and the problems they created. The younger guests discussed the latest balls, parties, films and film stars. Heated arguments raged about the relative merits of different films and their stars, the latest Parisian fashion, the marital and other prospects of various eligible young girls or young men who had recently returned from Europe or America and entered the 'market'. I was too small to join in the fray, but listened with interest. I remember some of the young men they discussed, who later became MPs, ministers, and a couple of them prime ministers – both friends who were eventually killed, one by a terrorist and the other by the revolution in 1979.

In later years, I often stayed in my room when mother had guests – unless they were friends I really loved. But she would often send for me or even come to my room herself.

'What are you doing cooped up here when Mrs So-and-so and her daughters are here and longing to see you?'

'Nobody is longing to see me, Mother, and I'm reading!'

'Well don't read! Whoever saw a girl buried in a book all the time – it'll ruin your eyes! Come and be with us for a while and slip away again – just to be polite!'

I would make my *acte de présence* and disappear. It is hard to be lonely if you are never alone, and I did not know what loneliness meant, or what a calamity it could be, until I came to Europe. Yet there was a price to pay for this cosy togetherness, which was loss of privacy. But looking back I wonder how much of our extolling of privacy and independence is an excuse for not caring enough about one another. Independence from what? From love and affection? Does anyone wish to be alone *all* the time? Does Greta Garbo *now* regret having said, 'I want to be alone!' I wonder!

When my father had guests, I used to go and sit beside him and listen to the conversation. But, after the age of 10, I was no longer allowed to, except when the party was mixed and my mother was present as well, and I missed the pleasure. Among my father's guests conversation ranged over philosophy, poetry, social events, and was all laced with anecdotes and jokes and witty repartees. Sometimes I sat in the adjoining room and listened, especially when some of Father's younger friends sang the *Mathnavi* or recited poetry.

Men expressed their affection verbally, with ornate protestations of eternal loyalty and friendship, while women were more physical – they touched and kissed and hugged a great deal; they told each other how much they loved one another. Of course, today such behaviour would elicit all sorts of grotesque pseudo-psychoanalytical interpretations and innuendos of sexual deviance. Nothing would be more inappropriate. They enriched their lives by giving friendship its due measure of love and tenderness, and took nourishment from a varied range of feelings. From their men, women expected security, love, protection for themselves and their children; but they relied on their women friends for affection, sympathy, companionship and practical help.

Following my parents' example, I grew up valuing friendship

as one of the most important human relationships. Luckily by the time I was older it was possible to have friends of both sexes. Of course, at a certain age, preoccupation with romantic love, mating and marriage eclipses all other concerns, but friendship belongs to a different area of the soul and it is more noble. 'Lovers come and go, but friends endure,' as Aunt Ashraf would doubtless have said! I cherish my friends more than ever, and depend on them almost entirely for my emotional well-being. Perhaps because, having lost the support system of my family by leaving my country and marrying a foreigner, I have had to rely on such affection more than most people. I have been very lucky in my friends – a claim I could not in all honesty make about my more romantic involvements ...

Country Life

Bientôt nous plongerons dans les froides ténèbres,
Adieu vive clarté de nos étés trop courts.

Charles Baudelaire

Every summer we took refuge from the torrid dog-days of the city in Damavand, a green valley tucked away in the deep folds of the Alborz mountains some fifty miles north-east of Teheran. The country was named after Mount Damavand, the highest mountain in Persia, whose cone-shaped snow-clad summit could be glimpsed on the far distant horizon wrapped in clouds. Once an active volcano, Damavand is now extinct and broods beneath perennial snows like a giant swathed in sulphurous fumes. It is the Olympus of Persian mythology, the abode of kings and heroes and mythical beasts: Zahak-the-Tyrant was chained to a prison-cave near its summit, after his defeat by Kaveh-the-Blacksmith whose leather apron became Persia's first flag. It is said to be the mountain of *Qaf* on which once lived the *Seemorgh*, the Bird-King in search of whom the birds undertook their perilous journey in Attar's *Conference of the Birds*.

For years, before I was born, my parents had migrated to Shemiran, a summer resort at the foot of the mountains some twenty miles north of the town. Reza Shah had built his summer residence there, followed by some of his courtiers and ministers, and a few foreign embassies. In later years, as the city shifted north, Shemiran became absorbed in the sprawling metropolis and its various villages and districts became affluent suburbs for the old and the new rich – especially the latter – who sold their town houses and moved 'up town'. But in those early days my parents rented a house with a garden there for the two hottest months of summer. All through the season, a stream of visitors, invited and uninvited, would go and stay with them. Sometimes they did not even know the people who turned up on their doorstep, armed with an introduction from the in-laws of a cousin of an old retainer of — and in desperate flight from the suffocating heat of the town. The expression for such tenuous relationships is 'I'm the sleeve of the sheep-coat of the cousin of ...'

My father accepted the situation without complaint, but my mother, who had to provide for and entertain everyone on her very limited resources, and in a suitably seigneurial fashion, finally rebelled:

'This is not a house,' she declared, 'it's a caravanserai!', and proceeded to find an alternative. Some of her close friends, notably the three eldest daughters of Ayatollah Kia-Noori (the leader of the Absolutists in the constitutional revolution of 1905), had properties in Damavand where they spent their summer holidays, and they suggested that she should give it a try the following year. So, as far back as I remember, we spent July and August in Damavand, camping in a *bagh* (an orchard or garden, usually with a peasant hut on it) in idyllic circumstances.

Preparations for the holidays started weeks ahead: the house was cleaned from top to bottom and treated with moth-balls; the furniture was covered with sheets and most of the rooms were locked up, and some old retainers came to house-sit – in later years it was Ali and his family. While flour, fruit and vegetables could be bought fresh in the country, other provisions had to be taken from town: rice, pulses, condiments, spices … all were ordered from a Bazaar wholesaler and packed; essential furniture and kitchen utensils, clothes and linen were wrapped inside carpets; and finally the large four-poled tent Mother had ordered arrived in a lorry the day before we left.

The night before our departure we always could hardly sleep with excitement, and we sat up in our beds on the roof talking until late. At dawn we were roused by the sounds of last-minute packing in the garden below. We would look down from the edge and see the bus waiting outside the front door, the huge carpet bundles being heaved up to its rack by Ali and the driver's mates. We would dress and breakfast quickly while Mother made last-minute recommendations and muttered prayers of protection against imponderable calamities, and finally we would get into the bus and set off. We each had our best friends coming to stay for a week or two during the summer, but always took Cousin Mohammad with us for the whole period. He was between my brothers in age, and a great friend of both. His mother had died when he was a child and his father had remarried, and Cousin Mohammad had adopted us as a second family. He went to the *lycée* with my brothers and was like a third brother for my sister and me, 'only much nicer!' Everybody loved Cousin Mohammad: he was gentle and courteous, with a quiet, dead-pan sense of humour, and very clever. He got scholarships all through his education and the best grades, and he was always ready for whatever adventure we got up to.

The bus called briefly at the 'Garage' – the bus terminal – to fill the back seats with passengers – mostly peasants returning to the country with their empty poultry-baskets and bundles of new clothes they had bought with their meagre profits. A journey that today takes little more than an hour took the whole day at that time, with a stop for lunch. The road, which was not yet surfaced, was full of potholes and striped with deep furrows made by lorries and other vehicles during the muddy winter months. You could see road-workers at regular intervals spreading pebbles with their long-handled rakes and spades, filling the holes and evening the ground. They would stand on the side and wave as the bus went past amid clouds of dust, their heads covered with white handkerchiefs tied into makeshift caps.

I sat beside Mother in the front as she turned the beads of her rosary and murmured prayers to protect us from the journey's hazards. Soon we left town and, after some ten miles of flat wilderness, reached the first low hills. Top-heavy with baggage and overloaded with passengers, the bus crawled uphill at a snail's pace, producing no breeze to temper the heat. Green and carpeted with wild flowers in the spring, the hills were now parched, covered with dry thorn-bushes and stones. Only the play of light and shadow on the rocks relieved the monotonous fawn. Presently we would reach *Hezar-Darreh* – A Thousand Abysses – so called because the road coiled around the vertiginous mountains, with deep precipices on one side and the sheer rock face on the other. Now and again an accident would occur and a vehicle go over the edge. Looking out of the bus window you could see little shrines at the bottom of the canyons marking the spots where people had perished. In later years, a new asphalted road was built through the mountains which shortened the journey and removed the dangers of A Thousand Abysses, but then car crashes increased in proportion to traffic and took even more victims.

'*Allah Akbar!* [God is great!]' shouted the driver's mate, to keep up the passengers morale as we approached the Perilous Pass.

'Praise be to the Prophet and His people!' echoed the male passengers whenever another vehicle approached and had to manoeuvre past.

Eventually we would emerge from the pass and stop for lunch at a roadside tea-house. It was a little oasis, with a tiny stream that came down the slopes and disappeared into the ground a mile or so down the canyon, and a few poplars and willows and oak trees in whose shade they spread a rug for us to sit. Mother did not trust the tea-house food and took our own, warmed by Nanny over a brazier provided by the tea-house owners. After lunch, quantities of tea were consumed while the driver rested and the peasants sat in the shade and smoked their long-handled *chopoqs* (pipes). Then we were called back to the bus for the last lap of the journey.

At dusk we reached the tip of the valley, where a stream ran alongside the road, bordered with poplars and willows. Gradually the narrow passage opened out to reveal fields and meadows and orchards and woods, surrounded by high mountains. On the far horizon loomed 'The Lion's Head', 'The Doves' Cradle', 'The Sleeping Giant' – names we had given to various hills, inspired by their rock formations. Then at last the bus hooted and stopped on the brow of a hill, outside the front door of our house, which was set back from the road and screened by a row of trees. Our excitement knew no bounds: we had arrived at the Promised Land and the next two months would be the happiest of the year.

We rented our *bagh* from Mashdi Abdollah, the village baker, whose wife, Soltan, was Nanny's sister. He had two sons, Hossein and Akbar, all others having died in infancy. The elder worked with his father at the bakery, leaving home before dawn and only returning late in the evening; the younger helped his mother in running the farm. With a large orchard, a couple of cornfields and the bakery, Mashdi Abdollah was considered rich by local standards, especially since he had so few mouths to feed compared to other peasant families, but you wouldn't know it: he had a reputation for being rather stingy and saving all his money. Towards the end of his life he had accumulated enough wealth to be eligible for haj (the pilgrimage to Mecca) and acquire the title of *Haji*. But in those days he and his family seldom ate anything save yoghurt, bread and soup, and they patched their clothes until there was nothing left of the original cloth.

Throughout the summer, Akbar and his mother picked the fruit, smoked the apricots and plums, dried the berries and raisins on the roof of the hut, and packed and dispatched them all to town for sale. By October, when the fruit trees were denuded and the harvest was done, the family left the *bagh* and went back to live in the village, above the bakery.

Mashdi Abdollah had built his hut himself. It consisted of two rooms, surrounded on two sides by a wide veranda. The walls were uneven and there were no windows, just a latticed opening made by criss-crossing the mud bricks. But life in summer was lived in the open air, so most such peasant huts were simple shelters for provisions, or against sudden showers in early autumn. There was a little kitchen at the end of the veranda, with a couple of brick braziers and a raised clay oven for baking bread. Underneath the oven there was a space for all of Soltan's chickens and roosters, who spent the day free-ranging over the property, but at night were gathered and crammed inside the dark enclosure to be protected from 'the wicked fox'. We bought their eggs, which Soltan gathered every day, still warm and covered with little feathers, and brought to the breakfast table. Mashdi Abdollah had built a very primitive lavatory at the back of the hut for our benefit, since the peasants themselves used nature – the nearest stream acting as a bidet!

We thought our *bagh* was the loveliest in the whole village. It was conveniently near the road yet set back from it; it was a couple of miles outside the village and the crowds of holiday-makers, yet not too far to be inaccessible; above all it had a running stream. One of the three streams that watered the valley curled around the veranda between the hut and the clearing in which we pitched our tent, and flowed parallel to the road towards the end of the cultivated area and the Jewish cemetery in Gilliard. A little bridge made with branches and mud connected the hut to the orchards and to paths leading to neighbouring farms. Beyond it was the expanse of grass on which our 'sitting-room' – the big tent – was geared up. A centenarian walnut tree rose beside it and spread its branches in a wide circle above lesser trees and saplings, like a colossus protecting its domain from the burning sun. From one of its thick horizontal branches Akbar and my brothers hung a long swing as soon as we arrived, using a piece of flat wood for a seat. In full flight it afforded a view over the surrounding land, and both children and adults used it all the time.

One of the first things we each did was to cut some long, straight willow branches to make into walking-sticks. The ground everywhere was uneven and steep, and a stick often helped climbing, pushing back stinging nettles from paths, and holding up branches overhead. We decorated the willow wands with a penknife by designing abstract patterns on the moist bark and cutting away the spaces in between. The result was often an ingenious and decorative green-and-white cylindrical patchwork. I wish I had kept a couple, as souvenirs – every stick was an original piece of primitive art! Akbar had become an expert in willow-carving, and his more elaborate and stylised canes could be sold for as much as five *toumans* (shillings) – a lot of money for him in those days. He was our mentor and guide in country pursuits of all sorts: small and wiry, he ran faster than a rabbit and climbed trees like a squirrel; he knew how to bake potatoes in the woods with a few twigs, how to make fire by rubbing two stones together or holding a piece of glass against the sun, how to shoot birds with a tiny catapult which he had manufactured from a piece of leather and some string. 'Never missed a bird!' he boasted, and often brought back wood-pigeons and quails, which he plucked and grilled over twig fires and shared with us. One summer, Cousin Mohammad gave him a Swiss Army knife, with all sorts of gadgets attached to it. Akbar regarded it as the most precious possession in the world, a source of infinite pleasure and mischief!

Damavand was a region of smallholders, of peasants owning pieces of land which they cultivated themselves. They worked hard and scraped a living from a cornfield, an orchard, a meadow, a few head of cattle or sheep. They supplemented their income by selling their dairy products to holiday-makers in summer, and by taking winter jobs in the village or in town, mostly as navvies on building sites.

Our peasant neighbours would come and pay their respects as soon as news of our arrival reached them, bringing presents of fruit and cream and honey. We bought their produce throughout the summer.

Next to us on the left was the Old Weaver, an ancient widow who lived with her son and his family. While they worked the land, she sat at her loom at the back of their hut and wove all day. She produced a species of calico with blue borders, which she sold as dishcloths, wrappings, napkins, table-cloths, etc. She was the only peasant woman there who still wore a *sheliteh* – a heavily-pleated short skirt which looks like a ballerina's tutu. They say that a Persian Shah visited France in the nineteenth century and was taken to the ballet; he loved the whole thing so much, especially the dancers' tutus, that on his return he had similar outfits made for his harem women. Later, the fashion spread all over the country. Certainly, nineteenth-century paintings of court women show them wearing something like the tutu over baggy trousers. Other authorities say that it was the tutu that was inspired by the oriental fashion catching on in Europe. At any rate, the Old Weaver wore a *sheliteh*, the only time I ever saw one. I sometimes went to see her, fascinated by her weaving – the way she coordinated her feet and hands, pushing the shuttle through the treads and combing the warp down while moving the machinery with her toes, for hours on end. Occasionally she would get up and disappear into a closet where she kept her cloth, and bring me a saucer of cream with sugar and a piece of bread to dip into, by way of a treat. I would reciprocate and take her some sweets and biscuits brought back from the city. One summer when we arrived, Soltan told us that the Old Weaver had died of old age the previous winter. I went to her hut to see if her loom was still there, but it had gone, and in its place was a new cow, whose milk was sold to us every day for breakfast by her daughter-in-law. Her son had also acquired a donkey, who lived in peaceful coexistence with the cow and occasionally came to visit Soltan's she-donkey for amorous purposes.

That year, rumour spread that a bizarre creature had appeared in the region which abducted small children. No one had seen it but from its spoors they had deduced that it was something between a wolf and a bear! My mother immediately 'pushed the panic button' about me, keeping me close to her at night. At an altitude of over ten thousand feet the stars were so bright that even on moonless nights you could see by their light, but Mother left a hurricane-lamp hung on a tree near the veranda to be sure nothing could move undetected, and perhaps discourage the 'child-snatcher'.

One night we were woken up by the sound of heavy footsteps upon the tiny wooden bridge.

'The child-snatcher! The child-snatcher! Help! Help!'

In a second, pandemonium raged and everyone was up lighting lamps and picking up sticks and kitchen knives to combat the beast! And there in the middle of the little bridge was the next-door donkey, evidently having broken loose from its shed to come and pay a visit to Soltan's she-donkey! It looked very surprised, unable to move back or forth, wondering what all the fuss was about. Everyone fell apart laughing. Put off by noisy interruptions, the donkey eventually decided to go back home, but Soltan was longing for a foal and, grabbing his mane and encouraging him with a stick, she led him to his paramour. After that night we did not worry about the 'child-snatcher' any more.

To the right of our *bagh* lived Mashdi Ahmad-the-farmer and his family. He had so many children that we lost count of them – his wife seemed permanently pregnant. The older boys helped their father on the land, and the girls were married off as they came up to 14 or 15. The eldest son, a youth of 19 or 20, used to come along the path at the back of our tent several times a day to open a tiny dam which let the water from the stream flow towards their fields. Invariably, after an hour or so, he would come back and close the gap with some pebbles, as the scarce, precious water had to be shared with strict economy and fairness among the farmers.

One day at dawn we woke up to heart-wrenching screams of woe coming from the direction of their hut – male and female voices wailing and crying, calling God and the Prophet to come to the rescue – anguish that could only signify one thing: a death in the family. We sent Ali to find out what had happened. It emerged that Mashdi Ahmad's eldest son, the one who diverted the water, had died suddenly. It sounded like peritonitis – acute stomach pain, nausea, high temperature. But the symptoms had suggested no more than a bad indigestion, produced by eating too many unripe apricots, which they had thought would soon pass of its own accord. Instead the boy had died in the night. There were several doctors among holiday families all round us, so why had they not called one? Alas, these poor people were not used to consulting doctors – there was only one in the whole valley – so they had just allowed nature to take its course. In most cases, this procedure worked perfectly, but occasionally it led to tragedies of this kind. Soon, a crowd of people emerged from the woods, carrying a coffin on their shoulders and going in the direction of the village, chanting, 'There is no god but God. Verily we come from God and to Him we shall return.'

Everyone rallied round the family with moral support, food, money, clothes ... A couple of weeks later life was back to normal, except that Mashdi Ahmad's second son took over the task of diverting the water from our stream, while his wife lost her rosy complexion and stopped having babies.

That was the only sad incident I remember from our Damavand days. Otherwise our summers were as evenly happy and unblemished as the cloudless sky. Some of my mother's best friends lived in the surrounding *bagh*s whose children and grandchildren were our playmates. Although the strict chronology of those magic days is blurred, I remember how we turned every activity into an adventure, every walk into an 'expedition', every climb into a mountaineering feat. Each morning after breakfast we would go down to the river, where we would find our friends. We would go for long walks in various directions, eating blackberries and picking wild herbs and flowers on the way; we would visit the *ghaleh* (fort), a peasant community on the other side of the river high in the mountains, or just play balls and skipping until it was warm enough for the boys to have a swim in the dam. This dam was either built anew or repaired – depending on the state in which the winter floods had left it – at the beginning of our holidays. All day, a dozen boys, led by Akbar and my brothers, would collect rocks and stones and build up a wall in a wide part of the river between two high banks. Slowly the water would rise and pour over the stones, making a pool of some five or six feet in depth. Soon quantities of trout gathered in the cold limpid water. We devised all sorts of traps to catch them, but they were too crafty to be tickled. Eventually we gave up, and just enjoyed looking at them flashing silver and gold and gambolling among the swimmers. Of course girls could not swim in those days – it would have horrified the peasants and been against the rules of modesty – but the boys dived from the dam and swam while we sat on the bank and watched them.

Shortly before midday we made our way home. On the way, we would fetch our drinking water from the spring, a furlong or two down river, in a place where rain-water, seeping through the hillside, emerged from the rocks into a basin hidden in a grove of poplars, beeches, and plane trees. The water was so cold that we could not bear keeping our hands in it for more than a few seconds, and so limpid as to glint like glass. Often hot, sweaty and parched after a morning's 'expedition', we would reach the spring and cup our hands to drink the delectable icy water as if it were the Spring of Eternal Youth – the very *Kowthar* of the Garden of Eden promised the righteous in the Holy Book. No drink I have ever drunk since has seemed so thirst-quenching and delicious! In my memory, that spring has become a metaphor for happiness residing in the simplest pleasures of life, the quotidian redeemed.

We filled our big pitchers and climbed back home. Sometimes on the way I would stop and buy fresh herbs for lunch from Zeynab, the village blacksmith's wife: radishes, chives, mint and taragon ... Zeynab had very beautiful children, all with straight black hair, large dark eyes and rosy cheeks, like exotic dolls. I loved them and usually held the baby – she always had one in her arms – while she cut the herbs and tied them in neat little bunches. One of her little girls, aged about 4, was particularly lovable – bright, coquettish and affectionate. Sometimes she would follow me up the path and I would pick her up and take her home on my back for lunch. Many years later on a trip to Persia, I went to Damavand for the day and found my way to our old haunts. Nothing seemed changed, the same paths and fields and orchards, their borders marked by brooks and short hedges. There was a young girl cutting herbs in Zeynab's garden who, seeing me approach, stopped, looked for a second and rushed forward to embrace me, calling out my name. Despite the years, my changed appearance and dark glasses she had recognised me. 'How could I forget?' she said. 'You remember how you used to carry me on your back up the hill to your house and give me lunch?'

'The heart has its reason which reason ignores,' said Pascal – perhaps it also has a memory which transcends mere remembrance.

Lunch being the main meal of the day, we often had guests, or took some of our friends home with us. After lunch, everyone had a siesta – even the hard-working peasants downed their tools and tied their animals in the shade for a few hours – it was simply too hot to do anything. The sun hung vertically like a ball of molten gold in the evenly blue immaculate sky; the whole country seemed quivering beneath its implacable gaze. Later on in the season, some of these resting peasants would sit on their threshing ploughs pulled by bullocks round and round the corn-stacks, just dozing.

'Be my guest!' they would say as we went past while they were eating their lunch under a tree – bread and cheese, cucumber and fruit ...

'Thanks! God grant you long life,' we responded, using their own expressions. Too young to require a siesta, we would go to the bottom of the orchard, spread a rug and play cards or backgammon. Sometimes, we girls would take advantage of the siesta break to bathe in the stream undetected.

By four o'clock the heat had abated and the valley came back to life. We had tea-parties or went visiting friends. Sometimes we went in a group to the village, where a bridge over the river led to a wide expanse of fields and meadows on which holiday-makers assembled. There were no cafés but plenty of makeshift stands selling barbecued corns-on-the-cob, fresh walnuts, ice-creams, white mulberries ... At sundown we would head back towards home and dinner.

More often we climbed the hill opposite our house. Half way up the slope there was a huge white flat rock, like a carpet, on which we sat to enjoy the scenery. Sometimes we children climbed all the way up to the summit, whence the view stretched over the whole valley and beyond. Rows and rows of mountains all around, an undulating fawn *moiré*, with the city road to the

Caspian Sea weaving through it like a snake. You could see caravans of gypsies moving slowly along the road, with camels and horses and mules, their bells a-jingle, echoing through the valley. Someone would surely quote:

'Oh Caravan! Go slowly, for you are taking away my
   Beloved ...'

In the foreground was the emerald-green valley, with the river meandering through it. We would make 'monuments' on the top, with rocks and stones, and find them delapidated the following year by winter storms. Once, an eagle had nested in a stone quadrangle we had left. We saw it wheeling anxiously above, wondering who the intruders were.

Slowly we would climb down and join the others on the white rock, to talk and joke and sing and enjoy the scenery and the cool evening breeze before being summoned to dinner.

Presently a sweet melancholy would spread over the valley as the sun slipped over the far-away mountain ridge in a riot of colours. What an Eden-like scene! All creatures preparing for the night – flocks of sheep, goats and cattle moving towards their sheds, peasants gathering their tools, lights appearing among the trees like fallen stars ... We could see Nanny and Soltan like two little coloured dots lighting the *tanoor* (clay oven) to bake the bread. They would send us a snack of fresh loaves with yoghurt and herbs and cheese.

As soon as the last rays of the sun disappeared on the horizon and a milky light diffused the valley we would hear a curious hoot: 'Haq! Haq!' – a forlorn melancholy sound, like a musical note that echoed through the night. It was probably made by a species of owl, but no one had ever seen it, and it's onomatopoeic name had created several legends around it. *Haq* means 'truth', as well as 'right', 'justice', 'fairness', depending upon the context. So this creature was known as 'the bird of truth'. Nanny said that it was a wicked man who had stolen the crop of a widow and her orphan children, and so God had punished him by turning him into a bird with a grain of wheat stuck in his throat, and till the end of time he would cry '*Haq, Haq*' – 'Justice', 'Equity', 'Truth' – to clear his gullet, but in vain! On the Day of Judgement he

233

would become a man again and answer for the wrong he had done. Like the nightingale, we always heard its call, but never managed to see it among the trees, so we believed what Nanny said.

Soon Ali would light the lamps and take the samovar to the tent, then come out and gesticulate with his arms to indicate that dinner was ready.

On moonlit nights, friends would walk to us from all over the valley after dinner, and we would sit on the Rock until late. So luminous was the moon at that altitude that when it shone full, the stars paled and vanished from the sky around it, until it disappeared behind the mountains. Otherwise we would see the Milky Way and all the different constellations as bright as diamonds strewn on black velvet.

It was always with reluctance that late at night we finally came down from the Rock and scattered in different directions towards our homes. What did we talk about, I wonder now? All those hours of conviviality, and I can't recall a word! But I do remember the feelings, the general well-being and the landscape as it went through various stages along the season. And I remember the songs I sang to entertain our friends – many of which I would record decades later in London, though at the time such a possiblity never occurred to me.

Once when the moon was full, we took a picnic and went to the Moon Lake, some six or seven miles behind the mountains on the other side of the river. So bright was the night that we needed no lamps or torches but took a hurricane-lamp, just in case, for the return journey. It took us two or three hours to reach the tiny oasis, tucked away among the hills, with a round pond of stagnant rain-water bordered by some trees. The full moon hung like a lantern and reflected in the water, quivering occasionally with the breeze. Not a sound anywhere to break the deep silence of the oneiric scene. We were inclined to whisper, as if intruding on Nature's dream. We sat down, consumed our food and enjoyed the scene. Then we made our way back over the stony paths, through hills and woods. By the time we reached home, the moon had disappeared behind the mountains and it was pitch-dark. Everyone was asleep, so we quietly slipped into bed, feeling proud of having finally reached the Moon Lake!

There was much activity at harvest-time, at the end of summer, on moonlit nights: you could see peasants winnowing their corn all over the valley, and clouds of chaff drifting in the wind. All night they worked, taking advantage of the breeze, and by dawn they had separated the grain and put it into sacks to take to the mill. Not a single machine in sight! Everything was done as it had always been done, from time immemorial, with toil and hardship, at the mercy of Nature's whims. It was a catastrophe if autumn rains were early, before the harvest was in, or if spring hailstones hit the fruit.

One evening sitting on the Rock, we saw the clouds gathering overhead and heard the distant rumbling of the storm. Presently a few drops of rain fell on our heads, followed by many more. We rushed down and sat on the veranda waiting for the shower to die down. It was time to pack up and go back to town. By the beginning of September, most families had left. Every day you saw buses, loaded with luggage and passengers, going past our front door. Finally one day a bus came for us. We knew we would spend the rest of the year in anticipation of next summer.

Last Years

❦

I have a feeling that wherever I may be in
future, I will be wondering whether there
is rain in Ngong.

Isak Dinesen

Over the years, more Teherani families bought property in
Damavand and built themselves summer villas. These were
simple bungalows whose flat roofs we could see amid the
profusion of greenery from the hill opposite our house. We never
bought anything. We could not afford it, and anyway we only
liked our own – Mashdi Abdollah's – *bagh*, which he did not wish
to sell. But it mattered not, since we had security of tenure every
summer. Mashdi Abdollah was often offered a much higher rent
than we paid him, but despite his reputation for stinginess, he
always refused, saying that the Master and his family had
priority.

Suddenly we were adolescents. Some of us were entering the
University in Teheran, others were leaving for colleges abroad,
in Europe and America, yet others were getting married, while
the younger ones like myself were preparing for their baccalaureate. Every summer, one or two friends were missing, and we
would remember them and talk about them when we gathered
on the Rock at dusk, wondering what they were doing at that
very moment 'on the other side of the world', or if they were
telepathically thinking of us.

Some of the old families ceased to come to Damavand
altogether, because their lives changed, or because, not having
any property, they did not feel obliged to spend every summer in
the same place, while one or two new people were added to our
circle of friends. Among these was the family of Colonel Deen.
They owned a couple of orchards and some fields down by the
river, but there was no building on them, so, to live in, they
rented a two-roomed hut from the farmer on the other side.

Colonel Deen had previously been posted to other parts of the country, which explained why we had not seen him in Damavand before. Then recently he had retired and settled in Teheran, and had decided to spend the summer in Damavand and see to his property. He knew my father, and came to visit him upon arrival. He was delighted with the valley as a whole and his own orchards in particular, and he was planning to build a holiday villa for his family. The next day he brought his wife and children to make our acquaintance, and soon we were friends.

The Deens had six children of various ages, ranging from the eldest son who was my brothers' contemporary at the *lycée*, to the youngest who was a toddler. They were unusual, we thought, because they did not belong to our social milieu, and their mother was Russian. She spoke Persian with a heavy accent and her behaviour did not conform to the formal, stylised social manners we were used to. Her family had fled from Russia at the time of the revolution in 1917, and settled in Azarbayejan, where later Colonel Deen, then a young officer serving in the town's garrison, had met her. He had fallen in love with her at first sight and pursued her until her family had consented to his marriage proposal. You could see how beautiful she had been – high cheekbones and a lovely bone-structure, dark brown eyes and hair, creamy complexion – even though age and six childbirths had taken their toll.

Colonel Deen's eldest daughter, Mimi, had just entered the School of Fine Arts at the University with my brother Nasser, and they had become friends even before we met the rest of the family. Though not beautiful by Persian classical criteria, she was tall, handsome, exotic, and attractively European-looking. She wore make-up, which we were not allowed to do, and which enhanced further her aura of sophistication. She spoke with a soft, slow voice and was reserved and aloof, quite the opposite of our other friends, who on the whole were extrovert and exuberant. She became my 'older friend' and role-model; we were soon each other's confidants, exchanging secrets, dreams and aspirations.

At the University, Nasser had immediately attracted attention – the talented student who was going to be a famous painter. He had met a number of other budding artists and intellectuals, some of whom had become his close friends and frequented our house. One summer, he persuaded four of his closest friends – all would-be poets and writers – to come and spend their holidays in Damavand. They camped in an apricot orchard on the far side of the river, at the distant end of the valley, but they spent most of their time with us. Together we went for walks and expeditions and sat on the Rock in the evenings endlessly discussing politics, poetry, literature, art, with the passionate intensity of youth. It was the time of Prime Minister Mossadeq and the nationalisation of Persian oil, of the international embargo that followed and brought about economic bankruptcy. Our adolescent turmoils coincided with these political crises, and every day there were huge street-demonstrations in large cities, clashes with the police, expressions of patriotic fervour, etc. . . . The intelligentsia were as divided as the rest of the population: into Nationalists who backed Mossadeq and had the support of sections of the clergy, and the Communists who opposed them. We were all Communist sympathisers, although we were not politically educated enough to realise the implications. We just liked the lofty internationalist ideals. Many books have been written about this oil crisis and its aftermath in the Middle East. We were just extras on the scene and were not quite aware that the slogans we shouted would produce far-reaching echoes. For although Mossadeq's crusade failed in Iran, he set an example which was followed in other countries with greater success – the national-isation of the Suez Canal, the acceptance by the Western powers that oil had to be paid for like other commodities, and which in turn produced counter-stratagems to get the money paid for it back somehow, in particular through the sale of arms, etc. . . .

No longer children, my sister and I were urged to be very mindful of our reputations, to avoid being seen alone with boys and so provoking gossip. But there was no mistaking love's stirring – it was in the air all around us. All the boys in our group were secretly in love with either my sister or with Mimi. They expressed it with almost imperceptible signs: a way of looking at them, or offering a pretty wild flower picked on one of our walks, or a gentle billet-doux accompanying a gift book. They would not have been bold enough to do anything more. But times were changing and the fact that we could all meet and talk and somehow get our feelings across was enough to feed our romantic longings. I was too young to participate in this subtle game actively; with my plaited hair and my studious air I did not stand a chance. Yet my heart was full of yearning and my dreams focused at various times on one or other of the young men who came into our orbit. I was confused: one day I wanted to break away from the restrictive confines of family and society, to go to Europe and be free to carve a new destiny for myself, the next day I was in love with a young poet and wanted to marry him and be conventionally happy ever after. I confided my uncertainty and confusion to Mimi, who gently backed my plans to go abroad, vicariously sharing my dreams of adventure and artistic fulfilment.

Many a morning after breakfast I would go down to the river and meet Mimi: we would walk along the bank in the shade of trees, the spongy soil carpeted with forget-me-nots and daisies, and talk endlessly about our feelings and our dreams. She would show me the love-letters and poems she had received from her score of admirers.

One of her beaux lent her a hand-wound gramophone and some records. Often we would climb up the steep slippery path to her house, which stood on the high ground where the valley opened out and flattened into cornfields as far as the eye could see. There was a row of willow trees by the stream that ran at the foot of the hills and we would sit in their shade and listen to music: Beethoven, Brahms, Schumann, Chopin, Lehar, Rimsky-Korsakov, Tchaikovsky ... the most romantic pieces by the most Romantic composers. Mimi painted the landscapes around from different angles while I lay on the grass reading. At noon, her mother would send someone to call us for lunch, then we would have a siesta on the shady side of the veranda, and afterwards go to our house where we all congregated for the long cool sunset hours.

One winter evening, when we were back in Teheran, a

messenger came to announce that Colonel Deen had died suddenly of a heart attack. We all rushed to his house to be with his family and to support them. His widow was shattered – how to bring up six children alone? Only two of them were barely out of their teens. During the week of mourning ceremonies we met Mrs Deen's family, her old mother who did not speak a word of Persian after forty years in the country, her sisters who had married 'Christians', her brother who had never been at their home before. Mrs Deen coped with everything at first, but gradually her mind gave out and she began to suffer from acute depression. In the end she was confined to a psychiatric hospital where she eventually died. But by then her children were grown up.

I still cannot believe that my parents actually allowed me to leave home. Given the turmoil of the country, they probably thought that I would get involved in left-wing politics and perhaps bring dishonour to them. Or perhaps they thought I would become a free-thinker and therefore 'loose' in my comportment? Or was it that the climate was changed so much in favour of Westernisation that they felt they had no choice? Or perhaps they simply wanted me to develop and express my own self? At any rate it was decided that I would go to France after my baccalaureate. My eldest brother Nassir had joined our Foreign Service and was already in Germany: he could keep an eye on me from there.

Our last summer all together in Damavand was melancholy. Many of our friends were absent: Cousin Mohammad had finished University and taken a job with the oil company at Abadan refinery. He would end up as Under-Secretary of State for Health. Nassir was in Europe as a junior diplomat, and other cousins and friends were scattered all over the world as students or young married couples. Soon after I left Persia, my sister married a young diplomat, and they were posted abroad. Then Nasser finished University and came to settle in Paris. Thereafter, my parents ceased going to Damavand for the summer, as did many of their friends whose households had also been depleted. Instead they had air-conditioning installed in our town house.

The oil boom of the late fifties and sixties made a number of people rich enough to have holiday homes, and it soon became fashionable to go for the summer to the Caspian Sea – in a few years the whole coast was bought up and 'developed'. A surface road shortened the journey to Damavand to little more than an hour. 'It could almost be a suburb if it were not snow-bound in winter.' And eventually this happened.

Over my student years, I travelled in Europe, all of it so green and lush, and some of it breathtakingly beautiful. But, in my memory, Damavand is the loveliest spot on earth, the lost paradise of childhood. Sometimes, on a summer evening, I think of those days and, if I close my eyes, I can see it vividly, as if it were only yesterday that I had left it – the whole green valley as seen from the top of the hill; the clump of trees at the far end where Mimi and I exchanged dreams and confidences, the 'umbrella willow' in whose shade Father used to sit and read, the silver river meandering below and rising to a blue lagoon by the dam; the spring glinting gold in the shaded poplar grove, the song of the invisible nightingale, the cry of *Morghe-Haq* – the Bird of Truth – as the moon rose ...

It was agreed that I should make the journey to Europe with a friend who was going to University in Germany. My father prayed in my ears and held a Qoran over my head as I went out of the door. My mother, Aunt Ashraf and Aunt Batool, Zahra and Ali, all came with me to the airport. In those days it was not the huge international centre that it became in later years – it was just a track with a two-roomed building as terminal. It was crowded with the passengers of our one plane, all leaving for Europe, and their relatives. At the far end I caught a glimpse of Pari, the friend I was travelling with – she was crying. It suddenly hit me: I was leaving home for the first time in my life; I was going to a foreign country, full of strange people; I would be very lonely, I would miss my family and friends desperately ... My face was awash with tears, and I turned round to clutch my mother. Floods of tears were streaming down her face and with her usual intuition she knew exactly what was going on in my head. 'Don't go!' she said softly. 'What does it matter?' But I didn't dare! What a let-down it would be for my school-mates who had encouraged me in my plans, and my teachers – I just did not have the courage to change my mind. All my future life was shaped by that one piece of cowardice. I would have to be very brave from then on to make up for it.

Finally the passengers were called to the plane, and I wrenched myself away from my mother. I did not know how hard I would have to work ever after to earn a fraction of that love from others, which was given to me freely without asking, and which I was leaving behind and discarding carelessly. I looked out of the window as the plane took off and circled around the mountains, until I could see nothing but clouds.

Twelve hours later we landed in Paris.

Glossary of Persian Words

❦

aberoo	=	honour, dignity
abi	=	blue (literally 'colour of water')
alem	=	savant, learned, wise
andaroon	=	women's quarters in a seigneurial home
Aqa	=	gentleman, Mister, Lord, mullah (depending on context)
aqd	=	marriage contract
araq	=	Persian vodka
Aref	=	one versed in the esoteric doctrines of Islam known in the West as Sufism
aroos	=	bride, daughter-in-law
atar	=	perfume
bagh	=	garden, orchard, fruit-growing land
baghcheh	=	little garden
baj	=	tribute, extortion money, tax
baraka	=	blessing, grace
Bazaar	=	market (usually covered), City
bazaarcheh	=	little district-market
birooni	=	the male quarters of a seigneurial home
chador	=	veil
chopoq	=	hooka, long-handled pipe
dallak	=	one who washes, rubs, massages clients in a *hammam* (public baths)
Dash	=	diminutive of *Dadash*, (colloquially) brother
Erfan	=	knowledge of the esoteric doctrines of Islam, known as Sufism in the West
Farangi	=	originally French, by extension European, Western

ghaleh	=	fort, fortress, communal peasant house
hadith	=	saying of the Prophet Mohammad
Haft-Seen	=	a collection of seven items all starting with 'S' in Persian, and part of the New Year celebrations
haj	=	the pilgrimage to Mecca which a wealthy muslim must perform once in his/her lifetime
hammam	=	public baths, known in the West as Turkish Baths
joob	=	open canals in the streets for water, gutter
kadkhoda	=	village headman, mayor of a small town
Khanoom	=	Mrs; Miss; Lady
korsi	=	a low table covered with blankets, with a charcoal brazier underneath, used for sitting around in winter and keeping warm
madrasah	=	traditional Islamic college; school
mahram	=	legitimate; close relative in front of whom women need not be veiled
Mashdi	=	short for Mashhadi, one who has been on pilgrimage to Mashhad where Imam Reza, the Eighth of the Twelve Imams of the Shia sect is buried
Mujtahid	=	a very high ranking mullah who has the qualification through learning of interpreting the *Sharia* (Islamic Law)
najeeb	=	modest, virtuous, honest
najis	=	impure, not to be touched
noql	=	a sweet made with a sliver of almond coated with icing sugar, used for weddings and festivities in particular
Norooz	=	literally New Day, also Persian New Year which happens at the spring equinox on 21 March

pahlavan	=	hero, athlete, brave man
Pa-Lees	=	a mythical creature which licks the foot of sleeping travellers to drink their blood until they die
paroo	=	long-handled wooden shovel for sweeping snow off roofs
qaltac	=	cylindrical heavy stone, like a steam-roller, to run over a roof after snow has been swept off it and tighten the clay
qalyan	=	water-pipe, hubble-bubble
qaran	=	money unit, one tenth of a touman, and about one penny
rayat	=	peasant without land, virtual serf
riazat	=	suffering, asceticism, tribulation
Roo-Hosy	=	popular theatre staged usually on a *hoz* (pool) in the garden
sabzi	=	herb, greenery
Seyyed	=	descendent of the Prophet Mohammad through his daughter Fatimah and his son-in-law Ali, who is the First Imam of the Shia sect
Sharia	=	Islamic Law
Sheikh	=	a Sufi Master; a mullah who is not descended from the Prophet and wears a white turban instead of the black one worn by Seyyeds
Sherbet	=	a soft drink made with fruit essence and water
sigheh	=	concubine, temporary wife
soozani	=	literally needlework, usually a square of embroidered brocade for sitting on after baths
taarof	=	traditional exchange of compliments and pleasantries, to indicate respect and affection and hospitality
talabeh	=	literally 'seeker after knowledge', in practice a seminarist at a theology college
tareke-donya	=	a renouncer-of-the-world, nun, monk

| *Tazieh* | = | a form of sacred theatre, usually based on the account of the martyrdom of Imam Hossein, Third Imam of the Shia sect and grandson of the Prophet Mohammad |
| *touman* | = | money unit which is the equivalent of one shilling or five pence |